Social Movements and Protest in France

Edited by

Philip G. Cerny
University of York

 Frances Pinter (Publishers), London

First published in Great Britain in 1982 by
Frances Pinter (Publishers) Limited
5 Dryden Street, London WC2E 9NW

ISBN 0 86187 213 4 hardback
ISBN 0 86187 214 2 paperback

Typeset by Anne Joshua Associates, Oxford

Printed by SRP, Exeter

CONTENTS

Introduction:
The Politics of Protest in Contemporary French Society

The close interrelationship between expressions of political protest, the growth of social movements, and the broader patterns of political life — the behaviour of individuals and groups, on the one hand, and relations of authority and power in the state, on the other — has provided historians, sociologists, political scientists and assorted other pundits with a dominant image of France for nearly two centuries. This image, which has dominated fundamental perceptions of France through a wide variety of ideological perspectives — inextricably intertwined with themes such as revolution, democracy, stability or instability, liberty, and capacities for change and development — has guaranteed France a unique place among the older capitalist democracies. From the fulminations of Edmund Burke, the bourgeois critique of Alexis de Tocqueville and de Gaulle's denunciations of France's 'perpetual political effervescence', on the one hand, to the Declaration of the Rights of Man and Citizen in 1789, the powerful imagery of the Commune of 1871 and the spontaneous creativity of the Events of May 1968, on the other, the French revolutionary tradition has captured the attention of the world, representing either a warning of the nefarious consequences of instability and chaos, or the hope that democracy might still contain an immanent potential for human liberation through participation and the transfer of real power to the people.

The place of this revolutionary tradition within France itself is, however, highly problematic. In part, it has been absorbed into the dominant political culture. In this way, the fact that France can claim to have experienced the first 'modern' democratic political revolution serves paradoxically to reinforce the legitimacy of the state and its elected leaders. Thus revolution becomes an anachronism, revered in cultural memory and ritually re-enacted as a part of adolescent political socialisation, but essentially both outdated and utopian. The style and rhetoric persist, but the reality is circumscribed by fear; when the safety valve threatens to blow, as in May 1968, the *grande peur* returns and order is reimposed.

Furthermore, the revolutionary tradition has been historically and socially fragmented. In this way, the main cleavages of French society — those of class, religion, town and country, and ideology — have interacted with the revolutionary tradition in such a way as to create a multitude of diverse protest movements with little potential for common action except a sense that they represent ordinary people striking back against a monistic, distant yet tentacular, state. Thus it appears as the very *alter ego* of the state itself — incapable of organising any genuine revolutionary movement, and yet inadequate (and unwilling) to develop into a system of 'voluntary associations' so beloved of the philosophers of liberal democracy since de Tocqueville. Sound and fury abound, and occasional concessions are gained, but the main impact is absorbed by the state; when common action is achieved (however temporarily), and the state itself is threatened as a consequence — again as in May 1968 — the reaction is crude but ultimately effective.

And yet protest politics retains a vitality and a sense of historical purpose which belies the negative impression conveyed by the foregoing critique. The demise predicted by pluralist political scientists has not occurred, and, indeed, the relevance of protest would seem to find a new affirmation in the complex context of advanced capitalist society — not only in France but elsewhere. For we are here dealing not just with a revolutionary tradition, but with a renewal of the politics of protest through the emergence of new social, economic and political concerns in the last quarter of the twentieth century and with the development of new social movements whose objectives cannot be accommodated by the political party systems and structures of interest group bargaining characteristic of the advanced capitalist democracies. The purpose of this introduction will be to set out some of these problems and to relate them to other recent developments in French politics and society.

Protest, Democracy and Revolution in Advanced Capitalism

Protest stands in a shifting and poorly defined no man's land between the politics of revolutionary change and the pluralist functionalism of pressure group politics. It creates problems for both of these analytical paradigms, problems which are particularly relevant to state/society relations in the conditions of advanced capitalism — i.e., those characteristic of the so-called 'developed world' of Western capitalist liberal democratic nation states. Indeed, it is in the arena of political protest that the concerns of these two paradigms meet and overlap in a complex and striking fashion, encapsulating both the historicity and the pathology of these societies.

For both liberal–democratic and revolutionary theory, protest movements play a crucial and irreplaceable role in the unfolding of the course of historical development, for both have sought to undermine what they have seen as social and political structures run by the few for the few — societies based on expropriation, exploitation and repression — with structures run by, or at least for the benefit of, the mass of the people. The concept of 'the right of rebellion' (or revolution) developed in the seventeenth century, by John Locke in particular, and which so influenced Enlightenment thinking — not to mention the American and French Revolutions — in the eighteenth, heralded and inspired a process which smouldered and flared throughout nineteenth-century Europe and the Americas until the collapse of the remaining dynasties in the First World War, and then provided much of the ideological impetus for colonial independence movements well into the second half of the twentieth. For socialist theory, indeed, revolution became the key to understanding history — the inevitable stage where social structures derived from an earlier mode of production gave way to new structures which were immanent in fundamental changes in the mode and relations of production but which require a revolution in order to replace the obsolescent but entrenched and encrusted system of distributing power and wealth inherited from the previous revolutionary phase.

Political protest, in both cases, represented a necessary phase of development. It involved the expression of new demands — whether for freedom of expression, economic liberalism, the right to vote, the right to organise trade unions, government action on behalf of the poor or powerless, or control (or replacement) of the state itself by structures inherently more capable of creating fairness — which called for fundamental changes in the old system, and brought new groups from among the mass of the people into a process which was both political and metapolitical at the same time. Thus new groups expressing new and fundamental demands created a consciousness of the need for change — and of the potentiality for change. Furthermore, they created, usually *ad hoc* but later through imitation, structures of action — committees, unions, and parties (both participating and non-participating in the existing system) — which could have a more persistent impact on society. In many cases, it was argued that this new consciousness, acting through these new structures, had thus come to embody the immanent form of post-revolutionary society and would ultimately inherit the fruits and responsibilities of longer-term social transformation, although moral and strategic divergences (in the liberal–democratic case, populism *vs.* constitutionalism, and in the socialist case, syndicalism *vs.* the revolutionary party, were salient forms of this divergence) made the issue highly complex.

But no matter how important the politics of protest — as catalyst, vehicle or embryo — the advent of a higher stage of political or social development requires its transcendence. Inextricably intertwined with the process of rejecting an existing system, it is inherently incapable in and of itself of providing an ongoing mode of socio-political action in a new system. For the new system itself requires a conservative — not a disruptive — set of structures for the expression and fulfilment of the popular will; it requires stability, and stability itself is inherently a conservative value. Thus although protest is necessary and instrumental in the transcendence of the old order, it must equally necessarily be transcended — or indeed *transcend itself* — in order for the new order to achieve the sort of society for which it was instituted.

This transcendence can take place in two analytically distinct, although empirically bound up, ways. Either it comes about through the imposition of a new order, a new order which is embryonic in the revolutionary movement itself — like the revolutionary vanguard party or the dictatorship of the proletariat. This sort of development is open to two basic critiques: it may lead to just as much repression, but in the name of a new leadership rather than the old one; and it is vulnerable to counterrevolution, as the technicians of power deny their past and sell themselves to the new regime in return for the restoration (usually in disguise) of privileges. But at the same time, this course of action responds to criteria of organisational efficiency, necessary in the (presumed) chaos of the replacement of the previous order. Or it comes about through the spontaneous development of the immanent potential of the new order — as certain different qualities are achieved. These qualities may be those which are seen as necessary in *any* stable order, such as maturity, responsibility and an understanding of the limits of power (the basis of pluralist thinking, but also important to some revolutionary perspectives); or those which reach deeper into social mores, such as the development of community or worker control with the withering away of the state, and the emergence of wholly new forms of hierarchy (rotating or collective leadership, etc.) or even the removal of the need for hierarchy itself as new forms of consensus spontaneously emerge (lack of the *basis* for conflict after the end of the class struggle; or the development of consensual practices such as Habermas's 'discursive will-formation').

But, however the new order comes about, and whatever its inner nature, it is clear that protest represents an infantile phenomenon — *except in so far as it is harmless*, either as a safety valve or as a means of bringing to public attention issues and grievances which can then be conciliated, thus strengthening the social order itself! *Functional* protest becomes the only acceptable sort, except perhaps in that most problematic of social conceptions, the permanent revolution, usually associated with Mao Zedong's thought, in which it is still essentially functional but in a much more effervescent and ever-present form. Indeed, if protest politics is not trancended (or functionalised), then the danger of chaos or instability in the new order is opened up. For the liberal–democratic pluralists, instability inherently involves the danger of collapse and totalitarianism – a danger brought home to a whole generation of Western social scientists by the experiences of the 1920s and 1930s. For revolutionary theorists, instability raises the spectre of counterrevolution, of which fascism is the most virulent sort; the disarray of the many permits the return of the rule of the few. Unlike the Platonic problematic, however – in which the dispersion of power among the many (democracy) inevitably leads to demagogic dictatorship – both the liberal–democratic theorists and the revolutionary theorists believe that the new order can be stabilised by the circumscription of protest politics and the channelling of discontent into responsive but functional channels.

But despite their common democratic heritage, and the fact that a few thinkers (like Jean-Jacques Rousseau) made vital contributions to both perspectives, the liberal–democratic and the revolutionary paradigms are divided by opposing perceptions of bourgeois society, differing conceptions of human potential in terms of individual self-interest and social cooperativeness, and antagonistic aims for the future. Thus their postures towards contemporary advanced capitalist society are fundamentally at odds. At the same time, one of the characteristics of advanced capitalist society has been not only the persistence and recrudescence of protest politics, but also the encapsulation in protest movements of certain of the underlying problems and pathological symptoms of that society. And each of the paradigms in question has had to assimilate and interpret this phenomenon, a task which had led to a wide range of responses within each.

This is not the place to attempt a detailed interpretation of advanced capitalism. In its most simplified form, it differs from earlier forms of industrial capitalist society (with their limited constitutional state) along three interrelated dimensions – the economic, the political and the social. In the economic sphere, the most salient broad transformation has been the internationalisation and bureaucratisation of production and exchange; the nationalisation and internationalisation of markets, the concentration and rationalisation of firms, the development of 'scientific' managerial techniques, the increasing importance of capital relative to labour (particularly the development of new technologies), manipulation of markets (marketing, advertising, consumer values), the growing importance of credit and credit institutions for both production and consumption, the increasingly crucial numerical and strategic position of technical specialists (the 'technostructure'), and the emerging predominance of the service and information sector over both primary and secondary production, are among the most important elements of this transformation.[1]

In the political sphere, the most salient transformation has been that of the state from a structure which basically provided for national defence and internal security, on the one hand, and the maintenance of a framework of legal order to protect property and to stabilise and harmonise the conditions of production and exchange, on the other — although there is controversy as to whether this ideal-type limited role ever existed in fact, given the realities of imperialism and of the protection and subsidisation of special interests — to one of widespread economic and social interventionism. Among the new tasks, roles and activities of the state are the manipulation of business cycles (in the hopes of maximising steady growth), the creation of demand, the provision of a welfare state, the protection of key industries against bankruptcy through subsidy or public ownership, the guaranteeing of credit, control of wage bargaining, monetary and fiscal manipulation, and the stimulation of new technology; these new tasks lead to a bureaucratisation and technocratisation analogous to that in the economic sphere as well as an increasingly complex need to assimilate pressures from a more and more interpenetrated international economy. Agenda-setting by democratically accountable political parties becomes more and more problematic in such an environment, and the increasing cooptation of interest groups (corporatism) into a structured bargaining process tends to replace parliamentary debate as the main decision-making arena.

The social consequences of these changes are paradoxical. On the one hand, the individual is drawn into a wider and more integrated social and cultural environment; mass education and communications media dovetail with the dynamics of the consumer society, urbanisation and suburbanisation, and the integration of key socio-economic processes such as wage negotiation and the provision of social and public services, to create a social web the mediation of which — and the escape from which — is less and less under the individual's control. Yet at the same time, the values of that society — especially private consumption and personal gratification — create a level of expectations not only of material improvement but also of personal satisfaction which can easily lead to disappointment and alienation when it is not achieved. In these conditions, the level of integration and bureaucratisation of state and economic processes offers few outlets for the effective pressing of grievances which are not 'functional', i.e., which are not ultimately conciliable within the existing system (and which would not thus actually reinforce the system). What is functional or dysfunctional is, of course, determined by the imperatives of the system itself, and, ultimately, by the groups which already possess power and influence within the state and the economy. Therefore groups whose values and objectives are perceived as 'dysfunctional' by power-holding groups – more and more linked through technostructural considerations – can no longer look to the system even for a 'safety valve'. It will be screwed shut.

This situation can lead essentially to three reaction patterns. The first is to increase pressure within the system, with the hope of creating stronger countervailing pressures and thus giving greater protection to disadvantaged groups. This pattern is always present, although more attractive during periods of relative economic expansion, when a growing pie can be sliced in incrementally different ways. The second is resignation and sublimation, leading to a diffuse sense of futility which is internalised rather than externalised – although it often leads to diffuse activities such as absenteeism, crime and 'spontaneous' rioting. It has been observed recently in France and Britain, for example, that the return of mass unemployment has not led to widespread, organised mass protest, as had frequently been predicted from earlier experiences, but rather to a feeling of sickness among the workers themselves, who feel isolated, morally and psychologically weak, and punished by society in an unexpected and badly understood way.[2] The third pattern, of course, is the politics of protest.

It will be clear, from what I have said above, that protest, while in theory the most obvious and rational course of action in the circumstances – a view reflected in the flowering of literature on the causes and objectives of protest following the Events of May 1968 or analysing the American movements against the Vietnam War (as well as the Berkeley Free Speech Movement, etc.) – tends to be defused in two ways: firstly, by fairly effective 'carrot and stick' actions by the state and by the 'business community' (effective in relieving the symptoms of unrest in the short term, though incapable of treating the causes); and secondly, by the fragmentation of society and culture and the psychological isolation of individuals and primary groups, who sink into lethargy. Meanwhile, the 'silent majority', which does not escape the problems and tensions of advanced capitalism, blames them on other, competing groups – such as the trade unions, seen as 'holding the country to ransom', or on the more salient of the protest groups, seen as 'subversive' of the huge material and social gains already made by capitalist society (compared with feudal or totalitarian societies). Nevertheless, the protest which *does* erupt — whether it be in the form of student sit-ins, protests against the spread of civil or military nuclear power, the growth of regionalist or nationalist movements, the socially revolutionary demands of women, or the more violent forms of 'terrorism', such as airplane hijacking — is widely diffused through the mass media and has a strong psychological impact on both actual and potential participants, on the one hand, and spectators, on the other.

Furthermore, these movements have an immediate contemporary quality which leads to the raising of questions which would otherwise be submerged. Their aims and actions are both more complex and more variegated than more traditional forms of protest, which were aimed more directly at the oligarchies of state and economy, but which were defused by liberal democratic politics and economic prosperity. And it is in this context that both liberal–democratic theory and revolutionary theory have attempted to come to terms with the new protest. For it is clear that advanced capitalism means neither the transcending of older forms of conflict based on the unequal distribution of wealth and power — which are cast into new, dynamically different moulds — nor the preventing of the development of new forms of conflict stemming from advanced capitalism itself. But in this attempt to diagnose and prescribe for the problems of advanced capitalism, the old ambivalence towards protest *per se* once agains reasserts itself.

In the liberal–democratic context, the problem is, quite simply, defeating or repressing protest which aims at undermining the system as such ('extremism') while attempting to assimilate protest movements into the system by functionalising them. This functionalisation process can be seen as a search for pragmatic compromises between modifying certain characteristics of the system itself, more effectively assimilating groups into the system, and repressing 'deviant' responses. This search for compromise thus covers a wide range of forms of activity, reflecting ideological differences between 'tender-minded' and 'tough-minded' politicians (a search for 'political solutions' *vs.* the call for 'law and order') as well as between 'interventionist' and 'anti-interventionist' socio-economic perspectives (the attempt to integrate potential protest groups into the corporatist bargaining process *vs.* the belief that each group should look after its own interests in a more efficiently functioning social and economic free market). Thus conflicting approaches to protest are closely related to divergent perspectives on advanced capitalist society itself; however, these different approaches are concerned with the *means* to control and limit protest, and assume that its causes can be alleviated *within* the broad context of political pluralism and the mixed economy and that they have no historicity.

In the revolutionary framework, the problem is that of ensuring that protest does lead to a fundamental break with advanced capitalism in spite of its seemingly fragmented character. This process of transformation can be seen as an attempt to nurture − or even to create − historicity in an environment where the short-term cards seem to be stacked against revolution. Here, too, we see that this perspective on protest reflects a variety of divergent views on the necessary and sufficient conditions for revolution. On the one hand, there is the attempt to identify − and to focus activity upon − certain key points of contradiction and tension, i.e., those which both create revolutionary consciousness and embody the immanent form of post-revolutionary society. Thus conflict arises between those who, in traditional Marxist terms, see the conflict between capital and labour as the crucial contradiction − and who therefore tolerate protest movements only so long as they represent a definable stage in the unfolding of this contradiction under advanced capitalism − and those who see the conflict between capital and labour *itself* reflecting a deeper contradiction (or set of contradictions) bound up with the search for a more profound form of human liberation; in this second category, for example, can be found views of human liberation as ultimately involving sensuality (Marcuse), rational discussion (Habermas), the social relations of human reproduction (the Feminist movement), the quality of the natural environment (Touraine and the political ecologists), etc., all of which can be seen as involving highly problematic relationships with the traditional Marxist dialectic.

On the other hand, there is the attempt to develop forms of organisation which can (1) immanently embody, (2) consciously develop, (3) strategically lead and (4) politically and socially bring to fruition the revolution itself, thus initially establishing post-revolutionary society. This − the endogenous nature of a revolutionary social movement − reflects conflicts between those who believe that such a movement will develop in an essentially spontaneous form from the relevant contradiction(s), and those who believe that organised, strategic action is a necessary condition of success. For the latter, too, there is the debate between the model of committees or councils, closely representing the rank-and-file of the movement while coordinating their actions (the 'soviets' model), and the 'democratic centralist' model of the revolutionary party or syndicate, coordinating activity from the top. For protest to be revolutionary, then, there is the problem of how the fragmented and variegated protest movements characteristic of advanced capitalism can transform themselves into effective revolutionary movements – all the more problematic when one considers the ways in which earlier forms of 'revolutionary' movements – trade unions, Socialist and Communist parties, cooperative movements, etc. – have generally been integrated in one way or another into advanced capitalist society.

Thus both liberal–democratic theory and revolutionary theory have manifest problems in coming to grips with an empirical phenomenon which appears to be increasingly important to the ultimate success or failure of either paradigm. For the politics of protest, and the social movements which they reflect, represent a real and continuing product of advanced capitalist society. This can be seen in the mass media, where, despite the attempts of the media establishment to be 'balanced', the underlying *cri du coeur* is often perceived by spectators who see themselves in situations analogous to that of the protestors, and yet where the bogey of 'extremism' and 'subversion' can arouse great fears too. It can be seen in the disillusionment with established political parties, on the one hand, and the growing ideologisation of party politics, on the other, as consensus politics are found wanting in the context of economic crisis. And it can be seen in the way that protest tactics are readily used, not only by radical movements, but also by those who want their streets made safer or playgroup provision improved. These are eminently contemporary phenomena. And yet protest politics does not arise in a cultural and historical vacuum, and, given the fragmented and varied nature of protest movements under advanced capitalism, crucial elements of their structure and dynamics – timing, style, leadership, social and political resonance, etc. – can only be analysed in the context of the social formation in which they arise.

The Dynamics of Protest in France

As we have already observed, political protest has played an important role in creating and maintaining a certain idea of French politics among historians, sociologists, political scientists and other observers. In the words of Stanley Hoffmann, 'If we take a closer look at the French political system, we find that the universality of protest transcends all the distinctions made by political scientists'.[3] Indeed, the image of protest in France extends into analyses of the style of French party politics and political culture in general – what Alfred Grosser called 'nothing but opposition'[4] – although, relevantly enough for our purposes here, this image has been muted by the changes in the party system of the Fifth

Republic. In order to assess the importance of this claim of the centrality of protest politics in France, we shall briefly consider two key aspects of French social, political and economic development: the emergence of patterns of conflict and stabilisation in the nineteenth and early twentieth centuries; and the transition to advanced capitalism after the Second World War. We shall then examine what is currently the predominant school of thought concerning protest in France, that which focuses on the 'style of authority' in French society, before suggesting some further thoughts on the experience of the 1970s and the situation in the early 1980s.

The Events of May 1968 are both a requiem for the past and a portent for the future, for they marked the end of one long and eventful epoch in the history of protest politics in France and yet at the same time left signs indicating the outlines of a new epoch still in the process of becoming.[5] The key to this transition was the rapid transformation of France after 1945 from a complex state of 'uneven development' into an advanced capitalist society. The French revolutionary tradition was itself both a cause and a product of that history of uneven development. Although there is no space here to provide even a brief survey of French development,[6] it is possible to identify certain features of that process which are relevant to our concerns.

The French Revolution of 1789, although a bourgeois democratic revolution in its structure and objectives, neither brought to power a modernising capitalist class nor installed an effective liberal–democratic political system. Powerful groups from the *ancien régime* retained footholds in the economy (through ownership of land and other forms of capital), the state (through the retention of the essence of the pre-revolutionary administrative system, streamlined under Napoleon I, and through the army) and the social hierarchy (through local *notabilité* in many rural areas, through the church, and through a certain intermixing with newer upper-class groups, such as the Parisian *haute bourgeoisie* – a process which had begun under the *ancien régime*). The new middle classes were themselves divided between entrepreneurial and *rentier* elements. The mass of the population was still a peasantry, as no 'agricultural revolution' occurred to alter the basic structures of a feudal rural economy, although there was a small and growing industrial working class in the large cities and an artisan class in the smaller cities and towns as well. Protectionism, conservative management of family firms, the lack of integration of the national market, and a host of other features provided barriers to the development of any self-sustaining process of economic growth.

But while the social and economic substructure remained relatively stable during most of the nineteenth century – compared, that is, with Britain, the United States or Germany (France was a rich and developed imperial nation compared with the rest of the world) – the political picture was wholly different. Monarchical, democratic and imperial regimes succeeded one another; revolutions erupted; wars and colonial adventures were frequent occurrences. Political parties and political ideologies emerged and struggled for shares of power – different sorts of monarchism, republicanism, liberalism and socialism, always in ferment, especially in Paris. And the struggle between the church and the anti-clerical forces, one of the most profound conflicts to emerge from the 1789 Revolution, provided a focus for other conflicts as well – character-ising two social subcultures whose impact on patterns of voting behaviour, for example, has lasted well into the second half of the twentieth century. The political compromises which permitted the establishment in the 1870s of a conservative republican constitutional settlement – the Third Republic, which lasted until 1940 – succeeded only insofar as they froze the social balance of forces and prevented the political ascendancy of any one group or class – a feature of the parliamentary regime which was to be both its strength and, later, its weakness, as the social changes of the twentieth century turned equilibrium into immobility.

In this context, a dual struggle was required of every social movement which wished to establish its social, political and economic influence – and, once established, to defend its *positions acquises* against the others. Firstly, it had to establish its representativeness and legitimacy *outside of* the corridors of power. Before 1871, this meant direct action – revolu-tionary or, indeed, counterrevolutionary. After 1871, this meant con-fronting a system of authority rigidified at two levels: the political level, breaking into which meant often the formation of a new political party (usually of the left – which is called *sinistrisme*); and the administrative level, dominated by a closed, aristocratic elite (although open to incre-mental bargaining through the intercession of *notables*).

On the left, then, protest politics was ever present. Either it represented a truly revolutionary set of objectives, as with the Commune of 1871, or it was the inevitable first step in a process of entry into the established system. Trade unions and left-wing political parties have, indeed, vacillated between revolution and entryism – but in either case a contestatory *style* of politics was an essential part of the development, self-image and legiti-mation of such a social movement. It was as much demanded by the conditions of the system as part of the post-1789 political culture, and not only was it an accepted necessary condition of left-wing politics, but it was also mimicked by extreme right-wing groups such as the nationalist *revanchistes* of General Boulanger and the anti-semitic groups of the late nineteenth century, who were succeeded by the *Action Française* and the quasi-fascist leagues of the 1930s. It could even be suggested that this contestatory style created a powerful form of cultural *feedback* which further exacerbated the rigidities of the system in the face of the challenges of the 1930s and the onset of the Second World War — not to mention the collapse of the Fourth Republic in the 1950s.

At the same time, the social changes of the late nineteenth and the twentieth century created growing sources of conflict. First the rural exodus and the economic boom prior to the First World War; then the war itself and the destruction and social changes which sprang from it; then the Great Depression: all took place in the context of the growing rigidity of the state, the increasing resonance of the urban working classes, and the mounting impact of external influences, both political and economic, which eroded the barriers of protectionism and the internal equilibrium of *positions acquises*. The result was an intensification of the politics of protest, from the workers, the farmers, the *petite bourgeoisie*, channelled into movements of both right and left — both conflicting and converging, as in the anti-parliamentary riots of February 1934 — and increasingly sceptical of the capacity of both the state and the economic structure to meet the challenge of the time.

That the modernisation revolution in France was catalysed in the wake of the crushing defeat of 1940 — in both the corporatist structures of Vichy and the political renewal of Free France — is by now common coin. Similarly, it is well known that the transformation of France into an advanced capitalist·society was carried out at the instigation of the state — or, at least, of certain parts of the state administration, while the political institutions of the Fourth Republic encouraged patterns of electoral and parliamentary politics reminiscent of the *immobilisme* of the Third. And the contribution of the Gaullist movement and the Fifth Republic was to consolidate this transformation in a new political regime which, in turn, changed the face of party and electoral politics.[7] At first, however, these changes seemed to reinforce the traditional pattern of protest politics. The isolation of the Communists in their political and social ghetto of the Cold War, along with the pacifist neutralism of much of the tradition of the non-Communist left, on the one hand, and the fierce reactions of the displaced rural and petty bourgeois groups — particularly the Poujadists — along with the strong resistance of the army and of colonial settler groups to the disintegration of the Empire, on the other created protest movements which outwardly fitted the traditional model.

Because of the strength of 'anti-system parties' in the National Assembly in the 1950s, and the growing instability of the regime itself prior to the collapse of the Fourth Republic in 1958 — Governments falling every six months on average — analyses of French politics understandably emphasised the continuities of French political behaviour — and, in particular, the interrelationship of destructive, moralistic protest politics with the rigidity and instability of the state, leading to vicious cycles of immobility and chaos. This image was extrapolated into a general theory of French administrative culture — and thence to French politics and society as a whole, through the notions of patterns of authority and styles of leadership.[8] What such theories did help to explain was the ways in which the residual cultural constraints — on both power-holders and protestors — affected the timing and development of protest movements: 'The non-participatory style of authority not only escalates conflicts physically, but also perpetuates their traditional ideological aspects long after the social bases of their ideologies have disappeared.'[9] In this context, the Events of May appeared (to quote Hoffmann again) as 'a typical revolt . . .':

> The truth is that . . . the revolutionary movement itself carried within it the seeds of its own destruction, and it grew in such a way as finally to appear as one more display of traditional protest. Most striking was the rebels' inability to step outside the style of authority they were attacking.[10]

But the 1968 Events were more than the replaying of an old record. This is not to say that traditional characteristics of French protest politics were absent; indeed, the tendency of the French left — and significant sections of the traditional conservative and old colonialist right — to dismiss the Fifth Republic as a temporary phase of quasi-dictatorial *pouvoir personnel* under their old *bête-noire*, General de Gaulle, seemed to confirm the old image of the vicious circle. But other developments had long since undermined the centrality of the traditional model. The old conflicts had been overtaken by the events of a quarter of a century. The rural exodus had turned into a flood, and the face of the agricultural economy had been transformed, as France became an urban industrial society. The French national economy had not only become more integrated internally, but had had to open itself up to greater interpenetration with the world capitalist economy after the Second World War — a process had taken a further leap with the establishment of the European Economic Community. Concentration and rationalisation in industry relegated artisan manufacture to certain specialised fields. And the reconversion strategies of French elites, which emphasised technical qualifications and expansion-minded business management, changed the face of the class system.

The old *positions acquises* were swiftly undermined — although the broad structure of the class system as a whole was, if anything, strengthened as the old upper classes claimed the commanding heights of advanced capitalism.[11] These changes were bought with the prosperity of the new economic growth characteristic of the Western capitalist economies as a whole in the 1950s and 1960s, and which had begun in France under the Fourth Republic only to gain momentum under the Fifth. Thus workers (including newly proletarianised members of the labour force) found full employment and rising real wages; farmers received state aid and the protection of the Common Agricultural Policy; the welfare state was gradually extended; and industrialists and financiers found state backing through the *économie concertée*. Old social cleavages were retired from centre stage; state aid to church schools, plus a certain radicalisation of sectors of French catholicism (which were active in the changes in the Church as a whole in the Second Vatican Council), defused the religious issue. And the bipolarisation of the party system, along with the growing salience of competitive presidential politics from 1965 onwards, not only integrated the diverse groups of the right — and condemned the extreme right to impotence — but led to the beginning of a process of the restructuring of the left, a process which, despite great setbacks in 1968–69 and again in 1977–78, eventually led to the Socialist victory in 1981.

It is interesting that the 1968 Events sprang from an uprising of students, for this group in some way both crystallises the traditional dynamic of protest and foreshadows the newer, emergent forms of today. On the one hand, the students in 1968 represented one of the groups left behind by social change. The huge growth in student numbers after the Second World War, and the traditional nature of much of the curriculum in the French university system, meant not only that students — whose very entry into university often stemmed from hopes of improved social status and income — were channelled into more and more limited areas of employment opportunity, but also that they were at a serious disadvantage in status terms compared with the limited numbers of technically-qualified graduates of the high-powered *grandes écoles*. They included both displaced elements of old elites and frustrated aspirants to elite status — forged in an intellectual environment in which radical and revolutionary thinking were deeply entrenched. On the other hand, however, they also formulated their objectives around analyses of advanced capitalist society, developing an ideology and a style grounded in the rejection of the technocratic state and of consumer society, and structured around the development not of revolutionary organisations but of common action and popular control from the base. Despite the rapid growth of the student-centred movement, however, and the temporary ineffectiveness of the state in controlling it, it rapidly collapsed — less in the face of repression than in the face of the decision to call parliamentary elections, which undermined the movement's claim to democratic legitimacy.

In recent years, then, France has not been characterised by protest politics of the old style. Opposition party politics has very much been channelled into competitive pluralism, in a way which has, if anything, strengthened the legitimacy of the Fifth Republic.[12] Many groups which would once have defined themselves in terms of opposition to the state in general have now been integrated into the pressure group system as *interlocuteurs valables*. The Communist Party now has four ministers in a Socialist Government, and the *rupture* with capitalism is no longer merely a subject for intellectual debate but a question of public policy. Leading Socialist (and, indeed, Communist) ministers are technocrats trained in the *grandes écoles*, and the revolutionary theorist Régis Debray is an adviser to the President of the Republic. But does this mean that protest is dead in France, that the revolutionary tradition has finally been absorbed and integrated into advanced capitalism?

The answers which are presented in this book do not point in this direction. In essence, we can see two sorts of trends. Firstly, there is the trend towards integration, a trend which is more marked in the case of groups whose demands can be satisfied through a process of bargaining within advanced capitalist society. We can see this trend most clearly in the case of the Poujadists; however, the trade unions too are moving towards integration at the level of both politics and collective bargaining, although this integration is also creating tensions within the unions which may undermine this process somewhat. Secondly, there is a trend towards increasing conflict, particularly among groups whose demands create real problems for the economic prosperity or social stability of French society. The issue of nuclear energy, given the absence of indigenous oil or coal in France, is one which even the Socialist Government is unlikely to be able to resolve. And the demands and aspirations of Feminism — a fundamental transformation of the social relations of reproduction — strike deep into the structures of all existing societies, advanced capitalist or otherwise.

On the whole, however, most social movements with the potential to take protest action are torn between the benefits of negotiation and integration, on the one hand, and a sense of powerlessness in the shadow of advanced capitalism, on the other. They vacillate. While the Socialist Government decides not to build some nuclear power stations but to complete others, the ecologists wait and discuss. While the decentralisation of regional and local administration is set into place, the Breton and Corsican groups wait to see whether it will permit sufficient expression of regionalist aspirations. Students welcome the repeal of the *loi Sauvage* and the re-democratisation of university councils, but, along with other youth groups, react angrily to the new Government's decision not to reduce compulsory military service from one year to six months despite a campaign promise to do so. And the disarray on the right of French politics raises the spectre of increased tension within the police — the recent Auriol Affair involving the SAC being the tip of the iceberg — as well as the possible recrudescence of racism and neo-fascism.

Conclusions

But this vacillation and tension is not surprising. Rather than being simply a recycling of the French revolutionary tradition, or even of traditional forms of protest, French protest today reflects the structural tensions and contradictions of advanced capitalist society. It may occasionally draw inspiration and rhetoric from the French revolutionary tradition, but its objectives, structures and dynamics have far more in common with protest movements in other advanced capitalist societies than with traditional forms stemming either from French history or from specifically French patterns of social and political authority. We should expect — given that advanced capitalist society is manifestly not free from internal tensions and crises — that the social movements which lie along the 'fault lines' of contemporary French society (as elsewhere) will lead to the continued relevance and effervescence of the politics of protest. Indeed, an understanding of protest will be of enormous importance in identifying and analysing the significance and the dynamics of those fault lines. The question which we ask about protest must ultimately reflect not merely the problems of one movement or one society, but those of advanced capitalism in general, and of the potential of protest movements to affect its present or to transform its future. This book, in examining the way in which social movements and protest in France have survived the decline of the revolutionary tradition and emerged in new forms in the 1970s and 1980s, aspires to make a modest contribution to this effort.

Phil Cerny
Paris, September 1981

Notes

1 For an analysis of some of these theoretical questions, see Anthony Giddens, *Capitalism and Modern Social Theory* (Cambridge: Cambridge University Press, 1971).

2 For France, see Hubert Cukrowicz, *L'homme en lambeaux: les effets du chômage consécutif à un licenciement sur les hommes de trente à cinquante ans* (Lille: Institut de Sociologie, Université de Lille-I, 1981).

3 Stanley Hoffman, 'The Ruled: Protest as a National Way of Life' in *Decline or Renewal? France since the 1930s* (New York: Viking, 1974), p. 112.

4 Alfred Grosser, 'France: Nothing but Opposition', in Robert A. Dahl, ed., *Political Oppositions in Western Democracies* (New Haven: Yale University Press, 1966).

5 See P. G. Cerny, 'The Fall of Two Presidents and Extraparliamentary Opposition: France and the United States in 1968', *Government and Opposition*, vol. 5, no. 2 (Summer 1970).

6 See P. G. Cerny, 'The Political Balance', in P. G. Cerny and M. A. Schain, eds., *French Politics and Public Policy* (London and New York: Frances Pinter and St. Martin's Press, 1980), ch. 1; Stanley Hoffmann, 'Paradoxes of the French Political Community', in Hoffmann *et al.*, *In Search of France* (Cambridge, Mass.: Harvard University Press, 1963), pp. 1–117; and Georges Dupeux, *French Society, 1789-1970* (London: Weidenfeld and Nicolson, 1973).

7 See P. G. Cerny, 'Gaullism, Advanced Capitalism and the Fifth Republic', in David S. Bell, ed., *French Political Parties* (London: Croom Helm, 1981).

8 See Michel Crozier, *The Bureaucratic Phenomenon* (London: Tavistock, 1964) and *La société bloquée* (Paris: Seuil, 1970): cf. Stanley Hoffman, 'Heroic Leadership: The Case of France', in L. J. Edinger, ed., *Political Leadership in Industrialised Socities* (New York: Wiley, 1967).

9 Hoffman, 'Confrontation in May 1968', in *Decline or Renewal?*, op. cit., p. 160.

10 Ibid., pp. 174–5.

11 See Jane Marceau, *Class and Status in France: Economic Change and Social Immobility, 1945-1975* (Oxford: Oxford University Press, 1977).

12 See P. G. Cerny, 'The Problem of Legitimacy in the Fifth French Republic', paper presented to the Workshop on Normative and Empirical Dimensions of Legitimacy, European Consortium for Political Research, Joint Workshops, University of Lancaster, 28 March–3 April 1981.

1 Dissentient France: The Counter Political Culture

JACK HAYWARD
Professor of Politics
University of Hull

In May–June 1981 the Fifth Republic successfully survived another challenge to its existence, so the boast of the former President, Valéry Giscard d'Estaing, in 1978 that it had become the second longest-lived regime since 1789 was not destined to be the self-congratulatory prelude to one of those premature obituaries in which political opponents and publicists have been all too inclined to indulge. This may therefore seem to be a paradoxical moment at which to offer some speculations upon French political culture that dwell upon the destabilising effects of its dualistic character, themselves deriving from an increasingly discordant relationship between the constituent elements of the French state on the one hand and of French society on the other. There are undoubted dangers in seeking to plunge below the surface of the apparently incontrovertible facts of perceptible political reality into the treacherous depths of shifting attitudes on the part of the French people towards the state, its agents, procedures, functions and values. However, if we are to try not merely to describe the 'facts' but to understand and explain them, we need to draw back somewhat and place them in a wider context, both temporal and socio-cultural. So as not simply to take refuge in a rarified stratosphere of generalisation, it will be necessary both to deploy some general evidence that appears to be consistent with these speculations and to venture some preliminary analyses of particular militant movements that seem to exemplify the dichotomy between an acquiescent and a dissentient France.

A Dual Political Culture: Acquiescent and Dissentient France

In the updated, early 1970s version of his remarkable early 1960s article on 'The Ruled: Protest as a National Way of Life', Stanley Hoffmann asked whether protest in France, far from being 'dysfunctional' or subversive to the social order, did not on the contrary, play a vital part in saving the individual from becoming a mere cog in society, and in saving the French body politic from the Scylla of violent conflict and the Charybdis of oppression.[1]

The answer he gives is not wholly clear because having castigated the French style of protest as totalistically destructive yet demagogically defeatist, he goes on to assert that the safety valve function of such protest was appropriate to a stalemate society that has passed away under the pressure of socio-economic change and state interventionism. Yet he maintains on the one hand that 'Even Utopian protest is functional in such a system. But the system is no longer functional for society'; while on the other hand 'the old system, dysfunctional perhaps, is assuredly self-perpetuating. It survives cries of protest (as in 1968) by piecemeal adjustments that appease the protesters for a while and thereby also give many of them a stake in the system.' The latter (relativist) view would imply the partial survival of a stalemate society despite the crises engendered by foreign and domestic pressures, while the former view implies that there is a clear disjunction between the immobilism of the 1930s and the modernising dynamism of the 1960s. Hoffmann concludes that 'Between command and dissent . . . participation is ruled out' but in the final essay entitled 'The State: For What Society?' he argues that 'there is no new balance, no new synthesis' and that the 'changes in French society could be explained only by assuming that the State is neither so indispensable nor so much a cause of paralysis as Crozier's analysis suggests.'

As this last comment implies, Hoffmann's conception of the relationship between state and society in France, while it has much in common with that of Crozier, is far less rigid and impermeable than the model represented by *The Bureaucratic Phenomenon* and subsequently reiterated and elaborated in general terms and in case studies, particularly of the French regional reforms of 1964 and 1972. The stalemate society is no longer a historically determined phase in French socio-political development; it represents France's indelible socio-cultural character, which has survived the transition from an archaic and rural society into a modern, industrial society virtually unchanged. The system's survival derives from the mutual support of its interdependent parts, despite the fact 'The gap between the politico-administrative system and social reality is increasing all the time.'[2] The fatalism of this approach is implausible in view of the highly pessimistic nature of the diagnosis of what is actually happening because, in the case of central-local relations, it is admitted that 'The general evolution of French society is strongly undermining the working of the system'; so much so that 'the urban exception is already more impotant than the rural rule.' Yet the partnership between the chief actors in the Crozierian system — the bureaucrats and the notables — is based upon 'sharing a common experience, complementary interests and identical values' which result in a 'conflictual complicity between bureaucrats and notables' that guarantees an integrative capacity to change without changing.

The attempts by both Hoffmann and Crozier to apply their variants of the same socio-cultural model to the 'events' of May 1968 exemplify the problems of regarding protest as essentially negative and dysfunctional, while looking to a systemic crisis to break the grip of the status quo. This kind of model tends to demonstrate that radical reform is not possible, while revolution has left an historical legacy of rhetoric that is wholly unrealistic in the context of a twentieth-century, advanced industrial society. So, despite reservations, what is left but acceptance of liberal capitalist economic and political norms and institutions? Crozier, in particular, clearly wishes France to evolve in an American direction in terms of the style of authority relations which would be more appropriate to a country evolving rapidly into an industrial and post-industrial society. This is evident also in the right-centre, liberal conservative writings of former President Giscard d'Estaing and Alain Peyrefitte,[3] who scarcely conceal a fascination with their idyllic vision of an Anglo-American style of consensus, pluralistic politics, in which abrasive *choix de société* are simply not on the agenda. The unrealism of such hopes — perhaps as utopian in their way as the aspirations of the liberal socialists — exemplifies the utopianism of the *notables*, just as the protagonists of *autogestion* reflect the utopianism of the *militants*. However, before we consider these champions of a counter political culture, let us briefly explore the evidence of how a sample of French provincial public perceived of their place in the changing relationships of state and society in 1974. This study is based upon a survey commissioned by Peyrefitte when, as Minister of Administrative Reforms, he was considering how to make the reorganisation of regional instituions in 1972 less of a fiasco than it was proving to be.

The results of the public opinion survey were so shocking to the official mind that Peyrefitte ignored them — along with the analysis provided in the Crozier–Thoenig report that was also commissioned — in presenting his findings on decentralisation, although he did subsequently refer to them in his critique of *Le Mal Français*.[4] The aspects upon which I shall dwell are those that relate to the three foci of dissent from the 'established disorder' which I shall be emphasising in the latter part of my remarks. These are the authoritarian and alienating character of an over-centralised and hierarchical system; the inegalitarian nature — in terms of access to power as well as in incomes and wealth — of the exploitative relations between socio-economic categories and classes; and the priority given to quantitative and material goods — maximising consumption of market-able commodities — at the cost of a decline in the quality of individual and social life. Given the purposes of the survey and the auspices under which it was conducted, it is naturally upon the first of these three issues that most evidence from public opinion is forthcoming.

Four attitude groups were distinguished on the basis of replies to a questionnaire about their relationship to the administration, which can be reduced to two for our purposes: the 68 per cent who are acquiescent (including those who are content, 18 per cent; those who are willing to 'wait and see', 36 per cent, and the downright defeatist, 14 per cent) and the dissentient 32 per cent who regard their situation as intolerable and who are disposed — at least verbally — to react unfavourably to admini-strative authority. Dissentients — described as 'aggressive' in the survey — are, firstly, disproportionately strongly represented among the young as against the old: 43 per cent in the 21–34 age group; 32 per cent in the 35–54 age group and 22 per cent among the 55-plus age group. (This finding is consistent with what we know from other sources about the support that militant protest groups receive, with public attitudes towards the May 1968 events and with the contrasting generational dispositions to the kinds of issues raised by dissenters.) There is a modest tendency for dissent to increase with income but the most interesting variable is socio-occupational category. The most dissentient are the white-collar employees and lower level staff (44 per cent) and manual workers (39 per cent) at one end of the spectrum, with small shopkeepers and artisans (28 per cent), farmers (26 per cent) and the inactive (21 per cent) at the other end. It is the more 'modern' element, the young urbanised workers and employees, who are most inclined to give expression to dissentient sentiments.[5]

The index of apocalyptic attitudes, based upon two out of three responses to the question — things cannot go on as they are at present, there will be an explosion one of these days — shows a markedly higher score than the dissentient index proper; at 64 per cent, the 2:1 propor-tions are almost reversed. While there is some similarity between the two indices — workers (71 per cent) and white collar and lower level staff (66 per cent) emerging as particularly inclined to take an 'apocalyptic' view of the future — in this case the small shopkeepers and artisans are also inclined (at 66 per cent) to take an especially apocalyptic view of the future. This is plausibly attributed by the survey report to the fact that the processes of modernisation are threatening the very existence of many members of this category but their defeatism means that they are less inclined to voice dissentient sentiments. Curiously, the farmers — many of whom have been sharing the mournful fate of their fellow small-scale producers and distributors — seem to take a less pessimistic view of the future, which the survey attributes to the influence of their organisations upon the government and the fact that they are less isolated in the face of hard times. This is confirmed by the response to other questions. The farmers are inclined to see themselves as part of a society with close and stable interpersonal relations rather than as a mass; while unlike the small shopkeepers and artisans, the farmers have access to local notables and are prepared to take the initiative in contacting them.

Acquaintance with and willingness to have recourse to notables declines among the mass of the disoriented urbanised population, especially among the white-collar staff and employees, who seem to be the least likely to have access to local notables (see Table 1.1). The survey detects a radical change in political culture amongst a small minority of the urbanised mass,

Table 1.1 *Acquaintance with and Recourse to Notables by Socio-occupational Category (%)**

Socio-occupational Category	Acquaintance	Recourse
Farmers	94	84
Higher managerial and bigger businessmen	62	70
Small shopkeepers and artisans	60	60
White collar staff and employees	48	64
Manual Workers	55	64
Inactive	57	63
All	62	66

*Adapted from A. Peyrefitte et al, *Décentraliser les responsabilités*, pp. 96–7.

who adopt militant action through associations, rather than looking for salvation to the traditional notables. Far from shunning conflict and face-to-face relations, they accept that as agents of change they must regard conflict as legitimate rather than deal in the consensus stock in trade of the notable. However, while 94 per cent of respondents believed that associations of local residents, consumers, environmentalists and the like were an excellent development and 86 per cent considered that such associations were certainly increasing in number, 62 per cent stated that they would be surprised if they would be particularly effective. So, we are back with a majority political culture that looks to the notables to act in the traditional way with the state system, whether to exert influence or to take the decision and a minority political culture that stresses associated self help to overcome citizen powerlessness.

As Pierre Grémion (the most original of the members of Crozier's school) has indicated, there is no shortage of associations in France. Their predicament is that they find it hard to avoid either the strait-jacket of being absorbed or tamed by the 'bureaucratic-notable system' on the one hand, or being marginalised by exclusion from the system and thereby reduced to impotent if vociferous dissent.[6] In France of all countries, the attempts to create not merely a pluralist style of politics but one in which industrial democracy, self-management and self-government are to become the models for public activity, scarcely seem to be practicable objectives. The proponents of such a programme are seeking to dislodge not merely the 'bureaucratic-notable system' but also the 'political professionals' — the party activists as well as the party leaders — who have sought to monopolise the function of change agent.

It is the political parties — especially those of the left — that have seen it as their function to identify the cause of dissatisfaction; to have sufficient resources to formulate and publicise an alternative programme to substitute for the existing system; to build a winning coalition based upon its internal cohesion and alliance with supporting movements. While in its 'counter-society' role, the PCF has for periods of its history sought to canalise dissent in a partisan fashion and through a proliferation of specialised, satellite mass organisations to expropriate the sources of protest, the evolution of the party during the Fifth Republic has primarily been to accommodate itself to bourgeois-capitalist society rather than to emphasise its alienation from it. For its part, the post-1971 Socialist Party has sought to incorporate as many as possible of the new forces of dissent, including those we shall examine shortly. Finally, the various incarnations of the 'Gaullist' party have sought to attract elements among the *forces vives* who would accept collaboration with the system. Some notable 1960s successes were the attraction into the fold of farm leaders such as Michel Debatisse and Marc Becam or regionalist leaders such as Joseph Martray of the Breton CELIB.

The peasantry, which traditionally accepted exclusion from political involvement, sealed off latterly by organisations that controlled rural society and mediated on its behalf with the state and the commercial market, taking over the traditional role of priests and landowners, were faced with a choice after the Second World War. Confronted with rapid economic change in the countryside, would they adapt their corporative response into a pressure-group collaborative conflict with government? The majority took this line and followed Michel Debatisse, who reflected a right-wing evolution from the left-Catholic *Jeunesse Agricole Chrétienne*, via the *Centre National des Jeunes Agriculteurs*, through the conservative peak farm organisation, the FNSEA. The minority, where the peasantry had been politically organized, tended to move leftward, following champions such as the Breton Bernard Lambert, author of *Les paysans dans la lutte des classes*, which should be contrasted with Debatisse's *La révolution silencieuse, le combat des paysans* of a decade earlier. The development of Debatisse into an influential notable and the confinement of Lambert into an impotent activist exemplify the working of the system as described by Pierre Grémion. Marc Becam went even further by leaving his farm organisation post in South Finistère to become first an RPR deputy and then a minister. Thus, what began as a Social Catholic corporatist avoidance of contamination by politics has ended in an incorporation into the state policy of reorganising agriculture along semi-capitalist lines.[7]

The Activist Model in Operation: Three Examples

Rather than dismissing the protest movements as anachronistic and retrograde, disruptive and dysfunctional parts of the French problem of how to develop into a modern industrial society and what kind of modern industrial society it wishes to become, we propose to argue that they have often performed a positive and innovative function in trying to make modernisation a more elevated process than merely accelerating the flight forward. A former CFDT leader claimed in 1977 with some vehemence that

> none of the new ideas that have been transforming French society over the last ten years have come from the politicians; all, without exception, have been launched by small groups, intellectual for the most part, or have been spread from the collective experience derived from life or struggle. The parties have done nothing towards this; on the contrary, they have often acted as a brake.[8]

If we focus upon the movements that have offered an alternative conception of society and have popularised protest against three of the less attractive features of contemporary society — its authoritarianism, its inegalitarianism and its consumerism — as well as those that champion the defence of the cultural identities of submerged nations, we may go some way towards vindicating Julliard's claim that constructive innovation has been primarily a matter of militant initiatives from below. The notables have been too preoccupied with managing the system and protecting their privileges to question their basic assumptions. Because of its greater range, its greater influence and because it has had a major part in transforming the sclerotic SFIO into a dynamic Socialist Party — demonstrating its capacity to modernise in the political sphere proper — both in terms of its programme, its strategy and its personnel, let us begin with the CFDT and concentrate upon it.

Unlike the traditional parties of the left and the PCF-controlled CGT, the CFDT has not made the conquest of state power the be-all and end-all of its activities. Like the revolutionary syndicalists of the late nineteenth and early twentieth centuries, it sets great store by the need for social organisations themselves to have a capacity to bring about the desired social transformation. While not denying the need for political parties of the left to play an indispensable part in abolishing a situation character-ised by economic exploitation, social inequality and political alienation, the CFDT leaders are not prepared to concede this function to political leaders and confine themselves to improving the conditions of work and remuneration of their members. In this sense they reject both the Leninist model of the trade union acting as the industrial extension of a Communist party that is the vanguard of the working class and the Labourist model of the trade union as the parent and paymaster of its own political party, which becomes the political extension of the trade union movement. Although Jean-Daniel Reynaud's description of the CFDT's position as one of ' "total" trade unionism'[9] is doubly misleading in implying the union's capacity to assume comprehensive responsibility for all aspects of the life of the workers (whereas the CFDT does not have such an inordinate ambition) and yet seeks to shape society for more than just a narrowly defined working class, the denomination does capture the societal significance of the CFDT enterprise. (In the words of the CFDT's General Secretary Edmond Maire: 'the working class includes more than the wage and salary earners; all those who in contemporary society are conscious that society alienates and exploits them belong to it . . .'.[10]) Whereas the political parties at elections engaged in alarmist shadow boxing about whether the choice between left and right coalitions involved an implausible *choix de société*, the CFDT is clearly and explicitly in the business of devising an alternative society based upon the conception of self-management and self-government: *autogestion*.[11]

Now *autogestion* is one of those resonant but obscure (and almost untranslatable) words that make excellent mobilising myths but do not necessarily evoke more than unattainable aspirations. The way a CFDT spokesman presents the matter is that 'The definition of a self-managed society is a society instituting and building itself. If self-management is a *projet de société*, it is not a *modèle de société* to be achieved. Self-management is *both* a method and a direction of social change'.[12] The experimental and pragmatic way in which the CFDT conducted its evolution away from being an anti-class conflict, Catholic trade union into a protagonist of such conflict, via the advocacy in the late 1950s and early 1960s of 'democratic planning' (which could be interpreted in an incorporatist as well as in a dissentient sense) indicates how a grassroots movement discovers what needs to be changed and how it should be done by starting from specific practical situations. One of its leaders refers to the CFDT's 'sort of pedagogical method, which consists of launching ideas, accepting them as such and then gradually going more thoroughly into them, devising ways of applying them, living them and achieving them'.[13] Movement is proved by walking, rather than by a theory of movement.

In early 1965, the CFDT launched the idea of *autogestion*, though not until the 1968 May events did it become clear that the aspirations it embodied were shared quite widely among the adherents of the counter political culture. In subsequent years the CFDT, at first in informal association with the PSU and then with the Socialist Party, worked out the ideas that influenced — in conjunction with the Communist Party — the Common Programme of the Left. Neither the CFDT nor the PSU supported this Programme in 1972 because it reflected the over-centralist 'Jacobin illusion' and relied too much upon nationalisation rather than upon altering the methods by which industry was managed. The change in the CFDT's 'political partner' was in part connected with the close personal link between Edmond Maire, General Secretary of the CFDT, and Michel Rocard, General Secretary of the PSU from 1967-73, who joined the Socialist Party in 1974.[14] However, the PSU was not a political party in the full sense of the word. It was more a sort of intellectual pressure group, an ideological forcing house which, like the CFDT, has provided the reunified Socialist Party with many of its most active members. It has been actively involved not merely in the specifically *autogestionnaire* movement, but also in the regionalist struggle against internal colonialism and in the environmentalist movements, of which more anon. As an incorrigible protest movement, operating on the margin of the system, it refused to join in the Common Programme of the Left.

The CFDT also kept its distance from the Common Programme in the name of trade union independence, while not concealing its sympathy with many aspects of the programme. As well as its increasing informal links with the Socialist Party — maintained strictly at that level, notably by forbidding in 1972 the combination of office in trade unions and political parties or in national (but not local) government, to avoid creeping *notabilisation* — the CFDT was acquiring a more friendly relationship with the Communist Party, until the 1977–8 onslaught of the PCF on the PS. This had been helped by the PCF adoption of much of the CFDT terminology that it had previously ridiculed: *autogestion*, democratic planning and the reduction of inequality in earnings, although it is dubious whether this was more than a matter of political expediency. The PCF had, after all, no new ideas to put in the place of the old Stalinist programme which was repugnant to anyone other than its traditional voters and was proving less attractive to some of these and particularly to the intellectual wing of the party.

The Communist Party — and its leaders in the CGT — still tax the CFDT with falling victim to the reformist illusion that it is possible to change society without first seizing the state. However, the CFDT believes that the old reformist-revolutionary antithesis is a false one and that the PCF has ceased to be revolutionary in the old insurrectionist sense. Instead of the 'withering away of the state' being postponed *ad infinitum*, one of the attractions of the self-management approach to social change is that it reinstates, theoretically and practically, the liberal priority of society over the state not merely at the end of the historical process but throughout its duration. In the 1960s, the CFDT successfully resisted the Gaullist regime's attempt to inveigle it, through involvement in a planning process which would be made more 'democratic', into following the incorporatist road along which Debatisse has led the bulk of the farmers. Homeopathic doses of incremental reform to enable the system to 'change without changing' does not interest the CFDT. Nor does the transformation of the 'stalemate society' into a neo-Saint-Simonian order run jointly by public and private sector bankers and industrials, meritocratic bureaucrats and technocrats, scientists and technologists, social engineers and their supporting cohort of hack apologists and publicists, tempt them into the collaborationist embrace. Such *récupération* of dissent is resisted as firmly as the romantic adventure into anything other than a cultural revolution, aimed at changing the values, the purposes and the procedures of a would-be democratic society, economy and polity.

Although, as we shall see, attempts have been made to link autonomist protests with *autogestion* as its territorial-cum-cultural aspect, the main intellectual basis for the reassertion of regional identity within

France has been, since the early 1960s, based upon the internal colonialist model. The attractions of such a model, in the wake of the concern with overseas decolonisation in the preceding decade, are obvious. Although there have been movements of varying vigour in the seven minority areas — Alsace, the Basque country, Brittany, Catalonia, Corsica, Flanders and Occitania — let us use one of the most assertive of such regionalist movements to exemplify the challenge to a culturally repressive, politically and administratively over-centralised, and economically exploitative French state.

While regional protests in the post-war period initially took the form of a non-separatist, regional economic and cultural pressure group, the *Comité d'Etudes et de Liaison des Intérêts Bretons*, this highly effective organisation was practically destroyed by the French Government thanks to its 1964 regional reform, the 'betrayal of the notables' and cooptation of a key Breton leader, Joseph Martray, while another key leader, Michel Phlipponneau, joined the Socialist Party.[15] The 'internal colonialism' thesis had already been advanced by the leaders of the nationalist *Mouvement pour l'Organisation de la Bretagne* (MOB), which sought autonomy for Brittany and it was to be taken up more generally by the leader of Occitan nationalism, Robert Lafont.[16] In a series of books, Lafont initially took an apolitical regionalist line before he in turn identified regionalism with the *autogestion* wing of the Socialist cause in 1976 in a rather discursive discussion of *Autonomie, de la région à l'autogestion*, which despite his disclaimer, smacks of jumping on an ideological bandwagon.[17] Michel Rocard, in his PSU phase, took up the theme of decolonisation within France generally in the mid-1960s, arguing that the loss of freedom of decision in administrative, political, economic and financial matters was even more important than economic and cultural deprivation. 'It is the nature of decision-making power that is at issue. We must examine the conditions of autonomous development.'[18] However, Rocard saw the remedy in the relatively conventional terms of decentralisation and democratisation, although he advocated increased local participation at the grassroots level to deal with the most immediate concerns of everyday life. In Brittany, this approach to the problem of regionalist protest was adopted by the *Union Démocratique Bretonne*, after it broke away from MOB in 1964.[19] It moved close to the new Socialist Party in the 1970s and won thirty-six seats in twenty-eight communes at the 1977 local elections on United Left lists. However, its poor showing in the legislative elections of 1978 (it secured less than 2 per cent of the vote in the seats contested) demonstrated that when it put up its own candidates, the UDB was not a serious political force in terms of public support.

The official failure before the Socialist victory in 1981 to move significantly in the direction of acknowledging the need to decentralise power, notably by creating directly elected regional councils with elected regional executives, has meant that there has been no choice other than that between submission and more or less violent demonstrations of resentment. The blowing up of tax offices and other official installations, as well as rhetoric about the practice of cultural and economic genocide, has been the stock in trade, since 1966, of the right-wing *Front de Libération de la Bretagne* (FLB)[20] and there have been similar challenges to the French state in Corsica. These miniscule movements have not managed to acquire more than nuisance value and have been used by the Breton and Corsican notables as a lever to extract economic concessions from Paris, their price for restoring calm. The big question mark for the future is whether the political parties of the left have the will to overcome their traditional Jacobinism and to concede a measure of self-government to peoples such as the Bretons or whether the expressions of dissent will be dismissed as hiccoughs caused by France's unduly prolonged national indigestion.

Turning in conclusion to a manifestation of dissentient France that has achieved notoriety more recently than the regionalists and the autonomists, environmentalist groups have been coming into existence in the mid-1970s at the rate of fifteen to twenty associations per week. A survey in Autumn 1977 of the attitudes of environmentalist activists suggests that just under a fifth of them adopt a strictly apolitical attitude towards ecological issues while over 50 per cent identify themselves with the left – though usually not with a major left-wing party – and 20 per cent did not reply. (The surprisingly good electoral results achieved by the environmentalists in the 1977 local elections and their more disappointing performance in the 1978 and 1981 elections were indicative that their attempt to move from a cause pressure group into the partisan field proper was a failure, although they may continue to play a significant part in local politics.) Over 70 per cent regard themselves as close to the *autogestion* group of movements but '*autogestion* is felt as a confused need, a sort of dream, without yet being aware of how it can be put into practice'.[21] Fifty per cent consider that links with trade unions are desirable, the union favoured being the CFDT. More generally, as a leader of the Paris branch of Friends of the Earth put it,

There exist within the left centrifugal, anti-statist, anti-productivist movements, inheritors in large measure of the anarcho-syndicalist tradition: PSU, CFDT, non-violent movements, regionalist and autonomist movements, etc. For years, it is with all these people that the environmentalists have been fighting, side by side. This '*auto-gestionnaire*' movement is the natural ally of the environmentalists.[22]

Fred Hirsch has demonstrated that even if one discounts the more extravagant manifestations of such movements, there is a general reason for the inability of both the political system and the market in advanced industrial societies to meet the expectations that they have generated. He points out that the 'mismatch between current expectations and resources is qualitative rather than quantitative', so simply dwelling upon the latter aspect

> has obscured the extent of the modern conflict between individualistic actions and the satisfaction of individualistic preferences ... The traditional liberal opportunities, which are still held out as a prospect attainable by all ... are available only to a minority. Tensions and frustrations have inevitably resulted ... Economic liberalism is ... a victim of its own propaganda: offered to all, it has evoked demands and pressures that cannot be contained.[23]

Hirsch has shown that the increase in the provision of material goods and services has been accompanied by a reduction in quality, while 'positional' goods and services or social relations — the particular concern of environmentalist groups — are absolutely or socially scarce and are subject to congestion and crowding. The frustrations produced by such social scarcities and qualitative deteriorations will not be remedied by an accentuation of commodity fetishism, whereby the market is required to produce even more of the specific commodities and services that it can do efficiently.

The sort of conflicts between the French state and sections of French society on which we have dwelt will doubtless be dismissed by many observers of the contemporary scene as more or less exotic by-products of the process of rapid modernisation which France has been undergoing. Some will regret that the French people in 1981 accepted the pseudo-*choix de société* they were offered and refused to resign themselves to the mixture as before. Others will look to the victorious Socialist Party, which owed its revitalisation in the 1970s in no small measure to the input in ideas and personnel from the protest movements, to undertake the task of trying to install some of these 'new men' in power to implement some of these ideas. The success of the former opposition parties in removing the right from office provides an opportunity for some of the politically imaginative movements constituting dissentient France to exert greater influence upon the institutionalised left, by exploring the boundaries and potentialities of the existing political and economic system. 1968 showed that action at the societal level alone was unable to do more than modify the deep-seated values of the system with consequences emerging at the surface only in the longer term. 1978 showed that action at the state level alone was not able to bring about short-term change in public policy. In 1981, has France at last engendered the appropriate mediating movement, linking 'state' and 'society' in the process of synchronising change in social values and state action with public support? Despite its highly significant role, the CFDT has been too weak to assume this task hitherto. And the Socialist Party, once in power, may be tempted by traditional social-democratic remedies of reform 'from the top down'. It remains to be seen whether it can mobilise mass public support for comprehensive social change by linking the somewhat esoteric call for *autogestion* to the solution of the public's immediate and pressing problems. Meantime, the effervescences and eruptions occurring within the counter political culture will merit at least an occasional glance from those whose eyes are habitually focused upon the conformist activities within the confines of the 'bureaucratic-notable system'.

Notes

1 S. Hoffmann, *Decline or Renewal? France since the 1930s* (New York: The Viking Press, 1974), chapter 5, p. 133. Subsequent quotations, ibid., pp. 143–4, 449, 473.

2 Michel Crozier and Jean-Claude Thoenig, 'L'importance du système politico-administratif territorial' in Alain Peyrefitte et al., *Décentraliser les responsibilités. Pourquoi? Comment?* (Paris: La Documentation Française, 1976), p. 14. Subsequent quotations, ibid., pp. 12, 6. For other statements of this position, see Michel Crozier, *La société bloquée* (Paris: Editions du Seuil, 1970), and Michel Crozier et al., *Où va l'administration française?* (Paris: Les Editions d'Organisation, 1974). For a more general criticism of the Hoffmann and Crozier conceptions of protest, see Sidney Tarrow, 'From Cold War to Historic Compromise: Approaches to French and Italian Radicalism', in chapter 4 of S. Bialer, ed., *Radicalism in the Contemporary Age* (New York: Praeger, 1977), pp. 221–31.

3 See two political best-sellers of 1976: V. Giscard d'Estaing, *Démocratie française* (Paris: Fayard, 1976) and Alain Peyrefitte, *Le mal français* (Paris: Plon, 1976).

4 See pp. 441–3. See also Peyrefitte's introduction to *Décentraliser les responsabilités*, op. cit., pp. 1–11.

5 In *Décentraliser les responsabilités*, op. cit., pp. 25–32, Elie Sultan and Clarence Preiss, 'Les citoyens et l'administration' a COFREMCA survey conducted in July 1974 in the Allier, Hérault and the Somme. Subsequent quotations, ibid., pp. 50–71, 92–3, 99.

6 Pierre Grémion, 'L'autogestion politique', *Projet* (April, 1977), p. 413. See also his *Le pouvoir périphérique: bureaucrates et notables dans le système politique français* (Paris: Editions du Seuil, 1976), pp. 248–67.

7 See Suzanne Berger, *Peasants Against Politics: Rural Organization in Brittany, 1911-1967* (Cambridge, Mass.: Harvard University Press, 1972). See also John Ardagh, *The New France* (Harmondsworth: Penguin, 1970), chapter 4 on 'The Young Farmers' Revolt'.

8 Jacques Julliard, *Contre la politique professionnelle* (Paris: Editions du Seuil, 1977), p. 102.

9 J.-D. Reynaud, 'Trade Unions and Political Parties in France: Some Recent Trends', *Industrial and Labor Relations Review* (January, 1975), p. 212. For reservations in 1971 by a CFDT leader on the concept of 'total trade unionism', see *La CFDT* (Paris: Editions du Seuil, 1971), p. 181.

10 *La CFDT*, p. 177. For illuminating cultural contrasts between trade union strategies in France and Britain, see Duncan Gallie, *In Search of the New Working Class* (Oxford: Oxford University Press, 1978), parts 4 and 5 *passim*.

11 See the Report by the CFDT President André Jeanson to its 35th Congress in May 1970 entitled 'Perspectives et stratégie', published in *La CFDT*, op. cit., p. 130; cf. 125 ff. See also Edmond Maire and Jacques Julliard, *La CFDT d'aujourd'hui* (Paris: Editions du Seuil, 1975), chapter 7.

12 Pierre Rosanvallon , *L'âge de l'autogestion* (Paris: Editions du Seuil, 1976), p. 83.

13 André Jeanson in *La CFDT*, op. cit., p. 174.

14 Jean-François Bizot, *Au parti des socialistes: plongée libre dans les courants d'un grand parti* (Paris: Grasset, 1975), appendix 2, 'Chronique d'un renouveau idéologique: le socialisme autogestionnaire'.

15 See Michel Phlipponneau, *Debout Bretagne!* (Saint-Brieuc: Presses Universitaires de Bretagne, 1970), chapter 4; Joseph Martray, *La région: pour un Etat moderne* (Paris: Editions France-Empire, 1970), pp. 47-71. See also J. E. S. Hayward, 'From Functional Regionalism to Functional Representation in France: the Battle of Brittany', *Political Studies*, vol. XVII, no. 1 (March, 1969), pp. 48-75 and L. Quéré and R. Dulong, 'Mouvements sociaux en Bretagne', *Sociologie du Travail*, no. 3 (1974), pp. 247-64.

16 Ned Urvoas, 'Vers le Front Breton', *L'Avenir*, no. 44 (September, 1961), quoted in Jack E. Reece, *The Bretons against France: Ethnic Minority Nationalism in Twentieth-Century Brittany* (Chapel Hill: University of North Carolina Press, 1977), p. 244; cf. 191-2, 198-205, 212, 228-31. More specifically, for an application of the 'internal colonialism' thesis, see Jack Hayward, 'Institutionalized Inequality within an Indivisible Republic: Brittany and France', *Journal of the Conflict Research Society*, vol. I (August, 1977), pp. 1-15. On the appropriateness of the internal colonial model to France in general and Brittany in particular see Eugen Weber's engrossing *Peasants into Frenchmen: The Modernization of Rural France, 1870-1914* (London: Chatto & Windus, 1977), chapter 29.

17 (Paris: Gallimard, 1976), pp. 18-19, 76-7; cf. 12, 15. See his *La révolution régionaliste* (Paris: Gallimard, 1967), *Sur la France* (Paris: Gallimard, 1968) and *Décoloniser en France* (Paris: Gallimard, 1971).

18 *Décoloniser la province*, Rapport Général sur la Vie Régionale en France, Recontre Socialiste de Grenoble (1966), p. 18.

19 On the UDB, see Reece, op. cit., pp. 195-8; Renaud Dulong, *La question bretonne* (Paris: Presses de la Fondation Nationale des Sciences Politiques, 1975), pp. 26-8, 139-41, 204-5 and Daniel Chatelain and Pierre Tafani, *Qu'est-ce qui fait courir les autonomistes?* (Paris: Stock, 1976), pp. 95-111.

20 On the FLB, see Reece, pp. 200-20 and Ronan Caerléon, *La revolution bretonne permanente* (Paris: La Table Ronde, 1969).

21 Claude-Marie Vadrot, *L'écologie, histoire d'une subversion* (Paris: Syros, 1978), p. 204; cf. 198 ff. and chapter 3 *passim*.

22 Laurent Samuel, 'La tentation de l'apolitisme' (March, 1977), quoted by Vadrot, op. cit., p. 96. On the CFDT's environmentalist preoccupations, see CFDT, *Les*

dégâts du progrès, les travailleurs face au changement technique (Paris: Editions du Seuil, 1977).

23 Fred Hirsch, *Social Limits to Growth* (London: Routledge & Kegan Paul, 1977), pp. 9-11; cf. 26-7, 67, 89. For rather different analyses of the counter-culture phenomenon, particularly in the USA, see Theodore Roszak, *The Making of a Counter Culture, Reflections on the Technocratic Society and its Youthful Opposition* (London: Faber & Faber, 1970), chapters 1-2 and Daniel Bell, 'The Cultural Contradictions of Capitalism', in Daniel Bell and Irving Kristol, eds, *Capitalism Today* (London: The New English Library, 1972), chapter 2.

The author would like to thank the Nuffield Foundation for their help in connection with this study.

2 Student Activism in France: 1968 and After

CHRIS ROOTES
Lecturer in Sociology
University of Kent at Canterbury

Of all the societies which experienced radical student movements in the late 1960s, it was only France in which a student movement precipitated a national political crisis of such severity that it even briefly appeared likely to issue in the revolutionary overthrow of the regime. It is easy, in restrospect, to see that revolution was not a likely outcome; but the occasion in May 1968 when students erected barricades in the boulevards of Paris and fought pitched battles with the CRS still stands in popular imagination as the apogee of the international student revolt.

Yet if the French May is to be glamourised as the most impressive achievement among Western student movements, there are certain features of it which are anomalous by comparison with other Western cases. The French events were unusual in the suddenness of their eruption, the rapidity and extent of their spread from the metropolis to the provinces, and the precipitateness with which they declined. Not surprisingly, the student revolt has been interpreted in the light of the explosive character of other social movements in France and the attempt made to explain it in terms of the peculiarities of French culture and attitudes, particularly towards authority. Schonfeld, for example, depicts the 'explosion' as a *chahut* − a cathartic rebellion by people whose attitude toward authority, learned in the school system, is dualistic, embracing both need and fear.[1]

Other writers have suggested that the culprit is less the peculiarities of the French than those of the French social and political structure. The common element in the analyses of writers as diverse as Aron,[2] Crozier[3] and Touraine[4] is their insistence upon the peculiarly archaic structure of authority in what is, in terms of technology, a modern and advanced society: the contradictions between hierarchy and authoritarian rigidity on the one hand and the requirements of modernity on the other are inherently explosive. It is, they suggest, these features of French society rather than any peculiar characteristic of French student protestors which gave the May events their character and translated the protests of a few hundred students into the gravest national crisis since the Liberation.

Touraine in particular is at pains to dismiss the argument that the student movement ran deepest in France because it was there that it came closest to precipitating the overthrow of the government. Revolutionary explosions occur, argues Touraine, not where 'revolutionary' consciousness is most developed but in situations where the existing institutions are insufficiently flexible to be able successfully to negotiate conflict.[5] Indeed, Touraine goes so far as to claim that among industrialised societies the French situation was the *least* favourable to the formation of a student movement: as a semi-industrialised country France still had a semi-revolutionary labour movement, and a well-developed left-wing intelligentsia already existed to lead political and cultural criticism. The vacuum, the absence of opposition, which student movements were required to fill in authoritarian states like Spain and Greece where normal democratic opposition could not exist or in democratic ones like the United States or Germany where the ruling consensus left major political issues outside the arena of conventional politics, did not exist in France. Yet a student movement did develop and if it shook French society more than its German or American counterparts did their respective societies, it was not because of its 'natural orientation, which most often resembled those of other student movements' but because of the condition of French society.[6]

In order to evaluate some of the claims and counterclaims about the uniqueness or otherwise of the French manifestations of student activism, it is necessary to look more closely at the May movement, its antecedents and the reasons for its decline. Equally, it will be useful to consider the development of student activism in France after 1968 because for all that it declined it did not vanish entirely and it was, in 1976, once again to issue in demonstrations and strikes which closed universities and colleges across the nation.

I. The May Movement

Considering the avalanche of publications stimulated by the May events, it is remarkable that so little of it should have attempted any systematic investigation of the students who were the detonators of the crisis as distinct from the condition of French society at large. Compared with the accumulation of studies of roughly contemporaneous developments in the United States, the empirical social scientific investigation of the French student revolt was modest indeed: no survey specifically directed at student activists was conducted and no survey even of a broader cross-section of students was conducted before September 1968.[7] Moreover, despite the fact that student protest was at the time prominent almost throughout the industrialised world, little· attempt was made to compare the French events, their origins and sequelae with student movements elsewhere.[8]

In many respects, the student revolt itself was swamped by the political crisis it touched off. It happened to coincide with a period of much wider political disaffection among the population at large,[9] and especially once that disaffection had issued in massive strike action and political crisis, it is not too surprising that the concerns of students were dwarfed by comparison.

Yet the fact remains that the French 'explosion' occurred relatively late and took by surprise those observers of the American and German events who had so recently remarked on the singular peacefulness of French universities. The events of May were not, however, entirely without portents. In 1966-7 the University of Strasbourg erupted and announced many of the themes and slogans later to appear in the debates and on the walls of the lecture theatres of Paris. With the start of the 1967-8 year, rumblings of discontent were louder and more widespread, especially at Nanterre, and the May Day march attracted 50,000 participants, the largest number since the Algerian War. Yet still the outbreak of rioting in the Latin Quarter seemed to take everyone quite by surprise.[10]

Why did the French revolt occur so relatively late and not until the examples of the Americans and the Germans were clear before them? No doubt contingent political factors are a part of the explanation: there was no mobilising issue such as Vietnam provided in the United States. Furthermore, 1967 was an election year in which the left, as expected, did well and it was only when the implications of their defeat became clear — as they did with the onset of recession and the arrogation of powers of rule by decree to the Prime Minister, Pompidou — that extra-legal opposition was to be expected. The long and tortured history of French student organisations themselves was an ambiguous legacy, but probably an inhibitory one. Students had, through UNEF (*Union Nationale des Etudiants de France*), been a principal focus of opposition to successive administrations during the Algerian War and through the early sixties had conducted mass action campaigns against the inadequacies of government provision for education, but UNEF had, in the interim, been wracked by internal disputes[11] and considerably weakened. At the same time, the Communist student organisation had fractured and the extreme left *groupuscules* soon to loom so large in the demonology of France began to emerge. It is noteworthy that the student revolt began not at the traditional Sorbonne where both the UNEF and the *groupuscules* were strong, but at the new and relatively liberal Nanterre where they were weak. For all that there was something of a tradition of students performing the role of a political opposition in France, it was by no means the case that the revolt was planned or manufactured by UNEF or the *groupuscules*.

The 'explosion' of May 1968 was both unexpected and unpredicted. Much of its theory, its practice and its perspectives emerged only in the course of the largely spontaneous mobilisation itself. And yet, paradoxically, the events were also a culmination of processes of development which occurred within the student movement,[12] or at least within the far left part of it, during the years 1964 to 1968 when both UNEF and the UEC (*Union des Etudiants Communistes*) were riven by conflicts and disabled by crisis. The extraordinary social and political conjuncture of the May events produced a situation in which fleeting but recurrent themes within the student left could be made concrete.[13] Certainly the movement was not and could not have been created by any of the political groups which predated it, but for all that those groups became caught up in something not of their own making they were able, willy nilly, to contribute to it something of their own experience and to develop through it strains of theory that were hitherto only nascent within their own rather sectarian politics.[14] If, as Abboud correctly observes, May provided students with the opportunity to break out of the university ghetto, so too it provided the *groupuscules* with the opportunity to flower beyond the confines of their sects, and those which were least dogmatic and more open (like the *Jeunesse Communiste Révolutionnaire*) did so to best effect. Indeed, as Nairn observed, given the opportunity to cooperate in action, they were prevented from indulging in the internecine warfare of theoretical dispute which characterised relations among them in more normal times.

One of the contributions of both UNEF and the *groupuscules* was to the movement's rapid diffusion,[15] although in a society as centralised as France diffusion is not in any case as difficult to achieve as in so decentralised and spatially segregated a society as the United States. Nor is the spread to the *lycées* quite so remarkable when it is remembered that the *lycées*, at least the more important of them, more closely resemble good American junior colleges than high schools[16] and that the average age of *lycée* students was rather higher than that of secondary school students in Britain or the United States.

The events of May and June 1968 are too well-documented elsewhere[17] to warrant any further account of them here but some expansion is necessary upon two points which have been the subject of particular contention: the motivations of the mass of activists and the processes of the movement's decline.

Although the view most commonly encountered in the literature is that student activism in France was, as elsewhere, a politics of moral rather than material interests,[18] there have been a number of attempts to ascribe the principal motivation for involvement in the protests to anxieties about employment prospects (Schonfeld, Boudon[19]), to a corporate resistance to planned reforms of the university (Schonfeld) or to the quasi-class consciousness of an emerging social class (Touraine). In so far as these arguments are based upon the evidence of surveys or interviews, it is invariably upon interviews or surveys conducted well after the events themselves, asking questions ill-suited to the imputation of personal motives and failing to discriminate between respondents according to the degree of their involvement in the actual events.

Arguments to the contrary have also drawn upon survey evidence, most notably Inglehart's treatment of May 1968 as a prime manifestation of the post-materialist revolution which he believes is sweeping the younger cohorts of Western societies. In a July 1968 survey Inglehart found that young, middle-class people (from whom most students are drawn) were much more likely to give 'radical', non-materialist reasons for participating in protest than were older middle-class people or, more particularly, working-class respondents. Indeed, asked to select three choices of reason for protesting, 16 per cent of the whole middle-class group selected solely 'radical' reasons, compared with 2 per cent for the working class.[20] In a later survey, O'Connor found the same increased propensity to post-conventional moral reasoning among left-wing students in France as earlier studies had found in the United States.[21]

Far from being anxiously materialist, the May movement was almost whimsically utopian. The proposition that the small increase in unemployment and worsened job prospects for graduates fuelled anxieties about threatened affluence is supported neither by the magnitude of the shifts in the labour market or the changes in the fortunes of the groups mobilised, nor by the themes of the protest itself.[22] In short, there is nothing to suggest that the motivations of French student protestors were much different from those of activists elsewhere.

The precipitate decline of the French movement is another matter of controversy. Apart from those who have, like Schonfeld, seen in it symptoms of the peculiarly French syndrome of the *chahut*, arguments range wide as to its causes. Among the reasons Statera lists are official repression, the movement's failure to forge suitable links with the working class, and a failure of leadership which exacerbated sectarianism and led the movement to relinquish its utopianism and to subordinate itself to working class ideology.[23] Since repression is so frequently invoked to explain the failures of the left, it is worth examining the evidence closely. The most straightforward instance of repression after the exclusion of Daniel Cohn-Bendit from France was the proscription, in July 1968, of the revolutionary groups which had risen to prominence on the wave of student protest. The main victim of this repression was the Trotskyist JCR (*Jeunesse Communiste Révolutionnaire*): its leaders were arrested, its attempts to re-group were frustrated and its rank and file members were arrested when they attempted to hold meetings. By August, it was reported[24] that almost every day a Trotskyist leader was arrested upon leaving a clandestine meeting. Trotskyism was plunged into clandestinity and while clandestinity might suit the Maoists (who, it was alleged, had penetrated even the Communist-dominated trade union, the CGT), it clearly did not suit the Trotskyists. The result was that in the immediate aftermath of the revolt the Trotskyists were prevented from organising effectively to capitalise upon the mobilisation which had occurred.

It might be argued that the Gaullist Government had thus correctly estimated the danger of the forces ranged against it,[25] for its policy on the universities themselves was remarkably liberal — too liberal, in fact, for many Gaullists once the initial shock had worn off. That Education Minister Edgar Faure's reforms and proposals for *cogestion* (co-management) did not entirely satisfy student opinion is scarcely surprising, but the continued malaise within the universities evidently recommended sterner measures to the Government. Faure's own attitude hardened as he concluded that the students were wilfully violating the rules of the game which he had laid down.[26] With Faure's replacement by Gaullist 'baron' Olivier Guichard, even the residual concern with liberalisation and democratisation was extinguished in the face of opposition from defenders of the *status quo ante* and proponents of the technocratic dream of the reconstruction *à l'américaine* of the French higher education.

The effects of the repression of the JCR were, however, short-lived. By the summer of 1969, the Trotskyists had succeeded in re-grouping under a variety of names, the most important being the AJS (*Alliance des Jeunes pour le Socialisme*), and, operating through the '*comités d'action*' — an organisational form born of the struggles of May — they were well-placed to begin their self-imposed task of reconstructing UNEF.

Of other instances of repression, perhaps the most serious incident involved thirty-four students suspended in February from the Sorbonne for their part in the occupation of the rectorate. Since they were suspended for the whole of the academic year 1968-9, they were deemed ineligible for continuation of their deferment from military service. Amidst protests that the action was punitive, eleven of them were inducted into the army. Shortly thereafter the *Conseil Supérieur de l'Education Nationale* met to consider the students' appeals against their suspension and, after three days of hearings, acquitted eight and reduced the penalties against the rest to a reprimand, thus entitling them to re-enroll. The Prime Minister, however, declined to release the eleven from military service, insisting that it was not a punishment but a civic obligation. But under the weight of increasing popular protest, including that of the CSEN, an administrative tribunal was established to investigate the case. When it reported in July, it annulled the cancellation of the students' deferment describing it as *'entachée d'excès de pouvoir et intervenant sur le fondement d'une décision illégale'*. Ten students were promptly discharged from the military, the eleventh already having been released after embarking on a hunger strike.

Complaints of official repression continued, but after the initial spate of prohibitions this seems to have had the character of the routine harrassments by vigilant police, and the heavy-handed administrative ineptitude characteristic of a traditionally authoritarian state, rather than any systematic and calculated policy of repression. Such actions served to irritate but were insufficient seriously to intimidate. Scarcely surprisingly, they had the counter-effect of repeatedly fanning the embers of discontent.

The repression, then, was real but scarcely suffices to explain the decline. The other factors mentioned by Statera were all undoubtedly contributory, particularly because they inhibited the movement's ability to make new recruits and drove from the movement those of its existing activists who could not or would not take the path of sectarianism. These, however, were not processes peculiar to the decline of the French movement but ones which operated in all Western student movements.[27] Indeed, the peculiarity of the French movement was its extraordinary compression: in a matter of months it completed processes which in other societies took years. This compression is largely to be explained by the fact that French students, because of the coincidence of their protest with widespread disaffection elsewhere in the society, succeeded so remarkably where other Western movements failed — in actually producing a national political crisis! The depth of that crisis, the fears of civil war it aroused,[28] and the ultimately demoralising failure of the left to resolve the crisis to its advantage, all conspired to crush the utopian movement more quickly than elsewhere.

II. Après-mai: 1969-1975

The situation after the national elections of June 1968 was a profoundly changed one: the regime was clearly stronger and the opposition weaker. If the return of students to the universities in the autumn failed to result in the conflagration some feared, it was nevertheless punctuated by protests. The issues varied — here corporate, there civil libertarian, elsewhere more narrowly materialist, but typically a mixture of the local, national and often international — and the protests ranged wide, from Paris to the larger provincial cities, from the Faculties of Law and Letters to the technical colleges and the merchant marine colleges. In the student elections the left did well. In this and the years immediately following, violent clashes between left-wing and right-wing student groups became more frequent. Within the left itself, factionalism increased apace with Maoists, Trotskyists, Communists and other socialists increasingly in conflict one with another. The chief casualty of this contention was UNEF. Its April 1970 congress revealed this organisation as quite unable to contain within it such diverse currents, and thereafter the split was formalised. Clashes with the police, although violent, were sporadic and localised, and by the end of 1970–71 relative calm had been achieved.

By now the commencement of each new academic year had settled down to an almost ritual campaign against the rising level of restaurant and residence prices and the insufficiency of student grants. This owed much to the strategy of one of UNEF's successor organisations, *UNEF* (*Renouveau*), which, in line with its increasingly strong links with the Communist Party, emphasised the common struggle of university workers and students against a government which was starving the universities of funds. UNEF's appeal was, however, syndicalist and reformist, and by October 1972 the universities were generally peaceful. The events of 1968 were by now a '*guerre du papa*', the slogans were no longer fashionable, the Maoists had gone underground and the numerous Communists were opposed to any disorderly revolt. Students had, in one sense, less reason to protest: the universities were now more liberal and open, teaching was more flexible and more personal, and staff–student relations were better.[29]

Protest was by now no longer the special province of university students; since 1971 their actions had been overshadowed by those of autonomous movements of *lycéens* and *collégiens*. The month of strikes, occupations and demonstrations, which in February and March 1971 closed some thirty institutions, began as a spontaneous movement of solidarity with a *lycéen* being arrested, apparently as a matter of mistaken identity, on a charge of assaulting a policeman. Discontents with a school system only cosmetically reformed since 1968 clearly underlay the movement and became manifest in the later strikes, whose general theme was libertarian — the extension of the rights of responsible citizens to those who felt themselves the victims of the 'anti-youth racism' of French society.[30] In 1973 the average age of those completing the baccalaureate was nineteen years and eleven months. French secondary education was increasingly dealing with those who had the expectations of adults and who were bound to experience as repressive a system which treated them otherwise.

The demonstrations and strikes of 1973 were even more widespread. At their peak they involved *lycées* and technical colleges throughout France and brought a hundred thousand demonstrators into the streets of Paris, the immediate spark being the Debré law which envisaged the abolition of students' rights to deferment of their obligation to render military service.

For all its vastly greater scale, the mobilisation of 1973 had much in common with that of 1971. On each occasion competition between leftist groups was counted among the stimuli, and on each occasion the Communist-dominated UNCAL (*Union Nationale des Comités d'Action Lycéen*) had attempted to take over the leadership of the movement and to channel it into demands for increased public expenditure on education and had denounced the actions of those who sought to prolong the strikes. On each occasion many of the protestors scornfully turned their backs on leftists and Communists alike: the *'inorganisés'* would not submit to being lectured at or represented by the *'petits chefs'* of the political groups. If the movement, once launched, threatened to escape the control of the political groups, their role nevertheless should not be unduly minimised. The strike committees which organised the protests were largely manned by Trotskyists, probably because only they had the necessary organisational skills. The relations between the otherwise competitive sections of the left were relatively cooperative both because the Trotskyists were skilful to realise the limits of their power to direct what they had helped to unleash and because the Communists, in a smart about-face on their policy in 1968, chose not to boycott movements which involved participation with leftists. Instead, operating through the student unions which they effectively controlled, they attempted to steer the movement into the channels of 'responsible' participation in wider social struggles. The Trotskyists' quest for acceptance as a legitimate and responsible part of the left in national politics, particularly marked in the case of Krivine's Ligue Communiste, probably accounts for their ultimately moderating influence.[31]

The remarkable feature of the 1973 movement was the degree of common cause across a diversity of circumstances. Most important was the solidarity technical students demonstrated with *lycéens*. The Debré law would not have been to their disadvantage, since they could scarcely fear the disruption of higher education for which they were not being prepared. Certainly they had an abundance of material grievances — long hours, poor conditions and strict discipline among them — but the form of their reaction is instructive. Their chief tactic in the colleges was the mounting of counter-courses which questioned not the curriculum but its bureaucratic organisation. Their principal innovation was the re-arrangement of classes so as to abolish fixed timetables and to enable younger and less experienced students to be aided in their learning by older students who had already mastered the appropriate techniques. They thus achieved, however briefly, a practical demonstration of co-operative self-management. Small wonder, then, that the movement of technical students should have been seen as a potentially important link in the possible union of the student movement with that of the working class.[32]

In the spring of 1974 it was again the students of the *lycées* and technical high schools who took to the streets and if the demonstrations in Paris were barely half the size of those the previous year, the presence of the technical students was even more marked. The immediate pretext for the demonstration was Education Minister Joseph Fontanet's proposal for the reform of secondary education, but there is evidence that the real root of the mobilisation was less a draft law which very few students could have read than the continuing malaise of secondary education, and the momentum which the movement had gathered over the previous twelve months. The strikes appear, in contrast to 1973, to have been more sustained in the provinces than in Paris but everywhere there was increasing evidence of the distance between the mass of the disaffected and the political groups of the left: the groups were accused of seeking to manipulate the protests, of seeing the students as a 'field for manoeuvre'. The tactics of the unorganised majority of protestors inclined less and less to the carefully orchestrated demonstration and more and more to such individualistic protests as protracted absenteeism.

In March 1975 a wave of demonstrations and strikes again swept the system, this time in response to M. René Haby's proposals for the 'modernisation' of French secondary education. That the protests were neither as numerous nor as durable as those of the previous two years was attributed by some observers to the fact that the *lycéens*, more politicised than their colleagues in the technical schools, had learned from past disappointments that the spectacle of massive demonstrations and strikes did not, in the absence of detailed political organisation, produce enduring results. The movements' victory over the Debré law had proved to be Pyrrhic: the law had been reintroduced after the summer with what amounted to only minor drafting changes, and the Fontanet proposals had scarcely been altered by Haby at all. Faced with such disappointments, the political organisers of the *lycée* movement had adopted a strategy of which demonstrations were only a part, only a preamble to attempts to confront education spokesmen on television and to organise national conferences to discuss the issues and to co-ordinate future activity. Efforts were made to enlist the support of trades unions, parents' organisations and teachers, and the principal Communist and Trotskyist organisations sank their differences in the interests of mounting a united campaign. The 'blitzkrieg' of previous years had given way to a 'war of position'.[33]

Yet, despite the cold, over thirty thousand had marched in Paris: if the *lycéens* appeared to have attained the age of reason, technical students had not. Technical students were more prominent in the demonstrations than in previous years and a disproportionate number of the strikes occurred in the technical sector. The status of the technical schools as an ante-chamber to industrial work was manifest both in the large number of protests articulating local grievances concerning poor facilities, anti-quated and often dangerous equipment; and, more generally, concerning the restrictiveness of the college regime and the low level of political development of technical students' struggles. They remained, unlike those in the *lycées*, 'without memory'. Their consciousness was undoubtedly the product of their circumstances; the regime in the technical schools was in every way more restrictive than that in the *lycées* and the curriculum itself neither encouraged the conception of alternatives nor provided the opportunity for the development of politically relevant skills. The result was that political activists had even less impact on their comrades in the technical schools than did their counterparts in the *lycées*.[34]

III. The Revival of Protest: The 1976 Campaign

In the universities, by contrast, all was calm save for localised clashes between the left and the extreme right and occasional protests at the deterioration of students' financial position.[35] Indeed, by the summer of 1975, articles appeared in several papers remarking, and in some cases deploring, the silence of the students. The year 1974–5 proved the quietest in the universities since 1958 and the turnout in student elections was exceptionally low. A number of writers claimed to detect in the universities a new mood of serious commitment to studies hardened by increasing financial constraints in the form of an increase in the duration and extensiveness of part-time and vacation work, and an increased anxiety about eventual employment prospects, all untempered by any satisfactory social life. In such bleak circumstances, it was suggested, political activity, even political discussion, did not thrive.

The calm of 1975 had so deadened public interest in the universities that when demonstrations did occur after the *rentrée* of that year, they were generally ignored. The eventual collapse of a strike lasting over six weeks at Nantes was even attributed to its almost complete failure to attract the attention of the mass media.[36] Even the spread, by the end of February, of strikes and occupations to Paris and to provincial centres such as Amiens, Brest, Clermont-Ferrand, Dijon, Grenoble, Rennes, Perpignan and Toulouse aroused neither curiosity nor condemnation. The media, the political parties and apparently the public were pre-occupied with the local government elections. Even the leftist groups had largely abandoned the campus. Moreover, student protest had become ritualised to the extent that in some institutions the 'annual strike' was expected. Most university rectors, regardless of their politics, no longer saw occupations as grounds for calling the police and this newly acquired 'moderation' of response itself contributed to lowering the temperature of student protests.

Herzlich attributed this lack of interest to more profound structural changes. In the face of the increasingly apparent lack of fit between the contents of university courses and the requirements of the economy, the image of the university as a training ground of future *cadres* or even of a potent intelligentsia was in retreat. The marginalisation of the university, increasingly evident to students, their teachers and the public, encouraged a growing air of detachment from university issues even among those whom they might most have concerned.[37]

Whatever the reasons, no-one was prepared for the eruption which followed. The issue about which the protest was focused was yet again an Education Ministry proposal for the reform of university education. The junior minister, the Secretary of State for the Universities, M. Soisson, had drawn up a plan in conjunction with Education Minister Haby for the reform of the second cycle of higher education, designed principally to coordinate courses with the needs and opportunities presented by the labour market. The project envisaged first that the preparation of secondary school teachers should involve training in pedagogical techniques and should be removed from the direct control of the strictly academically-oriented faculties. Second, that representatives of prospective employers should be invited to participate in university councils to advise on the modification of the curriculum. Third, that a university would be permitted to require a student holding the diploma of another university to submit to a further examination before admitting him/her to study for the *licence*. And fourth, that the *licence* would be restored as the normal terminal qualification by introducing restrictions upon entry to the *maîtrise*.

For the Government, the proposed reform represented no more than a rational response to changed conditions. Secondary school teaching, the traditional destination of university graduates in Letters and Science, could not absorb the same proportion of a student body that in ten years had doubled to eight hundred thousand. Since the public sector could absorb no more than a third of these graduates, it seemed only reasonable to invite the private sector to suggest amendments to the curriculum to enable it better to meet their requirements. In fact, the project constituted the most radical reform yet proposed for French universities and since it raised the twin spectres of selection and the subordination of the universities to the interests of the *patronat*, it is scarcely surprising that it should have been greeted by vigorous denunciations from all the teachers' and students' unions. Yet nothing in the reaction when in December 1975 the project was first announced suggested the massive mobilisation which was to follow.

Nothing, that is, save the isolated case of the University of Nantes. The strike at Nantes began early in December when thirty-eight law students, although qualified for admission to study for an advanced diploma, were refused admission on grounds judged extremely questionable. Immediately, students in the faculty began a strike in support. Towards the middle of December the Soisson reform was added to the list of grievances. Only after six weeks was the strike called off and then because the strikers recognised that the battle against the Soisson decree could only be effectively prosecuted by means of national mobilisation. In the absence of any such mobilisation the general assemblies of the three strike-affected faculties voted unanimously, upon the recommendation of the strike committee, to suspend the strike and to organise a continuing campaign in the faculties on the basis of action committees, to campaign to alert all other universities of the threat prosed by the Soisson decree, and to seek the support of peasants, workers, teachers and the unemployed in a common mass movement.

None of this would have been remarkable had Nantes been a stronghold of left-wing student syndicalism, but it was nothing of the sort. The strike began in a Faculty of Law traditionally considered a conservative bastion, and spread to the Faculties of Science and Letters. If there was a left-wing tradition in Nantes it was very much one of the libertarian left: the level of support for the PCF was lower than anywhere else in France and, in the university, extreme-left groups and student unions were virtually non-existent.

Indeed relations between the left and the strikers were by no means cordial. Prominent Socialists and Communists on the faculty supported the *numerus clausus*, the CGT refused to be associated with a demonstration against the Soisson reforms, and UNEF (R), warning that the movement was at risk from the 'irresponsibility of provocative minority groups', was virtually excluded from the general assemblies. The Communist effort to contain and to lead the movement had been scornfully rejected.[38] Nevertheless, the maturity of the strikers' political analysis was noteworthy. Independently of the PCF's 'moderate' posture the students recognised the limits of their power and the conditions necessary to their success.

Although such conditions were common to many French university towns, the mobilisation grew only gradually throughout January and although it began to affect a number of provincial centres, it did not yet have the character of a national mobilisation. In most of these provincial protests strictly local grievances were mixed with the opposition to the Soisson reforms. A remarkable number included detailed proposals for the reconstruction of courses and made specific demands relating to facilities as well as raising more general questions of the orientation of higher education. It was only in February that the agitation reached Paris and it was there that UNEF organised on 28 February an 'estates general' of several thousand students, the dominant themes of which were unemployment, selection, opposition to the government, university autonomy and agreement by employers not to interfere.

The press, in reporting this growing activity, made much of its economic motivation but it seems largely to have missed its cultural dimension.[39] Debates took place on the contents of courses, the status of women, the army, justice, as well as the relationship between the university and the economy. Although all this occurred in the context of an attempt to mobilise opposition to the Soisson reforms and to popularise such opposition, the movement had an element of genuine cultural efflorescence that cannot simply be reduced to its strategic purpose.

By the beginning of March, fifteen faculties and thirty university institutes of technology were on strike. By 10 March, strikes and suspensions of classes were in force almost everywhere. As the movement gathered pace so it enjoyed the increasingly unambiguous support of the parties of the left. In March a series of progressively more massive demonstrations, some of them involving public sector workers and teachers as well, rolled through the streets of Paris. The Government, meanwhile, remained intransigent.

This was the biggest wave of demonstrations since 1968 and, as such, it naturally invited comparison with the heady days of May. The press was quick to point out the contrasts: the new movement lacked the utopian *élan* of 1968;[40] it was founded upon a fear of the future rather than the demand to shape it.[41] But in one respect the student movement was seen to have returned to the spirit of May: unlike the movements of the intervening years the violence of the protesters was now, as in May 1968, merely symbolic.[42]

These confident characterisations must have seemed premature in the weeks that followed. The list of strike-affected campuses continued to grow and the struggle was taken to the streets in a manner more forceful than that of orderly demonstrations. In Amiens students occupied the local Chamber of Commerce; in Lyons an employment centre was occupied; in Bordeaux barricades were erected in the streets. The same day demonstrators and police exchanged paving stones and teargas in St. Germain des Près and students smashed the windows of two big department stores in the rue de Rennes. These latter incidents were, however, marginal to two massive demonstrations which were remarkable both for their general moderation and their rejection of all attempts at leadership by both UNEF and the Trotskyists. Indeed it was strongly suggested that the vandalism was the work of known *agents-provocateurs* employed by the authorities to prevent the movement attracting the public sympathy that so sustained the May movement.[43]

The leaderlessness and resistance of the movement to central organisation led many to doubt that the mobilisation would survive the Easter vacation. Perhaps it was the students' demand to be taken seriously, and their resentment at the new Secretary of State's confident announcement that she (Alice Saunier-Seïté had succeeded Soisson in January) expected the fortnight's holiday to cool their political ardour, which renewed the students' determination. Perhaps the movement had deeper structural roots than any of the commentators believed. Whatever the reason, after the vacation the campaign continued with a renewed vigour which surprised everybody, and set some wondering whether May 1968 might yet be repeated.

By the second week of April some forty departmental UERs (*Unités d'Enseignement et de Recherche*) and IUTs (University Institutes of Technology) were on strike. Violence had erupted in Rennes,

Clermont-Ferrand, Toulouse and Grenoble. Rallies, street demonstrations and occupations of public buildings occurred daily. The movement was also achieving some visible success: some thirty university councils had voted to express their hostility to the reforms, and several university authorities denounced the Government's intransigence as provocative. Such success was still limited to the campus, however. No groups other than their teachers had been at all vocal in the students' support. Attributing this to the lack of public exposure of their grievances the action was in many places escalated and taken outside the faculties in order to attract more media attention. Thus Lille students interrupted an outside live broadcast to publicise the general assembly in Amiens, students in Rennes occupied the *palais de justice*, in Grenoble a national highway was barricaded, and in Brest students halted the express train to Paris.

None of these seems to have made much positive impression on public opinion for all that the media coverage of the strikes expanded massively. The press did, however, use its editorials to urge the Secretary of State to break her silence, to receive student delegations and to moderate the proposals. Curiously it was from the Trotskyist UNEF (*Unité syndicale*) rather than the more moderate UNEF (R) that Saunier-Seïté first agreed to accept representations. On 11 April, after a meeting with the President, she announced that a new effort would be made to explain to students the nature and purpose of the reforms but the Government categorically refused to abrogate them.

Meanwhile the four hundred delegates to the national conference in Amiens had voted, against the strong reticence of the Communist minority (only 15 per cent of the delegates), to call for a general strike throughout French higher education. At the same time it was reported from Bordeaux and Toulouse that students anxious to resume studying for the exams scheduled to begin in May were beginning to organise to counter the strike. Yet there was no evidence to substantiate the Minister's claim that the strikes were the work of tiny minorities of leftist political groups: massive votes, often by secret ballot, in favour of continuing the strike were reported in mid-April from all parts of France, and *lycées* and technical colleges, even in towns without universities, were beginning to join the strike.

The Secretary of State's television appearance did nothing to calm the situation. Indeed it impressed most observers with her lack of understanding of the situation, in terms either of the seriousness of the protestors or of the needs of the economy. A second wave of massive demonstrations took place throughout France on 15 April: some forty thousand marched in Paris, there were brief but violent clashes with the CRS

(*Compagnies Républicaines de Sécurité* — the specialised riot police); two hundred and twenty people were held for questioning but later released. The presidents of sixty-five universities met and, by a clear majority, declared themselves opposed to the proposed reform.

By the fourth week of April the strike had been extended yet further in the *lycées* and to some fifty *grandes écoles*. Even a private school in Paris had joined the strike. On 22 April, ten thousand *lycéens* demonstrated in Paris. The following day, some twenty thousand students did likewise and again there were clashes with the CRS.

The united front which the movement had exhibited thus far had, however, already begun to crack. It was widely observed that the Communists at the Amiens assembly had been decidedly cool towards the call for a general strike. UNEF had in the end agreed to one for fear of being cut off from the groundswell of the mass mobilisation, but the SNESup (higher education teachers' union) delegate had argued that a prolonged strike was neither possible nor welcome.[44] The unity of the movement had thus far concealed the quite different interests of teachers and students. The teachers were defending their right to manage the faculties, but for the students defence of the status quo was limited to the defence of the degree of liberty from the constraint of the market which the university afforded them. As was to become increasingly clear, the students' agreement did not extend to the defence of the power of the 'mandarinate' which presently controlled the faculties. In mid-April SNESup and, with more reservations, UNEF decided that the time for negotiations with the Government had come and began the process of disengaging themselves from the strike. The 'treason' of their compromise was immediately denounced, and when, on 26 April, UNEF called for a return to the campus, the call was widely ignored. UNEF was denounced for having negotiated with the authorities behind the backs of the students. Again fearing that it was losing touch with the movement, UNEF quickly published a communiqué announcing that it had not meant to call for a return to classes but merely for a return to the campus, in order that discussions on future strategy might take place.

Both SNESup and UNEF were concerned to 'save' the academic year in the face of the threat of cancellation of the exams which would have deprived students of a year's academic standing; but in fact the Secretary of State had determined that the exams should proceed, remarking that they would perhaps be more valuable than in previous years in discriminating amongst students.

In many places the strikes continued well into May, but although the defection of the teachers and the compromising of UNEF had unleashed with a new clarity the libertarian and anti-establishment forces that had hitherto been relatively submerged beneath the common banner of a limited grievance, the movement was increasingly dissipated by its internal contradictions. Moreover, the movement had achieved little: the Government had conceded almost nothing, the unions had failed to rally in the students' support and now even the teachers had deserted them. With the exams steadily approaching, the students began reluctantly and in many places only after protracted discussions and negotiations to abandon the strike. Although in many places some exams were postponed until the autumn, where they did take place, these proceeded without serious incident.

The strike had produced a mass mobilisation the strength of which nobody, including UNEF (R), had believed possible. At every turn, UNEF's attempts to take the movement in hand had been rebuffed. The students had clearly demonstrated that they were not prepared to subordinate their struggle to the electoral ambitions of the PCF. The other student unions and political groups had fared only a little better. The support of Trotskyists was generally accepted where they did not attempt too obviously to lead. The biggest, though still modest, gains were those of MAS (*Mouvement Action Syndicale*), an independent socialist organisation. Yet for all that they resisted the overtures of the political groups, the strikers recognised the weakness of their lack of a permanent organisation. At the Lyons assembly of the national mobilisation it was proposed to set up a form of permanent umbrella organisation which was yet not to violate the sense of the existing groups. Scarcely surprisingly, it failed to materialise.

IV. Interpretations of the Student Protest Movement

Most of the newspaper reports of the 1976 mobilisation interpreted it as above all a response by students to the increased hardships of their financial condition and to their anxieties about the prospects of finding work in a society wracked by high levels of unemployment apparently affecting the young disproportionately. The weight of this consensus of interpretation is too great to be ignored, but it needs to be examined critically.

Some journalists linked the outbreak of the strikes to the rent strikes in the student residences organised at the beginning of the academic year after the government had increased rents by 25 per cent. Furthermore they pointed to the campaign mounted by UNEF to protest against the impoverishment of the university and its students. Yet neither of these events was in any way novel. Rent strikes and restaurant boycotts had marked the beginning of every academic year since 1968 and none had ever sustained a general mobilisation. UNEF had campaigned almost exclusively for improvements in material conditions ever since it came under Communist control, not as a response to demands from below, but because such a programme best fitted the overall Communist plan of an integrated national movement built around the demand for economic reconstruction.

The press seems often to have failed to distinguish between the slogans of UNEF militants and the motivations of other activist students.[45] The slogan '*Non au chômage*' (No to Unemployment) was certainly raised by the well-organised UNEF cadres but there is ample evidence that UNEF's attempts to represent and organise their grievances were widely rejected by students. Moreover, the ostensible and articulated grievance of the demonstrators — the Soisson reform — was something about which many Communists were ambivalent. Their objection was less that there should be a better match between education and the needs of the economy, than that the reform would give the *patronat* rather than the labour movement the ultimate power to determine what those needs might be.[46] Had the students merely been concerned with unemployment, their objection to the spirit of the Soisson reforms and their simultaneous rejection of the Communists would have been scarcely intelligible. If, however, their rejection was the cultural and libertarian one, against the subordination of cultural and intellectual values to economic ones, and against selection based on the same principle, then the rationality of their action is not in doubt.

What the press, with the notable exception of the libertarian *Libération*, seems to have overlooked were the peculiarly cultural manifestations of the mobilisation: the corridors covered with paintings at Amiens, the '*fête-forum*' which Bordeaux students organised towards the end of the strike. Everybody who was there remarked on the animation of the campuses — the scent of freedom in the air that brought students out of the constraints and isolation of their specialised studies and into encounters with students from other disciplines.[47] If there was little of the great flamboyance of May 1968, nevertheless the movement had a dimension larger than the demand for redress of a limited set of grievances; and when the movement persisted even after the departure of those whose programmes had been so circumscribed, the libertarian and even utopian tendencies of the movement came strongly to the fore. The impression that these impulses were merely masked by the part the students' and teachers' unions had played in marshalling the movement in its early stages is reinforced by the findings of Touraine's investigation.

For none of the students he and his team interviewed was the fear of unemployment a major issue.

The possibility remains that economic anxieties were a powerful motivating factor, albeit at a more general and perhaps only semi-conscious level. Given the national economic recession and the frequency with which the press raised the issue, that would scarcely be surprising. Yet the evidence for such a motivation is slender at best. General surveys of student opinion which ask which of a variety of issues most concern students scarcely give the answer, since they fail to distinguish between those students who do take to the streets and those who do not; and, as we are constantly reminded, the activists are only a tiny minority (usually put at 5 per cent) of the total student population. Furthermore, even if, as Ardagh suggests,[48] about half of France's million unemployed in 1975 were young people and an 'alarming number were graduates', Marceau[49] has observed that the duration of unemployment for the young was very much shorter than for older workers. Nor, from such survey data as exist, is there much evidence that there was quite so much substance to the spectre of graduate unemployment in France as has often been suggested.

Amiot and Frickey[50] observe that the rather high level of youth un-employment in France was largely the difficulty of those without any work experience finding jobs within six months of leaving full-time educa-tion. In this graduates fared consistently better than non-graduates and, moreover, their promotion prospects once in employment were very much better. True, the situation did deteriorate between 1974 and 1976 and the positions in which graduates were then most likely to find employment were less exalted than those to which their counterparts of a previous generation might reasonably have aspired, but graduates were still in a relatively privileged position on the labour market.[51]

In the absence of leaders, organisations or anything more than token concessions from the government, it is not surprising that the movement did not resurface after the summer of 1976. The autumn of 1976 was almost unprecedentedly peaceful, its tranquillity disturbed only by a handful of local incidents and the ritual mobilisation of the major unions. The 1977–8 year was quieter still, and the anniversary of the 'explosion' of 1968, though widely commemorated in the press, passed virtually unnoticed in the universities.

One newspaper report of the tenth anniversary celebration at Nanterre of the birth of the 22nd March Movement described it as 'the saddest fête of all', a half-hearted homage to disappointed hopes. It was a picture which fitted well with a by now conventional wisdom that '1968 and all that' was an episode of history — that students had succumbed to the demands of the economy and to the normal politics of sectional material grievance.

Before the final demise of the French student movement is pronounced, however, it would be well to remember how often this demise has been wrongly asserted in the past; and an examination of the historical record makes it clear that the May movement did not vanish without legacy. Not only did the universities not return to tranquillity for several years after 1968, but just as peace seemed to have arrived, it was abruptly shattered. Moreover, the tactics of demonstration and strike spread in ten years from the Paris faculties and *lycées* to affect even technical colleges in small provincial towns. A legacy of a different kind is to be seen in the student unions and political groups which, however fractious, have a national identity and a relationship to the political parties quite different from that which existed before 1968.

To suggest that a movement has left legacies is not, however, to suggest that they are all positive or that the movement in itself has endured. Indeed, it is inescapable that movements did not have a continuous identity throughout this period. As Louis-Jean Calvet remarked in 1976, 'the student world has, since the fall of UNEF in 1965-6, been characterised by the fact that it mobilises itself exclusively by 'coups', punctual actions outside of which it reverted to its fluidity, its unorganised state and its apparent apoliticism'.[52] This oscillation between activism and apparent apathy exists in spite of the best efforts of politicised student unions to implant themselves. The unions endure, but are prominent only in the absence of any wider mobilisation of students. When such mobilisations occur, the unions are of only marginal significance.

Such a pattern is not peculiarly French. There are deep-rooted structural reasons why the sectional materialist politics of student unions have only very limited appeal to students.[53] The politics of the mass mobilisation about issues of principle, on the other hand, suits well the peculiar combination of concerns, circumstances and resources which characterise the student condition, conditions which are writ yet larger for secondary students. Nothing in the events here reviewed suggests that that condition has in this respect changed in any fundamental way.

Yet the mobilisation of 1976 was not identical with that of 1968. How are we to account for the differences? Georges Bensaid's attempt to put the movement of 1976 in the context of the developing relationship between university and society since the late 1950s is particularly noteworthy.[54] Bensaid sees the 1976 movement as the final confrontation between the old myth of the university and its contemporary function — between the idea of the university as the classroom of the country's elite and its actual function as a training ground for the intermediate technical and administrative functions of society. The elitism of the *grandes écoles*, manifest in both the social bases of their recruitment and the occupational destinations of their graduates, has always compromised the old image of the French university, but the rapid economic growth of the 1950s and 1960s did much to conceal the fact. The students who from 1958 to 1962 actively protested against French policy towards Algeria, although they too were drawn from the middle rather than the upper or working classes, knew that they were destined for elite positions and this gave them the confidence to enter uninhibitedly into political debate with the nation's rulers.

When the confidence and ambition which the growth and social promotion of the fifties and sixties engendered amongst the middle classes began to be revealed as illusion, their student children asserted themselves collectively so as to maintain their ascendant position and to avoid social demotion; this is how May 1968 is to be understood. By 1976, however, the battle was lost; the Soisson reforms were merely an attempt to rationalise the existing situation. Students no longer anticipated elite employment and were increasingly anxious about their chances even of obtaining secure middle-level positions. Their politics were adjusted accordingly. No longer did they presume to speak, as an elite-in-training, on broad matters of national policy; their protests now were sectional and more self-interested. But nor, from the vantage point of their reduced expectations, could they afford to identify with the struggles of a working class whose poorly-paid and dominated position they were struggling to avoid. Their political consciousness, then, resembled that of administrative and white collar workers with respect to the working class. Accordingly, UNEF, which sought to cement the unity of students and the working class, was vigorously rejected.

Such an interpretation is attractive, but in one respect at least it is wrong: the 'explosion' of May 1968 was not a response to suddenly reduced expectations but an expression of discontent with the quality of life under steadily improving conditions of material affluence; the May movement rode the crest of a still rising wave.

Bensaid saw in the movement of 1976 two elements: one of the left, linked to the working class through UNEF; and another consisting of the downwardly mobile *petite bourgeoisie*, frustrated and anxious and refusing to link themselves with the working class. The more lucid of the latter would, he suggested, come to see that their only choice lay with the organisations growing out of the working class movement. As for others, this is implied that they would move in the direction of fascism. As

Wieviorka points out,[55] such an analysis reflects nothing so much as the left's tendency to regard all who do not support them as political enemies. In this world of black and white there is no room for shades of grey, much less for colour. Unable to conceive of an autonomous student movement animated by distinctive interests of its own, the left was concerned to co-opt what it could under its own materialist banner and to consign what it could not co-opt to the dustbin of irrationality. The result is that, for all its attractiveness, Bensaid's interpretation remains a materialist reduction of a phenomenon infinitely more complex.

The movement may be better understood if the multiplicity of divisions within it are recognised. The militants of UNEF and the rival student organisations gave one, albeit fractious, dimension to the movement; organised extreme leftists gave another; those students with specific and sometimes rather narrow grievances such as those of some technical students gave yet another; and finally, the style and spontaneity of the movement came from the nebulous *'inorganisés'*, whose language was often reminiscent of the situationists of May 1968 and who rejected equally the revolutionary rhetoric of the leftists, the authority of the government and the reformist moderation of a UNEF conscious always of its part in the wider strategy of the PCF. In the absence of survey data, the class composition of these various groups can only be inferred.

Such a diversity of groups was, of course, also present in 1968. The case for the materialist interpretation could be saved, at least in part, if it could be demonstrated that the constituency had shifted in some important respect. Journalistic evidence on this point appears inconclusive. Although the bulk of the Paris press interpreted the 1976 mobilisation as one animated by the fear of unemployment and social demotion, the correspondents of the major British papers did not: both *The Times* and *The Guardian* focused upon the autocratic style of French decision-making as the major inspiration of the outburst.[56] Moreover, neither the one sociological investigation of the strikes at Amiens and Bordeaux nor the reflections of academics and students published by *L'Esprit*[57] some eighteen months later reveal economic anxieties as a major concern. Indeed, it might be more plausible to regard economic anxieties as a reason why students would not resort to a course of action likely to jeopardise both their future employment prospects and their chances of obtaining a degree. The two groups most exposed to such anxieties — final year students and those students of working-class origin organised by UNEF — do appear to have been underrepresented in the strikes.

One thing that clearly had changed between 1968 and 1976 was the political situation. In 1968 the left had only recently failed to unseat the

Gaullist majority, whereas in 1976 its win in the local elections encouraged many to believe that the left was at last on the road to power in the 1978 parliamentary elections. This situation had the effect of encouraging the parties of the left to tread extremely warily, and an explosive student movement was something which the left had every interest in defusing. Moreover, the replacement of the authoritarian and conservative face of Gaullism by the more liberal image of Giscard, together with the apparent imminence of the left's accession to parliamentary power, robbed the student movement of the role of an oppositional intelligentsia which it had been able to play since the Algerian war.[58] The fact that the mobilisation of 1976 failed, unlike that of 1968, to issue a general social mobilisation or a political crisis is not a product of any peculiar quality of the student mobilisation of that year but of the political conjuncture at which it occurred. If the 1968 'explosion' was in part attributable to the response to student demonstrations of a government so preoccupied with its grand design as to have taken the acquiescence of the students for granted — and so to have been taken by surprise — no such advantage accrued to the 1976 movement.

A number of commentators pointed to the failure of the 1976 movement to establish itself outside the universities as further proof of its character as a protest about purely sectional grievances. Yet it was clear from the beginning that the students in 1976 *did* attempt to carry their struggle beyond the universities — indeed, that they recognised that their success depended upon their ability to do so. Their efforts were frustrated, however, by the almost total lack of response with which they were met. Undoubtedly, the political situation had much to do with that. In the face of such difficulties, it is not surprising that the movement of 1976 lacked much of the utopian *élan* of that of 1968. By Touraine's strict standards, the mobilisation of 1976 was not a social movement just because it lacked such a sense of an alternative future. Yet, as Touraine observed of his interviews, there was evidence that the students, or at least those of them not committed to UNEF or the PCF, aspired to such a social movement; it was simply that internal divisions and contradictions themselves imposed on the movement by the social and economic situation prevented the realisation of any such ambition.

The negative role in all this of the student unions and political groups needs to be stressed. In large part it is in this respect that the events of May 1968 imposed an unwanted legacy on all subsequent student mobilisations, for they encouraged the development of a plethora of political groups, each contending for students' allegiances. Moreover, the shock of 1968 had prodded the PCF into taking students seriously at least to the extent of attempting to ensure that they were not again so embarrassed by a student-initiated radical social movement. Communists had, in consequence, assiduously farmed their student constituency, attempting to steer it in the direction of the same kind of syndicalist demands as they encouraged in the trade union movement. The chief effect of all these interventions was to politicise debates within the student community without politicising the mass of students themselves. Student politics took on the character of sectarian squabbles among groups more concerned with settling scores amongst themselves than with educating the student population for subsequent action. The result was that divisions within the activist fraction of the student population were increasingly formalised along sectarian lines and the old dream of an all-embracing student movement seemed ever more impossible to attain. It is perhaps significant that the campuses at which both the 1968 and 1976 mobilisations began — Nanterre and Nantes, respectively — were campuses on which the organised student left, including UNEF, was particularly weak. Nothing suggests that the development of the political groups since 1968 was in any way positive for the student movement.

Touraine did, however, see one positive development in the 1976 movement. Although it left neither words nor images to its successors, it more directly engaged the future than did the great revolutionary outburst of 1968 which had, after all, issued in a workerism that still drew on the past for its images of the future.[59] The movement may not have been able to transcend the constraints circumstances imposed upon it, but neither did it repeat the illusions of its predecessor.

Conclusion

What, in retrospect, is most striking about the recent history of student activism in France is the similarity of the processes of its development to those of other Western student movements. Beginning against a background of lack of formal access to power, the political discontents of a tiny activist minority were generalised by the vehicle of a civil libertarian and morally outraged response to what was perceived as official provocation and repression. Although the movement in its first wave revolved around charismatic figures, they were not leaders in the ordinary sense and certainly not controllers. Indeed the movement and its successors rejected both leadership and organisation and proceeded by largely spontaneous mobilisation. Sectarian revolutionary groupings crystallised out of the movement and tended to inhibit continued or further mobilisation. The 'workerist' turn of these groups, in particular, militated against the revitalisation of the student movement for it denied even the possibility of successful independent student initiatives. Instead, the utopian strain was submerged beneath indifferently received 'student syndicalist' campaigns conceived as the sectional counterparts of the struggles of the organised working class for better material conditions. But massive student mobilisations had never been founded upon narrowly, materially self-interested issues and when periodic outburst did subsequently occur, they were unorganised and spontaneous and largely focused upon moral, civil libertarian or cultural issues.

In greater or lesser degree, these have been the characteristics of student movements in all Western societies, in Australia and the United States as well as in France. The peculiar reputation of French student activism is derived from the extraordinary conjunction of circumstances which produced the 'explosion' of 1968. That only eight years later an even more massive mobilisation should have passed without any such repercussions serves to demonstrate that French students are not so different after all, and that the circumstances which in the past to amplified their protests were not so much deeply ingrained structural characteristics of French society as temporary and highly contingent political situations.

Notes

1 William R. Schonfeld, *Obedience and Revolt: French Behavior Toward Authority* (Beverly Hills, Cal.: Sage, 1976). Schonfeld sees the May revolt as having all the classic hallmarks of the *chahut*, but his account is seriously flawed by its mis-characterisation of the role of student leaders: Sauvageot, Geismar and, especially, Cohn-Bendit were not, as he claims, directive 'controllers' of the protests so much as the figureheads and symbols of a movement which explicitly declined leadership and formal organisation.

2 Raymond Aron, *The Elusive Revolution* (New York: Praeger, 1969).

3 Michel Crozier, *La société bloquée* (Paris: Seuil, 1970).

4 Alain Touraine, *The May Movement* (New York: Random House, 1971).

5 Touraine, op. cit., pp. 67–8, 224–30.

6 Ibid., p. 348.

7 Institut Français d'Opinion Publique, 'Sondage étudiants, septembre 1968', *Réalités*, no. 254 (November, 1968). However an IFOP poll of 1 July 1968 did, by surveying a national sample of all those over age 16, provide data on a large number of young people, some of them students. See Ronald Inglehart, *The Silent Revolution* (Princeton, N.J.: Princeton University Press, 1977), ch. 10.

8 The notable exception, but one that is neither contemporary with the events nor French, is Gianni Statera, *Death of a Utopia: The Development and Decline of Student Movements in Europe* (New York: Oxford University Press, 1975).

9 Philip E. Converse and Roy Pierce, 'Basic Cleavages in French Politics and the Disorders of May and June, 1968', paper presented to the 7th World Congress of Sociology, Varna, Bulgaria (September, 1970), especially p. 30. See also Melvin Seeman, 'The Signals of '68: Alienation in Pre-crisis France', *American Sociological Review*, 37 (4) (August, 1972), pp. 385–402.

10 Though not, incidentally, the police: M. Manotte, the then head of the Autonomous Police Federation, claimed on the BBC Europa programme on the fifth anniversary of the 'explosion' that it was clear to the police from the beginning of 1968 that something was going to happen at Nanterre. The only surprise was that the government was doing nothing in the face of evidence that something serious was happening.

11 For an account of these, see Nicole de Maupéou-Abboud, *Ouverture du ghetto étudiant* (Paris: Anthropos, 1974); also, A. Belden Fields, *Students in Politics: L'Union Nationale des Etudiants de France* (New York: Basic Books, 1969).

12 Statera (op. cit., p. 69) insists on the discontinuity of this development, chiefly because in the Algerian crisis the student campaign was channeled through the formal organisations of UNEF whereas in 1968 UNEF was itself engulfed by the movement.

13 Abboud, op. cit., p. 292.

14 As Nairn put it: 'Although the [ultra-left revolutionaries] certainly had some influence on its development, they were on the whole left behind by it.' Tom Nairn, 'Why it Happened' in Angelo Quattrochi and Tom Nairn, *The Beginning of the End: France, May 1968* (London: Panther, 1968), p. 127; cf. pp. 134–5.

15 For an excellent graphic representation of the diffusion of protest see Alain Delale and Gilles Ragache, *La France de 68* (Paris: Seuil, 1978).

16 Touraine, *The May Movement*, p. 255n.

17 Of works in English, cf. Roger Absalom, *France: The May Events 1968* (London: Longman, 1971) and Patrick Seale and Maureen McConville, *French Revolution 1968* (Harmondsworth: Penguin, 1968), which both provide useful accounts of the events.

18 For a review of these arguments see C. A. Rootes, 'Student Radicalism: The Politics of Moral Protest and the Legitimation Problems of the Modern Capitalist State', *Theory and Society*, vol. 9, no. 3 (1980), pp. 473–502.

19 Raymond Boudon, 'Sources of Student Protest in France', *The Annals of the American Academy of Political and Social Science*, no. 395 (May, 1971), pp. 139–49.

20 Ronald Inglehart, *The Silent Revolution*, op. cit., pp. 280–1.

21 R. E. O'Connor, 'Political Activism and Moral Reasoning', *British Journal of Political Science*, vol. 4, no. 1 (1973), pp. 53–78.

22 Suzanne Berger, 'Politics and Anti-politics in Western Europe', *Daedalus*, vol. 108, no. 1 (1979), p. 32; cf. F. Bon and M.-A. Burnier, *Classe ouvrière et révolution* (Paris: Seuil, 1971), for whom the movement was the leading edge of a *rising* class; as Abboud states: 'During the rise of the movement no "student demands" were raised ... Rather, in May, the students were preoccupied with giving voice to other social and professional groups, articulating their grievances and appropriating them.' *Ouverture du ghetto étudiant*, op. cit., p. 298.

23 Statera, op. cit., p. 220.

24 *Le Figaro*, 9 August 1968.

25 Certainly Régis Debray seems to think so. He describes the JCR, unlike the other sections of the student movement, as having 'some very good ideas' about how to seize power. See 'A Modest Contribution to the Rites and Ceremonies of the Tenth Anniversary', *New Left Review*, no. 115 (1979), p. 55.

26 *Le Nouvel Observateur*, 17 February 1969.

27 See Anthony Oberschall, 'The Decline of the 1960s Social Movements' in Louis Kriesberg, ed., *Research in Social Movements, Conflicts and Change*, vol. 1 (Greenwich, Conn.: Jai Press, 1978).

28 See Inglehart, op. cit., ch. 10.

29 *La Croix*, 21 October 1972.

30 Yves Agnès, 'L'ennui lycéen', *Le Monde*, 20 March 1974.

31 T. Pfister, 'Une lutte d'influence entre communistes et trotskyistes', *Le Monde*, 8–9 April 1973, pp. 5–6.

32 A. Khaled, 'Sursis ou pas, on n'ira pas', *Politique Hebdo*, 5 April 1973.

33 B. Le Gendre, 'Le vide', *Le Monde*, 20 March 1973.

34 See especially Guy Herzlich, 'Les collégiens ont pris leur autonomie', *Le Monde*, 14 March 1975.

35 The value of bursaries continued to be eroded by inflation and by 1974 only one student in six benefited compared with one in four in 1967–8. In 1974 alone the price of meals in student restaurants rose by 60 per cent. A UNEF inquiry alleged that 54 per cent of students were compelled to work more than fifteen hours per week in order to subsist.

36 L.-J. Calvet, 'La voie étroite des étudiants', *Politique Hebdo*, 11 March 1976, p. 44.

37 G. Herzlich, 'Les marginaux des campus', *Le Monde*, 6 March 1976, pp. 11–12.

38 B. Marquet, 'Patrons hors des facs', *Quotidien du peuple*, 27 January 1976.

39 Alain Touraine, F. Dubet, Z. Hegedus and M. Wieviorka, *Lutte Etudiante* (Paris: Seuil, 1978), p. 24.

40 *Le Monde*, 6 March 1976.

41 *Le Point*, 15 March 1976.

42 *Le Monde*, 6 March 1976.

43 André Keller, 'Barbouzes professionnels', *Libération*, 26 March 1976.

44 Touraine, *et al.*, *Lutte Etudiante*, op. cit., p. 322.

45 See, e.g., *Le Figaro*, 20 January 1976.

46 See Touraine, *et al.*, *Lutte Etudiante*, pp. 318–19 for a discussion of this.

47 Ibid., pp. 254–5.

48 John Ardagh, *The New France* (Harmondsworth: Penguin, 3rd edn., 1977), p. 511.

49 Jane Marceau, *Class and Status in France* (Oxford: Oxford University Press, 1977).

50 Michel Amiot and Alan Frickey, *A quoi sert l'université?* (Grenoble: Presse Universitaire de Grenoble, 1978).

51 There were, however, areas of more specific discontent and these do account for some of the variation in the range of strike-affected institutions in the first wave. The University Institutes of Technology (IUTs) were especially prominent, particularly in the first wave of protest. Chief among the grievances of their students was that when they graduated they were considered eligible only for lowly paid positions because the diplomas of these new institutions had yet to be recognised by industrial conventions. Bureaucratic disorganisation, then, appears to have been the more proximate cause of their discontent than the simple fear of unemployment or under-employment.

52 L.-J. Calvet, loc. cit. There is also a certain parallel with aspects of trade union mobilisation in France, which depends more on the 'social climate' than on organisational manipulation: cf. Martin A. Schain, 'Corporatism and Industrial Relations in France', in P. G. Cerny and M. A. Schain, eds, *French Politics and Public Policy* (London: Frances Pinter Ltd., 1980), ch. 10.

53 C. A. Rootes, 'Student Radicalism', op. cit., and 'The Rationality of Student Radicalism', *Australian and New Zealand Journal of Sociology*, vol. 14, no. 3, part 1 (1978), pp. 251–58.

54 G. Bensaid, 'Les majorités du campus', *Le Monde*, 15 March 1976.

55 In Touraine, *et al.*, *Lutte Etudiante*, op. cit., p. 320.

56 See reports and leading articles, 17 April 1976.

57 *L'Esprit*, November–December 1978.

58 See especially Touraine, *et al.*, *Lutte Etudiante*, op. cit., p. 245.

59 Ibid., p. 371; cf. Statera, op. cit., pp. 221–31.

The research on which this chapter is based was supported by grant no. HR 5981 from the Social Science Research Council. I am also grateful to Michel Wieviorka and especially Isabel Boussard for their helpful comments on the end-of-grant report 'French Student Politics 1968–1978' (January 1980).

3 The Integration of Trade Union Confederations into the Social and Political System

JEFF BRIDGFORD
Lecturer in Modern Languages
Newcastle upon Tyne Polytechnic

Trade unions as a social movement are continuously torn between the requirements of bargaining on behalf of their members within capitalist society and the need to change that society if their members are to achieve a form of social structure which corresponds with their contributions and aspirations. The events of May 1968 had a considerable impact on the way in which French trade unions were to consider the question of social and political change. In spite of the fact that syndicalism made up one of the traditional strands of trade union thought in France, the unions usually looked elsewhere for means of attaining their social and political objectives. Because of the plurality of the French trade union movement, more than one approach was advocated; some trade union confederations were content to negotiate for improved working conditions, while others emphasised the necessity of breaking with the present political system.

In this chapter we shall consider these two approaches. In the first part we shall study the ways in which trade unions have participated in the political process. We shall also study the ways in which trade unions have participated in the process of industrial relations. Both forms of participation have led to a certain integration within the social and political system. In the second part we shall consider the position of those who remain ouside this process of integration. We shall study the reaction of those elements of the trade union movement who oppose the participatory policies of the confederations and finally we shall consider the position of two groups within the working population, immigrants and women, who have been less than successfully integrated into the trade union movement. Thus despite the increasing social and political integration of recent years, the potential for protest to develop, and even to grow, is strong. But the coming to power of the Socialist Party in 1981 has created new conditions which will undoubtedly affect the unions' strategic and tactical position.

I. Trade Unions and the Social and Political Environment

Trade unions and the political system

During the seventies trade unions have remained somewhat removed from the formal political process. Although their representatives have sat, albeit intermittently at times, on a number of government bodies, such as the Economic and Social Committee, the Planning Commission or the Institut de la Statistique, they have not been co-opted on to government bodies as such, perhaps not surprisingly given that the right had been in power. They have had limited links with the legislature. Cayrol's study does not even mention trade union membership as a factor in political socialisation, although there are some ex-union officials who have become *députés*, for example, Georges Marchais.[1] When trade unions have involved themselves in the political system they have generally entered through their association with political parties. There has been disagreement about the desirability of having these links. The reformist trade unions, like the *Force Ouvrière* (FO), have strenuously denied dependence on political parties.[2] On the other hand, the *Confédération Générale du Travail* (CGT) has claimed to be independent but, as a number of observers have shown,[3] it has often been closely allied with the French Communist Party. The seventies began with two important developments for the left in general and for union-party relations in particular. The non-Communist left was revived in the form of the *Parti Socialiste* and in July 1970, the *Confédération Française Démocratique du Travail* (CFDT) opted for a socialist programme, *le socialisme autogestionnaire* (self-management socialism).

The focal point for union-party relations was provided by the decision of the parties of the left to agree upon a manifesto, the *Programme Commun de Gouvernement*, which laid down the foundations for an electoral pact, capable of ensuring better representation within the legislature. This step proved particularly important, since it meant that trade unions could relate to the whole of the left and not just to one particular party, thus reducing the possibility of factionalism, not only between the parties, but also between the trade unions themselves. Union reaction was mixed. Faithful to its position of independence, the FO chose to remain apart. The CGT, following its own logic, endorsed the agreement. Later on in the year a special number of *La Vie Ouvrière* was published, in which specific elements of the *Programme Commun* were shown to be similar to the policy positions of the CGT.[4] Henri Krasucki, the editor of the magazine and a member of the CGT's national bureau, explained that in the *Programme Commun* there were practically all the union demands on social affairs, workers' and union rights. 'How could the CGT fail to give its support to a united left, which takes into consideration the concerns of the union organisation and which responds to the most basic interests of the workers?'. Georges Séguy, the General Secretary of the CGT, was slightly more circumspect, maintaining in a radio interview that it was possible to support the *Programme Commun* without necessarily the parties as such.[5]

The CFDT's reaction was less effusive. Although the National Bureau described the signing of the *Programme Commun* as 'an important event', it put forward an independent line, claiming that 'it is not up to a trade union to decide on a programme of government nor exercise political power'. Moreover the CFDT criticised the contents of the *Programme Commun*, noting primarily that neither of the following were taken into consideration: public ownership of the mass media, and real decentralisation of political and economic power. Moreover, the CFDT claimed that the type of industrial development supported by the *Programme Commun* did not lead to any basic transformation in the quality of life in that there was a predominant emphasis on the demands of profitability and productivity.[6] The CFDT continued to demonstrate its wariness as to the parties of the Union of the Left. In January 1974, its national council proposed a variant to the Union of the Left, *l'Union des Forces Populaires*, which was defined as 'the union of all forces of the left, which would establish, on a class basis, a convergence between their strategies, thus making it possible to bring together those conditions necessary for the transition to socialism';[7] this union would include the Union of the Left and *'forces autogestionnaires'*, such as the *Parti Socialiste Unifié* (PSU) and the CFDT. It was a vague concept which was unable to impose itself on the Union of the Left.

The next stage in union-party relations came when the Union of the Left began to flounder. The CGT organised a campaign *Il faut que vive le Programme Commun* ('The Common Programme must survive'), reminding its militants of the particular relevance of certain points:

> 'As far as the principal question of nationalisation is concerned, the CGT would like to recall that it supported the *Programme Commun* from the beginning, particularly because it foresaw the nationalisation of the banking sector, credit and the insurance companies and also the nationalisation of the nine most important monopolist groups, together with their subsidiaries.'[8]

Thus the CGT aligned itself more closely with the Communist Party. More specifically it began to criticise the Socialist Party, for its position on nationalisation[9] and on tax reform.[10] In addition Georges Séguy made a number of speeches, criticising the calculations of the cost of the *Programme Commun* that the Socialist Party had made.[11] Given the reticence of the CFDT in supporting the Union of the Left, it could be expected that the CFDT would prefer to dissociate itself from the wrangling over the *Programme Commun*. The contrary was true. Edmond Maire, the General Secretary, put forward his position: 'We say to the Communist Party that its total refusal to consider the ten latest Socialist proposals seems unjustified ... Now that the Communist Party has become obsessed with the number of nationalisations, the following question has become much more important: has the PC changed its strategy?'[12] There is even evidence to suggest that the CFDT made a particular effort to repair the damage done by the *rupture de la gauche* in the latter part of 1979 and to bring about a compromise between the Socialists and the Communists,[13] perhaps fearing that electoral disappointment would have deleterious consequences for membership levels.

Another indication of the extent to which trade unions were prepared to become integrated into the political system can be seen by analysing the trade unions' behaviour at the time of the elections. Were the trade unions prepared to mobilise their support to vote for the Union of the Left? Some time before the elections of 1973 Georges Séguy explained that 'the next deadline for the workers was to be provided by the general elections'.[14] At the time of the elections the CGT militant was left in no doubt. The cover of *Le Peuple* read: 'Voting for the candidates of the *Programme Commun* is a way of extending union activity'.[15] Before the presidential elections in 1974, the CGT magazines carried a number of articles, pictures and cartoons supporting the candidate of the Union of the Left, François Mitterrand.[16] Conversely, at the time of the 1978 legislative elections, the CGT's appeal was more muted. The covers of its magazines were less exhortatory;[17] but whether this illustrates a more subtle approach to propaganda or a lack of enthusiasm is not absolutely clear.

As for the CFDT it chose initially to support the left in general, without stipulating the Union of the Left.[18] Between the two rounds in 1973 it noted with satisfaction the net losses of the right, and congratulated the left on its improvement.[19] A year later at the presidential elections, the CFDT's choice could have been complicated by the fact that one of its best known militants, Charles Piaget — the incarnation of *'socialisme autogestionnaire'* during the work-in at the LIP watch factory in Besançon — was going to stand. In the end, he decided not to, and the CFDT supported the candidacy of François Mitterrand.[20] As the 1978 legislative elections approached, the CFDT national bureau resurrected the idea of the *Union des Forces Populaires* and called on its members to vote for it. Interestingly, this time, the extreme left, ecologists and regionalists were excluded from this *Union des Forces Populaires*,[21] in spite of their impeccable *autogestionnaire* credentials. The *Union des Forces Populaires* had become the *Union de la Gauche*. Indeed, unlike the CGT, the CFDT chose to make its intentions quite plain; as the front page of its magazine stated, 'Victory of the left must be achieved *at any price*'[22] (my italics). As for the *Force Ouvrière*, it remained consistent with its own policy of independence. It gave no indication of how its members should vote, even during the presidential elections of 1974, when two of its militants were candidates.[23]

The members of trade union confederations have also at times campaigned for the victory of the left, particularly during the 1978 legislative elections. Georges Séguy then proclaimed that all the organisations with the CGT were mobilised to contribute to a victory of the left at the second round of the general elections.[24] The CFDT, too, demonstrated ways in which it had campaigned to help the left's electoral cause.[25]

It is perhaps not at all surprising that there should be such links between the CGT, the CFDT and the political parties. Apart from clear similarities between the policies of the CGT and those of the parties of the left as decided in the *Programme Commun*, and relative similarities between the policies of the CFDT and those of the *Programme Commun*, there was a certain overlay or convergence of personnel. The leader of the CGT, Georges Séguy, was a member of the Politbureau of the PCF; in the Confederal Bureau, eight of the sixteen members were also members of the Communist Party, as were 60 per cent of the Executive Commission and (according to Joanine Roy) 80 per cent of the secretaries of the national unions and of the *'unions départementales'*.[26] The leaders of the CFDT and the FO were members of the *Parti Socialiste*, although they did not hold any important post in the latter's hierarchy.[27] According to a survey carried out at the Brest conference of the CFDT only 33.5 per cent of the delegates were also members of a political party — a reduction of 7.5 per cent since the last conference — but it was the *Parti Socialiste* which was the most popular.[28] Although figures are not available for the number of PS members who did in fact hold important posts within the CFDT it would seem nevertheless that the CFDT had fewer links with the PS than the CGT had with the PCF.

Unlike the reformist trade unions, the CGT, and more recently the CFDT, have played a distinct part in the workings of the political system, at least through their association with political parties. There is considerable convergence between the *Programme Commun* and the CGT's policies, and to a lesser extent between it and the CFDT's policies. The CGT and the CFDT have both made an effort to mobilise their members and campaign for a victory of the left at the elections. When the Union of the Left began to disintegrate, the CGT and the CFDT continued to ally themselves with the political parties, although individually: the CGT supported the PC and the CFDT the PS.

The trade unions and the pattern of industrial relations

The seventies witnessed a perceptible, though partial, transformation in the pattern of industrial relations, which was to some extent as reflected in the greater emphasis laid on the process of collective bargaining. The events of May 1968 showed up the inadequacy of the existing procedures for collective bargaining (as introduced in the 1950 law) and the sub-sequent *'accords de Grenelle'* were to serve as something of a model for future agreements. Two important modifications to the procedures were made: on the one hand *contrats de progrès* were introduced; and on the other, the law was amended. Jacques Delors, the adviser on social affairs to the would-be reformist Government of Gaullist Prime Minister Jacques Chaban-Delmas, was responsible for introducing *contrats de progrès* — collective bargaining agreements within the public sector. The first contract at the *Electricité de France* fixed salary increases for a two year period both in terms of the productivity of the industry and in terms of the gross national product. The 1950 law was modified with three specific aims: to allow agreements to be conducted, not only at the national, regional or industry level, but also at plant and inter-industry level; to increase the categories of workers allowed to make bargaining agreements; and to simplify the technical procedures for making these agreements.[29] As shown in Table 3.1, there have been a significant number of actual agreements signed in the public sector.

Agreements varied in importance. The national agreement for the chemical industry covered 350,000 employees, whereas that of the button industry only covered 1,500 people. Regional or local agreements could cover from a few hundred employees to 650,000 in the engineering industry in the Paris region; and whereas in the primary sector nearly all wage earners were covered by a bargaining agreement, there were many gaps in the tertiary sector, particularly in the retail trade and the hotel and restaurant industry.

There have also been a number of inter-industry agreements on vocational training (1970), maternity pay (1970), and guaranteed income in case of redundancy (1972). What these lists of agreements omit to mention is that they are not necessarily signed by all the trade union

Table 3.1   *List of Agreements in the Public Sector*[30]

	1970	1971	1972	1973	1974	1975	1976	1977	1978
Civil Service	–	A	A	A	A	A	A	–	A
Social Security	A	A	A	A	–	A	–	A	A
ELF/SNPA (oil)	–	A	–	A	–	A	A	A	R
Air France	A	A	–	A	–	A	A	–	A
Aéroport de Paris	–	A	A	A	A	A	A	–	A
SNCF (railways)	A	A	–	A	A	A	A	A	A
RATP (Paris transport)	A	A	A	A	A	A	A	A	R
EGF (electricity/gas)	A	R	R	R	R	R	R	A	R
Charbonnages (coal)	A	A	A	R	R	R	R	A	A

A: Agreements
R: Renewal of Agreement

confederations. In an earlier study, Pierre Dubois showed that there have been a significant number of occasions where one or more unions did not sign the agreement — which admittedly, however, tended to become the agreement for the industry if it was signed by at least one representative union confederation.[31]

What were the positions of the trade union confederations with regard to collective bargaining? The reformist unions, FO, CFTC (*Confédération Française des Travailleurs Chrétiens* — the Christian Democratic union) and CGC (*Confédération Générale des Cadres* — the main white-collar union), fully support the principle of collective bargaining. At its 13th conference the FO confirmed its wish to see salary negotiations in the civil service sector respected in their entirety. It considered that collective bargaining was the best means of ensuring trade union independence and the permanent evolution of social guarantees.[32]

The traditional opposition of the CFDT and of the CGT to the capitalist system has normally precluded any negotiation with the *Patronat* (employers) and the state[33] and Birien has shown that in theory the CFDT would not accept agreements with social peace clauses nor any conceptions which would link a salary increase to the productivity of the plant, to the economic situation in general, or to the increase in the retail price index; and that the CGT insisted on a scheme which guaranteed the purchasing power of its members. However, the CGT and the CFDT were not always consistent in their approach.

The CGT and the CFDT will therefore reject propositions which deny the possibility of another social system and which aim to integrate them into the present-day system. Consequently they reject clauses which index salaries to the evolution of the GNP (Gross National Product) and above all to that of the plant; any improvement in the lot of the workers must not be linked to the prosperity of capitalism . . . this sort of position would immediately imply class collaboration and the acceptance of the aims of capitalism. Consequently they will not sign at RATP (in 1971, 1972 or 1973) nor in the mines. However in opposition to this doctrine, the CFDT signs the EGF agreement in 1970, 1971 and 1973; and the CGT signs it in 1971, 1972 and 1973.[34]

During the mid-seventies there was a reduction in the number of agreements registered by the Ministry of Labour, from 1,659 in 1975 to 1,426 in 1976 and 950 in 1977,[35] and yet the CGT, perhaps the most hostile trade union confederation, stated that even in 1977, these agreements covered a large sector of the working population — 11 million people.[36] Why are there fewer signed agreements? According to Despax, 'the state wanted to limit the inflationary effects of an excessively liberal policy of salary negotiations and so it showed itself to be prudent in its interventions; the *patronat*, too, played a game of wait-and-see; as for the trade union confederations, they based their hopes on the victory of the Union of the Left and on the implementation of the *Programme Commun*'.[37]

However, as soon as it became abundantly clear that the electoral hopes of the CGT and the CFDT in 1978 were to be confounded, they changed their strategy.

The very evening of the second round of the elections, Georges Séguy, the General Secretary of the CGT, called for a renewal of negotiations. In order to draw attention to a new policy orientation, the CFDT asked to see the President of the Republic. The President and the Government seized the opportunity. After an appreciable fall in the number of agreements in 1976 and above all in 1977, a new period of negotiations was starting up.[38]

The Barre Government (1976–1981) attempted to promote the idea of collective bargaining, with the support of the CNPF (*Conseil National du Patronat Français* — the employers' organisation). The reaction of the trade union confederations was interesting. The FO maintained its enthusiasm.[39] As for the CGT, according to Despax it had 'continued to remain reserved and distrustful, while all the same taking part in the negotiations procedure . . .'[40] Lucien Chavrot, the CGT general secretary for industrial claims, maintained that the CGT had not modified its position. However he added, 'when a possibility for serious negotiation appears, one that will give results at whatever level, we're ready to take part'.[41] At the end of the year, in a report to the Confederal Bureau, Georges Séguy alluded to 'a sterility which is due to the absence of a real bargaining procedure, not only in the civil service, but also in the nationalised industries, and for the most part, in the private sector'.[42]

The CFDT's position seemed to change even more radically. According to Despax again: 'Edmond Maire confirmed that his confederation would henceforth remain within the framework of trade union activity and would attempt to obtain, in industry-wide negotiations, "significant progress" '.[43] The member of the CFDT's Executive Commission who was responsible for industrial claims had the following opinion: 'A new content must be given to collective agreements ... we have re-emphasised their importance because it seems that this type of negotiation should make it possible to deal with many of the workers' present-day problems: the working week, jobs, wages, union rights, and working conditions'.[44] At the CFDT conference in 1979, Edmond Maire advocated negotiating as a form of union activity and later he even defended its relatively meagre results.[45] In 1978, a number of important agreements were reached, the most spectacular of which was signed by all the trade union confederations and the national employees of the engineering industry, covering four million workers.[46] Crouch has argued that: 'collective bargaining is not an established aspect of industrial relations ... Despite the vast number of initiatives and policy stances adopted by the various groups involved over the past few years, most commentators seem to agree that the essential framework of a contestative industrial relations system in which negotiations and bargaining at all levels play a relatively minor role remains'.[47] It is true that contracts are not legally binding, that agreements are weakened by trade union pluralism, that there are no peace clauses and that the agreements are of undeterminate length.

Crouch's view is valid, particularly within the framework of his own comparative study, which shows that collective bargaining is practised more in most other Western European countries. However he fails to appreciate the change that has taken place during the 1970s in France, above all in the trade unions' attitude to collective bargaining and more importantly their readiness to participate in it. This change became all the more apparent once the CGT and CFDT had changed their strategy as a result of the failure of the parties of the left to gain power during that decade.

Jean-Daniel Reynaud has written: 'In the public sector as well as in the private sector, the development of negotiation has led to an increase in the number of opportunities for meetings. Even if no agreement is made, then deception is made more difficult, if not impossible'. Having explained that there was a certain reluctance to enter into negotiations after the onset of the recession in 1974, he continued: 'The most surprising thing is that this reluctance is not more noticeable. Two and a half years of recession have not managed to destroy the web of relations that has been built up'.[48]

During the seventies the trade unions were increasingly drawn into the process of collective bargaining, even though the CGT and the CFDT had initially chosen a different strategy for political change and even though the economic recession had exacerbated the conflict between capital and labour. Although the number of signed agreements has fallen, trade unions have still been involved in the machinery of collective bargaining. Moreover, because of the centralised nature of collective bargaining practice in France, it is the leadership, whether at national or regional level, which negotiates. As the rank and file is more or less excluded from this process, there is an opportunity for tension to build up within the trade union organisation. It is to this subject that we shall now turn our attention. We shall consider whether the rank and file have been integrated into the social and political system to the same extent as the leadership.

II. Integration, Cohesion and Potential Sources of Protest

Trade union confederations and their own members

The previous comments on trade union confederation attitudes to integration into the political system or into the collective bargaining process tend to reflect the position of the leadership. However, the confederations are not monolithic and these policy developments and the ensuing activities have not always obtained the support of all elements of the confederation, at least according to statements made to national conferences. Trade union confederation conferences were held at the end of the decade (CGT 27 November–1 December 1978; CFDT 8–12 May 1979; FO 17–20 June 1980).[49] Formal opposition was minimal at the FO and also at the CGT, but quite considerable at the CFDT. The principal resolution of the FO conference was approved by 99 per cent of those entitled to vote. In the CGT, the *rapport d'activité* and the *document d'orientation* were approved by approximately 96 per cent. At Brest, the general report of the CFDT conference was only approved by 56.7 per cent of those entitled to vote. (31 per cent voted against and 12 per cent abstained.) The *politique d'action* for the next three years obtained 63.4 per cent of the vote, and a resolution on *structures et fonctionnement démocratique* was approved by 69 per cent.

Opposition was to revolve directly around recent developments *vis-à-vis* political parties and collective bargaining, although not exclusively. At the CGT there was no particular opposition to the leadership's alignment with political parties, in general, only to its links with the PCF.

Several examples show that the CGT has aligned itself with the PCF. Apart from the question of the subsidiaries [to be nationalised], the conclusion of the meetings between the CGT and the parties of the left and the aggressiveness towards the PS in the speech of Georges Séguy at Angoulême which was a mixture of false conclusions and half-truths, I particularly want to draw attention to Georges Séguy's speech at Gentilly (in which he supported the PCF) and the agreement of 13 March.[50]

This same theme was also developed by speakers representing other union sections — Finances, Toulouse and Insee for example.

Angot (Métallurgie) considered that this action had divided the confederation, while Villette (Mobiloil–Gravenchon) explained that it had caused the CGT to be heavily criticised. In a thinly veiled statement, Feuilly (SNJ–CGT) and Goume (Métallurgie) complained that the PC was over-represented within the leadership whereas the PS was heavily under-represented. This point was conceded by Georges Séguy in his opening speech when he said that 'the composition of the top union institutions did not always properly reflect the diversity within the CGT and its constituent strands of thought'. This criticism was partially accommodated by increasing the number of Socialists on the Executive Commission to seven (out of a hundred!). This readiness to accommodate a large group of the critics could explain why there was less formal opposition to conference's votes. There was also criticism of the CGT's attitude to elections in general by Angot (Métallurgie) and to the *Programme Commun* in particular by Elophe (Syndicats Cheminots, Strasbourg). This criticism, too, was admitted by Georges Séguy in his opening speech: 'The fact that, during this period, we have referred increasingly to the *Programme Commun* and less and less to the CGT's own programme has contributed to a situation of confusion.'

In the CFDT, there was no overt criticism of the confederation's relationship with political parties. In general the criticism was directed to the confederation's *immobilisme* prior to the legislative elections. Henry, speaking on behalf of thirteen unions from Loire-Atlantique, opposed the interpretation according to which the attitude of the CFDT encouraged the workers to follow a wait-and-see policy before March 1978. Opposition centred round the CFDT's recent espousal of collective bargaining. 'The confederation has overvalued the possibilities for negotiations', said Tiersin, speaking on behalf of eight unions of the EDF Rhône-Alpes and added: 'Lately the activities of the Executive Commission have caused us a number of problems. After March 1978, they urged the organisation to negotiate without being in a position of strength [Bourne-Chimie Grenoble and six other unions]. The behaviour of the confederation over the last year has given the impression that a more flexible attitude will induce the *patronat* to yield; it was a mistake.' He goes on to resurrect the old syndicalist tactic of the general strike, as does G. Laurent (Syndicat de la Banque des Bouches-du-Rhône). Indeed the only opposition expressed at the conference of FO advocated the use of the general strike (Ditcadet, Municipaux Toulouse). Lambert (Sécurité Sociale), too, advocated the use of the strike weapon and prefaced his remarks by explaining that he wished to dissociate himself from the majority reformist tendency within the confederation. However, it would be unwise to over-estimate the feeling of opposition with the integrationist FO. Serious opposition to the CFDT's strategy of gradual improvement in its members' working conditions through the process of collective bargaining was voiced in an amendment proposed by the PTT-Loire to the resolution on the *politique d'action*. It called for a clean break with the logic of capitalism and was only defeated by 41 per cent to 51.3 per cent of the votes.

The only other serious point of criticism within both the CFDT and the CGT was not directly linked to attitudes towards integration with the social and political system; rather it concerned the theme of the confederation's internal democracy. According to René Doz (CGT-Grenoble): 'I have seen more or less the same procedures: no discussion of positions or of the decisions of the CGT, no discussion concerning our own industrial claims, nor about who to elect as *délégués du personnel* or for the different committees . . . Poor information, no communication, and decisions are made on high . . .' Gérard Deseagne (SNI-Aérospatiale, Paris) alluded to the malfunctioning of the principle of democratic centralism. Interestingly two unofficial candidates tried to stand for the CGT Executive Commission elections. It was only after a second count, this time by secret ballot, that they were allowed to become members. Within the CFDT, Georges Dufaud (Hacuitex Annecy and twenty-two other Hacuitex unions) called for an improvement in the confederation's democratic process. 'The local unions should be better represented where there are any changes in confederal views. We oppose the fact that initiatives within the organisation are by small committees. It is not possible to criticise democratic centralism in others, when it exists within our own organisation'. Another speaker, Jeanne Couderc, represented sixteen unions in the Paris Region opposed to the suspension of certain local unions (Usinor–Dunkerque, BNP Paris, Lyon-Gare), as did Jean-Louis Monnereau (SGEN-Lyon). They had been suspended by the leadership because they had pursued policies which diverged from the official confederal line.[51]

It is unclear whether these points of criticism have been directly responsible for the reduction in membership figures. In the CFDT, membership declined in 1977 and in 1978, by 0.06 per cent and 3 per cent respectively. The CGT lost 7.8 per cent of its members during a three-year period up until April 1979.[52] However, Floquet (SNADG-Finances) was quoted as saying that in his union 'since the beginning of the year five hundred workers have given up membership and 3,000 subscriptions to the union (out of a total of 25,000) have not been renewed; these are the consequences of a deep dissatisfaction with the attitude of the CGT during the election campaign'.[53] And even Georges Séguy himself suggested in his opening speech to conferences that the bitter disappointment which followed the great hope of a victory of the left had hit the CGT's recruitment campaign. The results of the *élections prud'homales* (for the mixed conciliation boards for industrial disputes) show that over the decade the CGT has lost a considerable amount of support, whereas the FO has made small gains and the CFDT has made quite substantial gains.

However, disenchanted ex-union members have explained what led them to leave the union, the CGT. The Confederal Bureau had refused to reply to their communications. They were, also, not prepared to distribute CGT tracts which were hostile to the *Parti Socialiste*. They rejected the attempts by the *union locale* of the CGT to discipline them. Their candidate for the local regional organisation was eliminated because of their contestation; and they had sent off 13 resolutions to the 40th Conference at Grenoble, which had been eliminated by intermediary bodies. In addition, they criticised the language of the CGT and the fact that it had become less revolutionary and more social-democrat. Finally they stated that 'in the local branch of the union a few years ago, being against the *Programme Commun* unleashed tirades of abuse. Now some of us are wondering if the CGT was right to support it . . . Some of us think that the CGT is no longer revolutionary and the majority consider that the parties of the left should not be able to run the union.'[54] These remarks exhibit various dissatisfactions with the way in which the CGT has become integrated into the social and political system.

The most consistent theme in the remarks made by twenty-two militants from Renault-Billancourt who were excluded from the CFDT is that the confederation was following the CGT in its integration into the existing social system; it accepted the logic of capitalism and no longer campaigned for a complete change of society.[55] Some ex-union members decided to set up their own union, the *Syndicat Démocratique des Banques*.[56] This disaffection has important repercussions for potential members. In another article in *Partis Pris* a number of young workers explained why they refused to join a trade union. They considered that trade unions were too closely identified with the political and social system and were consequently unable to put an end to capitalism. Moreover, unions were rigid institutions which were not interested in new or different ideas.[57]

The FO has met with little internal criticism of its activities. However the CGT and the CFDT have been criticised, specifically because of the ways in which they have been integrated into the social and political system. They have also been criticised for the lack of internal democracy which can be partly attributed to the leadership's increased importance, due to its role in the process of collective bargaining. The CGT and the CFDT have lost members. The former has also lost support at the *élections prud'homales*, whereas the latter has gained. There is a distinct divergence between the leadership and some elements of the rank and file. Some have left the unions, some have chosen not to join.

We now turn from individual members to the groups which the trade unions have less than successfully integrated into their structures.

Women and immigrant workers

The number of women in employment has risen to 8,809,800, i.e. 32.3 per cent of the working population.[58] According to figures obtained in October 1976, approximately 1,470,000 immigrants were employed in France,[59] that is approximately 7.8 per cent of the working population. Women tend to be employed mainly as unskilled or semi-skilled labour, or as office workers,[60] tending to predominate on the production line in the textile, leather, footwear, electrical assembly, paper and printing industries.[61] Two-thirds of immigrants are employed as labourers or as unskilled workers. These make up 30 per cent of the labour force of the building industry, 30 per cent of refuse collectors, street cleaners etc., 25 per cent in the machine and vehicle construction industry, 17 per cent of the rubber industry and more than 16 per cent of the engineering industry.[62] They have an inordinately high percentage of accidents at work.[63] Both groups are badly paid: the women, in spite of a law passed in 1972 designed to ensure equal pay for equal work,[64] the immigrants particularly because of an intricate and iniquitous system of bonus payments.[65]

Moreover, although immigrants pay the same social security contributions as do French workers, they do not have the same rights to social benefits. They are not entitled to the same family allowances if their children live abroad, nor maternity allowance if the child is not of French nationality, nor the same old age or disability pensions if they return to their country of origin, nor again grants for the children to study, and so on. Given the trade unions' traditional record of defending the underdog, one could perhaps have expected them to take an interest in the plight of women and immigrants — all the more so, if for less noble reasons, as far as the latter group is concerned. Immigrant workers have recently obtained improved trade union rights. They can be *délégués syndicaux* (as of 27 December 1968, and with fewer restrictions from 11 July 1975), are eligible to stand for the elections to *comité d'entreprise* (since 27 July 1972), and are now eligible to vote in *élections prud'homales* although not to stand for election.

What attitude do the unions have towards the two groups? In their comparative study, Baudouin *et al.* have described the attitude that the unions have to immigrants, who are considered primarily as units of labour.[66] The reformist unions see them as threats to their own members' jobs. In a television interview in 1973, André Bergeron, the General Secretary of the FO, declared that the present number of 1,700,000 immigrant workers must never be exceeded. He bemoaned the fact that 850,000 were unemployed in France and yet 2 million had been called in from abroad.[67] At their 1980 conference, FO delegates passed a resolution which included a description of the conditions which would need to be fulfilled if the process of immigration were to be reversed.[68] The CFDT and the CGT have tended to consider immigrants as potential allies in the class struggle, because, as Georges Séguy has explained, if capitalist exploitation is merciless for French workers, it is ferocious for immigrants.[69] Consequently it was on this basis that they were prepared to integrate immigrants into the trade unions.

The CFDT and the CGT have occasionally undertaken trade union action on behalf of immigrants — demonstrations[70] or more rarely strikes[71] — which have been of limited success and, as Juliette Minces has pointed out, distinctly unusual.[72] Equally the CGT and the CFDT have shown that they are by no means always ready to take part in action on behalf of immigrants.[73] The CFDT, for instance, refused to support the *Mouvement des Travailleurs Arabes*, claiming that 'to strive to organise immigrant workers separately from their French comrades, as has been argued, is to raise an obstacle against solidarity, contribute to lack of understanding, and make the necessary common fight on the job front more difficult'.[74]

What is more, the trade union would have lost complete control over whatever action was planned. In addition, the CGT has recently begun to follow the traditional line of the FO (and incidentally the new line of the PCF). At its fifth national conference on the problems of immigration the CGT decided to demand that all immigrants should be refused entry, regardless of their educational level or of their country of origin.[75]

On the whole, however, it would seem that the CFDT has been more flexible in responding to some of the needs of the immigrants. It has been able to organise groups which have shunned the CGT, such as the sub-contracted immigrant labourers on the Paris Metro.[76] Nonetheless trade unions for the most part have been less than successful at understanding the problems specific to immigrant labour. They originally tried to fit the immigrants into a framework which was not totally suitable.

> The trade unions tend to concentrate on the work place and thus to neglect all the problems which the immigrant workers face outside — segregation of housing, coercive administrative controls, a cultural desert — and so the trade unions do not seem to provide the best response. They see only one of the daily realities of the immigrant workers, and in this sense they are not really the anti-capitalist tools that they claim to be. They lose a bit of their credibility.[77]

Attitudes to women are quite instructive. The CGT has assimilated women's liberation to the class struggle and the need for a complete transformation of capitalist society. Liberation is to be achieved through economic independence which itself is contingent on the right to work. The CGT has also espoused a series of demands concerning tax, wages, professional training, working conditions, hours of work, pensions, child-minding facilities, and so on.[78] At the beginning of the 1970s, the CFDT national conference followed a similar line of thought, associating women's liberation solely with the class struggle. By the time of the 1976 conference, however, a change had taken place. Not only did the CFDT condemn discrimination against women, but it also advocated the right to work and freedom through economic independence. Moreover, it questioned the predetermination of roles and the division of labour between men and women, and put forward liberal policies on contraception and abortion. It has also subsequently advocated the introduction of a thirty-five hour week, the insufficiency of which has met with criticism:

> contrary to what the CFDT claims, I don't think that the 35 hour week will make it possible to achieve a better distribution of tasks between

men and women. It would perhaps make it easier for women to be integrated into work, but it's hard to see how a reduction in the length of the working week will persuade men to take on tasks that they don't take on at the moment.[79]

The trade union confederations have set up certain structures to accommodate women's interests. The CGT and the CFTC (forerunner of the CFDT, and also the name of a small rump union) set up official women's committees immediately after the Second World War; it took until 1969 for the FO to follow suit. However, in the CFDT for example, these groups were not only destined for women members, but were mixed. As Martine Storti has explained: 'There is a problem concerning the Women's Committees. Officially each national union has a women's committee. But don't be mistaken, organised autonomy for women is unacceptable. These committees are mixed and often, at least at the national level, headed by a man'.[80] There has been no opportunity for the women to set up their own committees formally. Edmond Maire has explained that 'no autonomous action should be taken by women or for women',[81] in this way reducing the lure of factionalism and ensuring maximum union control. Only the CGT has chosen to publish a specialist magazine for women, *Antoinette*. As for immigrant workers, the CGT has set up a confederal committee on immigrant labour. The CFDT has recommended that local working parties should be set up, and that a national and confederal committee should be set up too. The FO has set up study groups on immigrant labour. The unions also publish foreign language newspapers — the CGT have six, the CFDT three and the FO one.

To what extent have women and immigrants been integrated into trade union movements? In the CGT 25 per cent of the rank and file members are women[82] and there are 25 per cent approximately on the Executive Commission and three on the Confederal Bureau (out of sixteen). Although no precise figures are presented, the impression is that the percentage of women members is relatively low. In the national and regional committees the percentage varies between 10 and 20 per cent: however, the number of full-time officials is even lower. At the confederal level, now that Jeannette Loat has left, there are no women on the Executive Commission (out of thirty-one) nor on the Confederal Bureau (out of ten). At Brest in 1979, the CFDT conference voted to encourage women to take part in union activities. It was decided that the question of a quota-system for women would be studied, and the recommendations of a working party report would be discussed at the next conference. At the FO, the number of women members seems to be relatively low: 'No women are secretaries of *unions départementales*, there's only one at the confederal level. We're only here for the photo'.[83] Trade unions are loathe to give figures on the unionisation of immigrants, since, this, in itself, could be interpreted as a racialist initiative. However, the CGT has claimed that 6.3 per cent of its members were immigrants.[84] Precise figures are not available for the number of immigrants who are full-time officials or members of national or confederal committees. However it would seem that 'even within the confederations themselves, immigrant workers are up against an unfavourable power struggle, the consequences of which can be felt down to branch and plant level'.[85]

The trade union confederations have been slow to recognise the specificity of the demands of women and immigrant workers. Only the CFDT has made a particular effort, towards the end of the last decade, to advocate policies and undertake actions which demonstrate a limited awareness of this specificity. None of the confederations has been successful in integrating immigrants into their structures. Only the CGT has been able to integrate a relatively high proportion of women members and permanent officials.

Conclusion

During the seventies it would seem that the trade union confederations have become increasingly integrated into the social and political system. Although the reformist trade unions such as the FO have remained separate, the other trade unions have identified more and more with the parties of the left. The CGT has continued to support the PCF, while a new phenomenon has occurred as the CFDT has haltingly and then more enthusiastically supported the cause of the *Parti Socialiste*. It could also be suggested that the style of industrial action taken by these two confederations during the seventies, with the emphasis on national twenty-four-hour strikes, instead of on local plant issues — thus mobilising maximum support and providing direct opposition to the government and its policies — was also conceived so as to help the cause of the political parties and assist their coming to power. To argue that such behaviour does not lead to integration into the political system is to forget that the Socialist Party and by now the French Communist Party too are no longer anti-system parties. They are also well integrated into the political system.

As to the attitude of trade union confederations to the process of collective bargaining, there have been some interesting developments. The reformist unions have maintained their positive stance. The CFDT and the CGT have also signed a considerable number of agreements, in spite of their reticence at allying themselves with capitalist or state capitalist enterprises. Since the failure of the left to be elected in 1978 these two confederations have become increasingly interested in the process of collective bargaining. This process is by no means complete. They have refused to submit to a government pay policy or to conciliation or arbitration procedures, although, of course, they have participated in government bodies such as the National Planning Commission (intermittently), the Economic and Social Committee, the *Institut de le Statistique*, as well as a large number of bi-partite committees on unemployment payments, social security benefits, and so on. This tendency has increased the power of the leadership to the detriment of the rank and file.

Aspects of this process of integration have been contested within the trade union confederations themselves. The CGT has rarely been criticised, though, for its links with political parties in general — more for its links with one particular party, the PCF. In the CFDT there has been some criticism of the leadership's *recentrage*, its more reformist way of attaining trade union objectives, but there has been virtually no criticism of the confederation's integration into the political system. Perhaps this relatively low level of opposition results from the existence of consensus between the attitudes of the rank and file and of those of the present day leadership. In election surveys it has been shown that most, although not all, members of the CGT and the CFDT vote for the parties of the left,[86] and Gallie has shown that most, although again not all, of the rank and file are not as radical as the 'revolutionary' declarations of the leadership would suggest.[87]

And yet there are undercurrents of disaffection with trade union activity. This can be found amongst a minority of members and amongst those who choose not to join trade unions, whether they be individuals who are disillusioned with the conservatism of certain aspects of the trade union movement, or groups such as women and immigrants whose specificity has often been neglected by the confederations themselves. If the trade union confederations continue along this road towards increased integration into the social and political system, it will be interesting to see what the reaction of the rank and file will be: equally it will be interesting to see whether immigrants and women workers will be integrated into the union structures or whether they will be obliged to look elsewhere for the defence of their own specific interests.

Postscript

At the time of writing, one particular event has had significant repercussions on the process of trade union integration into the social and political system in France — the election of François Mitterrand as President of the Republic and the election of a Socialist majority to the National Assembly. In spite of the split within the Union of the Left and of the disappointment with the 1978 legislative election results, the CGT and the CFDT have still campaigned for the parties of the left: the CGT with less enthusiasm than before, the CFDT with even greater enthusiasm. Since the elections, moreover, one trade union leader, André Henry — the leader of one of the teachers' unions, *Fédération de l'Education Nationale* — has been brought into the Government and a number of trade union officials have been invited to join ministerial *cabinets* or governmental organisations. The rank and file have not reacted as they did at the time of the Popular Front in 1936. There has not, for example, been a wave of factory occupations to force the government to introduce new social legislation. The trade union confederations have responded favourably to the government's offer of negotiations on the increase in the SMIC (the official minimum wage), family allowances, rent rebates and pensions. They are also negotiating a reduction in the length of the working week.

It would be surprising if the new Government did not attempt to lay greater emphasis on collective bargaining, and not only because Jacques Delors, the advocate of *la politique contractuelle* in 1969, is now a member of this Government as Minister of Finance, the key post in the economic policy field. It would also be surprising if the Government did not associate the trade unions with its plans for nationalisation and economic planning. It would seem likely that the trade unions would respond favourably to such an initiative. It could also be argued that even the CGT would participate, particularly now that a handful of Communist ministers has been appointed to the *Conseil des Ministres*. But should the Government decide that wage rises must be limited in order to make the rest of its economic policy work, or should specific groups among the rank and file be disappointed by particular policies or by the overall performance of the economy, then the broad systemic potential for autonomous rank and file action[88] could be catalysed into forms of protest which the integrated confederations would find it hard to control.

Notes

1 Roland Cayrol, *et al.*, *Le député français* (Paris: Colin, 1973).
2 For an understanding of the position of FO for example, see 'Contre toute emprise politique', *FO* magazine, special number, 21 November 1979.
3 Cf Gérard Adam, 'Eléments d'analyse sur les liens entre le PCF et la CGT', *Revue Française de Science Politique*, vol. 18, no. 3 (June, 1968), pp. 524-39. David Hine, 'The Labour Movement and Communism in France and Italy' in Martin Kolinsky and William E. Patterson, eds, *Social and Political Movements in Western Europe* (London: Croom Helm, 1976), pp. 178-210. Jean Ranger and Gérard Adam, 'Les liens entre les PCF et la CGT: éléments d'un débat', *Revue Française de Science Politique*, vol. 19, no. 1 (February, 1969), pp. 182-6. George Ross, 'Party and Mass Organisation: The Changing Relationship of PCF and CGT', in D. Blackmer and S. Tarrow, eds, *Communism in Italy and France* (Princeton, N.J.: Princeton University Press, 1975), pp. 504-40.
4 18 October 1972, pp. 40-1.
5 See *Le Monde*, 18 October 1972.
6 Printed in *CFDT Syndicalisme*, 21 September 1972.
7 Printed in *CFDT Syndicalisme*, 31 January 1974, pp. 5-9.
8 Statement published by the Confederal Bureau, printed in *Le Peuple*, 1-15 October 1977, p. 2.
9 See R. Guibert, 'Tout est encore possible', *La Vie Ouvrière*, 9-15 January 1978, p. 17.
10 'La Fédération des Finances CGT fait des réserves sur les comptes du PS en matière fiscale', *L'Humanité*, 27 February 1978.
11 See, for example, *Le Monde*, 19-20 February 1978, p. 6.
12 *Le Monde*, 28 September 1977, p. 11.
13 See, for example, articles by Jean-Pierre Dumont and by Thierry Pfister in *Le Monde*, 7 February 1978 and 10 October 1977 respectively.
14 See the article by Raymond Gelly in *L'Humanité*, 28 November 1972.
15 1-15 February 1973.
16 See, for example, the supplement to *La Vie Ouvrière*, 8 May 1974.
17 See *La Vie Ouvrière*, 6 March 1978 and 13 March 1978.
18 See for example *CFDT Syndicalisme*, 28 December 1972, p. 1.
19 *CFDT Syndicalisme*, 8 March 1973, p. 1.
20 *CFDT Syndicalisme*, special number, May 1974, pp. 6-7.
21 Resolution of the National Bureau, reprinted in *CFDT Syndicalisme*, 16 February 1978, p. 5.
22 *CFDT Syndicalisme*, 16 March 1978, p. 1.
23 See the statement by FO in *FO* magazine, June 1974, reprinted as an annexe to J.-P. Bachy, 'Les syndicats et l'élection présidentielle', *La Nouvelle Revue Socialiste*, no. 3 (1974), p. 64.
24 In an interview with Agence France Presse, 16 March 1978, reprinted in *Le Peuple*, 16 May 1978, p. 27.
25 'Toute la CFDT mobilisée', *CFDT Syndicalisme*, 16 March 1978, pp. 9-12.
26 *Le Monde*, 2 December 1978, p. 37.
27 Indeed, the CFDT's official policy forbade overlap between such organisations. For further details see the text adopted by the National Council (January 1973), reprinted in *CFDT Aujourd'hui* (March-April, 1975), p. 102. Also Jean-Pierre Oppenheim, 'La question du cumul des mandats politiques et syndicaux à la CFDT', *Revue Française de Science Politique*, vol. 25, no. 2 (April 1975), pp. 317-36.
28 See *CFDT Aujourd'hui* (January-February, 1980), p. 29.

29 For more details, see Gérard Adam, Jean-Daniel Reynaud, and Jean-Maurice Verdier, *La négotiation collective en France* (Paris: Editions Ouvrères, 1972).
30 Adapted from a table in *Les institutions sociales de la France* (Paris: La Documentation Française, 1980), p. 766.
31 Pierre Dubois, *Mort de l'Etat — Patron* (Paris: Editions Ouvrières, 1974), pp. 192–3:

Table 3.2

EDF–GDF	1970	CGT rejection
	1971	unanimous agreement
	1972	CFDT rejection
	1973	unanimous agreement
	1972	unanimous rejection, but later unanimous agreement at the end of the year
	1973	unanimous rejection, but later rejected by CGT and CFDT only
Charbonnages	1970	CGT–CFDT rejection
	1971	unanimous agreement, but rejection later in the year by CGT and CFDT
	1972	CGT–CFDT rejection (unanimous agreement on reduction of working hours)
	1973	CGT–CFDT rejection
RATP	1970	unanimous rejection, but at the end of the year rejected by CGT and CFDT only
	1971	CGT–CFDT rejection
	1972	CGT–CFDT rejection
	1973	CGT–CFDT rejection
Renault	1970	unanimous agreement
	1971	CFDT–FO rejection
	1972	unanimous rejection
	1973	unanimous agreement
Fonction publique (civil service)	1970	unanimous agreement
	1971	unanimous rejection; at end of year rejection by CGT–CGC and part of CFDT
	1973	rejection by CGT–CGC and part of CFDT
	1973	CGT–CGC rejection

32 Reprinted in Jean-Louis Birien, *Le fait syndical en France* (Paris: Publi-union, 1978), p. 135.
33 For more detail on this aspect of CFDT and CGT ideology see Birien, op. cit., pp. 99–100 and 118–20, and Hubert Landier, *Les organisations syndicales en France* (Paris: Entreprise Moderne d'Edition, 1980), pp. 60–71.
34 Pierre Dubois, op. cit., p. 194.
35 M. Despax, 'La négociation collective: France', in *European Conference on Labour Law and Industrial Relations* (Deventer, The Netherlands: Kluwer, 1978), p. 363.
36 For further details see *Le bilan social de l'année* (Paris: Confédération Générale du Travail, 1979), pp. 88–94.
37 Loc. cit.
38 Jean-Daniel Reynaud, *Les syndicats, les patrons et l'Etat* (Paris: Editions Ouvrières, 1978), postface, p. 178. Also *Le Monde*, 21 March 1978.
39 See the comments of Antoine Flaesch, Confederal Secretary of the FO, in 'Questions aux syndicats', *Projet* (November, 1978), pp. 1043–58.

40 Op. cit., p. 365.
41 In 'Questions aux syndicats', op. cit., p. 1049.
42 *Le Peuple*, 1–31 December 1978, p. 10.
43 Op. cit., p: 365.
44 Alain Mercier in 'Questions aux syndicats', op. cit., p. 1049.
45 Reprinted in Edmond Maire, *Reconstruire l'espoir* (Paris: Seuil, 1979), pp. 45 and 81.
46 For details of the agreement and the reactions, some reluctant, of the trade union confederations, see *Le Monde*, 21 July 1978, pp. 1 and 22.
47 In Colin Crouch and Alessandro Pizzorno, eds, *The Resurgence of Class Conflict in Western Europe since 1968*, vol. 2 (London: Macmillan, 1978), p. 212.
48 See Jean-Daniel Reynaud, 'Nature et rôle de la convention collective dans la France actuelle', *Revue Française de Sociologie*, vol. 19, no. 2 (April–June, 1978), p. 185.
49 For details concerning the conferences, see *Le Peuple*, 15 November and 1–31 December 1978; *CFDT Syndicalisme*, 17 May 1979; and *FO Hebdo*, 25 June 1980. All information in this section comes from them unless otherwise stated.
50 Letter published in a CGT magazine by M. Thouroude (*Syndicat des Employés de la Sécurité Sociale*, Ille-et-Vilaine) printed in *Le Monde*, 7 October 1978, p. 34. Ironically, one of the reasons this criticism came to light was the confederation's effort to initiate an open debate on all aspects of union policy prior to the Grenoble Conference.
51 For more details of these exclusions, see *Libération*, 9 March 1978, p. 5, and 20 April 1978, pp. 4–5.
52 Hubert Landier, op. cit., pp. 75 and 79 respectively.
53 See Joanine Roy, *Le Monde*, 30 November 1978, p. 33.
54 Jean Tighit, 'Pourquoi quittons-nous la CGT', *Partis Pris* (January, 1979), p. 12.
55 'Renault–Billancourt: des exclus de la CFDT parlent', *Partis Pris* (November, 1978), pp. 6–10.
56 'Un nouveau syndicat a la BNP', *Partis Pris* (January, 1979), pp. 13–16.
57 'Nous refusons d'appartenir à quelque chose ou à quelqu'un (des non syndiqués)', *Partis Pris* (January, 1979), pp. 18–21.
58 *Yearbook of Labour Statistics* (Geneva: International Labour Office, 1980), p. 27.
59 *Problèmes Economiques*, no. 1697 (25 June 1980), p. 18.
60 See survey carried out by L. Thevenot, *Economie et Statistique*, no. 91.
61 See 'Travailleuses pour une libération', *CFDT – Information* (1979), p. 22.
62 Jean Benoit and Patrick Sery, *Dossier e . . . comme esclaves* (Paris: Alain Moreau, 1980), p. 26.
63 Ibid., p. 237.
64 Table 3.3   *Net Salaries for 1976*

Occupational category	Monthly wages (men) (F)	Monthly wages (women) (F)	Wages gap between men and women (%)
Higher executives	8 934	5 628	37.00
Middle management	4 514	3 136	30.50
White-collar employees	2 865	2 189	23.60
Manual workers	2 381	1 683	29.30
Service workers	2 192	1 744	20.40
Others	3 725	3 414	8.40
All categories	3 194	2 121	33.60

Source: CFDT – Information, *Travailleuses pour une libération*, loc. cit.

65 Juliette Minces, *Les travailleurs étrangers en France* (Paris: Seuil, 1973), pp. 221–46.
66 Thierry Baudouin, Michelle Collin, and Danielle Guillerm, 'Women and Immigrants: Marginal Workers', in Crouch and Pizzorno, eds, op. cit., vol. 2, pp. 71–99.
67 See Jean Benoit, op. cit., p. 341.
68 *FO Hebdo*, supplement to no. 1634, p. 18.
69 *Lettres ouvertes à Georges Séguy* (Paris: Confédération Générale du Travail, 1975), p. 53.
70 See, for example, *Libération*, 7–8 June 1980, p. 7.
71 See, for example, Jean Benoit, op. cit., p. 245.
72 Op. cit., p. 327.
73 See, for example, *Le Monde*, 19 November 1977, p. 48.
74 Reprinted in Baudouin, *et al.*, op. cit., p. 96.
75 *Le Monde*, 22–23 November 1980, p. 26.
76 *Partis Pris* (June, 1980), pp. 9–15.
77 Jean Benoit, op. cit., p. 338 (Report by Denis Jacquet, one of those responsible for the CFDT research group on immigration).
78 Sixth National Conference on 'Women Wage Earners Today', GFT, 12–13 May 1977.
79 Rosine Martin, *Partis Pris* (November, 1978), p. 16.
80 *Libération*, 2 February 1978.
81 *Libération*, 4–5 February 1978.
82 Jean Birien, op. cit., p. 89.
83 According to Huguette Mouten, *Libération*, 19 June 1980, p. 7.
84 Jean Birien, op. cit., p. 89.
85 Juliette Minces, op. cit., p. 327.
86 Cf. *Le Nouvel Observateur*, 28 May 1973; *Le Point*, 29 April 1974; *Le Nouvel Observateur*, 10 June 1974; and *Le Matin de Paris*, 27–28 October 1977.
87 Duncan Gallie, 'Trade Union Ideology and Workers' Conceptions of Class Inequality in France', *West European Politics*, vol. 1, no. 3 (October, 1978), pp. 10–32.
88 For a consideration of the potential for rank and file action, see Martin A. Schain, 'Corporatism and Industrial Relations in France', in P. G. Cerny and M. A. Schain, eds, *French Politics and Public Policy* (London: Frances Pinter Ltd., 1980), ch. 10.

4 Poujadism and Neo-Poujadism: From Revolt to Reconciliation

ROGER EATWELL
Lecturer in Social Sciences
University of Bath

Introduction

The dominant mode of approach to the transformation of protest and social movements has been the institutionalisation/goal-displacement model. This analysis, deriving from Robert Michels and Max Weber, holds that as a movement attains an economic and social base, and as its original charismatic leadership is replaced, a bureaucratic structure emerges, together with a general accommodation to society. The movement thus becomes more like a formally organised pressure group, seeking influence within a pluralist system rather than working against it. Such a development has been difficult for groups representing small business in advanced societies during the post-war era. The pre-eminent economic trend has been towards economic concentration and larger business units: accommodation would mean the acceptance of extermination or suicide for the artisan, small shopkeeper and other marginal producers!

In no country has this problem been more apparent than in France. During the Third Republic 'la France des petits gens' (the France of the small man) had been central to popular political mythology, but since 1945 France has undergone an economic miracle which has made her one of the world's great industrial powers. This development has been accompanied by periodic outbursts of violent protest from the marginal social groups threatened by this trend, in particular from artisans and small shopkeepers. In the 1950s, Pierre Poujade led his UDCA (*Union de Défense des Commerçants et Artisans* — Union for the Defence of Small Businessmen and Artisans) into a spectacular campaign of direct action, electoral success and even *putschist* activity. Since the late 1960s, Gérard Nicoud's CIDUNATI (*Comité d'Information et de Défense — Union Nationale des Travailleurs Indépendants*) has continued this pattern of violent confrontation between government and small businessmen.

Although the movement has shown no signs of following Poujade's virulent entry into the parliamentary arena, Nicoud's endorsement of the clown Coluche's candidature for the presidency in 1981 on the surface appeared to be hardly a sign of accommodation to the system!

A dictionary of modern French political vocabulary would undoubtedly classify the word *'Poujadisme'* as highly pejorative. *Poujadisme* today conjures up images of economic marginality, of a backward, narrow mentality, blindly resisting economic progress. *Poujadisme* further denotes a language of violent abuse, a demagogic damning of politicians and the state, a purely destructive protest. It cannot be denied that classic Poujadism of the 1950s exhibited many of these features. The campaigns of Nicoud and the CIDUNATI seem to have followed this pattern. However, the current connotations of the word *Poujadisme* are in many ways a travesty of the original movement — and its successor. Poujadism and Neo-Poujadism can be located within a more honourable French tradition, the defence of the little man. Much of this unrest stemmed from strongly felt grievances, both economic and institutional — a sense of injustice in an uncaring society.

Moreover, the present meanings of the word fail to take notice of the changing pattern of artisan and small shopkeeper politics since the 1950s. The recent revival of interest in the importance of small business has offered new hope for accommodation. Even before this, the emergence of a less authoritarian administrative approach to intermediary groups, together with the stronger governments of the Fifth Republic, had helped produce a reappraisal of protest. Where protest is still used, its purpose is to seek specific concessions rather than to attack the whole system, or to remind the state of the need to maintain contacts with representative groups. Current French usage of the term *Poujadisme* provides no indication of these important developments — a reflection of the neglect in both France and elsewhere of any serious study of the nature of, and changes in, small shopkeeper politics during the last generation. *Poujadisme* therefore seems doomed to remain a highly negative term, rather than a word encapsulating the way in which the general pattern of small business-state relations in France since the Fourth Republic has changed from revolt to reconciliation.

I. Poujade and Poujadism

The social prelude to Poujadism

Stanley Hoffmann has written that French society from the Revolution until the immediate post-1945 period rested on a minimal consensus around a 'stalemate society', which tended to 'preserve largely pre-industrial values and attitudes and to dilute or delay industrialisation'.[1] Popular mythology defended this *'France des petits gens'*, even celebrating it as an ideal. According to David Thomson, 'freedom and equality were translated into terms of individualism, economic independence and social equality'.[2] This outlook found its most self-conscious expression in the Radical Party, whose importance in the unstable governments of the parliament-dominated Third Republic helped ensure the continuation of the 'stalemate society' until the Second World War. Change was further blocked by the popular taste for protest, itself in part a product of a centralised and authoritarian administration. This tendency to protest was reinforced by the prevalence of weak and fragmented pressure groups. French individualism militated against strong organisation; moreover, French constitutional theory was hostile to intermediary groups, stressing the direct relationship between citizen and state. This constitutional theory further reinforced the weak party system, and the lack of esteem in which politicians were held — though periodic scandals and corruption were even more important factors in the low repute of the *'République des camarades'*.[3]

In many ways the Fourth Republic seemed a case of *'Plus ça change . . .'*.[4] However, beneath the political surface France after 1945 was changing rapidly, undergoing her second great revolution. A new technocratic elite was acting as midwife to France's entry into the industrial age, laying the foundations for rapid economic growth to succour a suddenly increasing French population. The number working in agriculture began to decline dramatically: in 1946 this sector had accounted for 32.7 per cent of the workforce, but by 1954 this was down to 26.5 per cent.[5] The population living in towns began to rise. Real industrial wages grew by an annual average of 6.2 per cent during 1951–6, having fallen 11.7 per cent on average during 1946–8, and been static during 1949–50. For most workers, and for the growing numbers of the new middle class, life in France was unquestionably becoming more comfortable.

For the new technocracy, symbolised by the creation of the École Nationale d'Administration (ENA), these developments reflected France's reconciliation with progress. The groups threatened by this economic development were predictably less happy. Farmers and small business-men, especially artisans and shopkeepers, were the most adversely affected by these changes. Both had tended to benefit from wartime shortages and the high prices which continued even after the war ended, but by the early 1950s the prices of many farm products were falling, while the growth of multiple shops heralded the end of this golden age for shop-keepers. Both groups were also affected by tax changes after the war. For a generation before the 1940s, opposition to taxation had prevented France from balancing the budget. In the words of a famous aphorism, France was a land of excessive taxation, fortunately tempered by fraud. In 1952–3 the government sought to introduce harsher penalties for tax evasion, and more strict controls on assessment. As by this time post-war inflation had been brought under control, it was no longer possible to pay taxes the customary year in arrears with depreciated currency (inflation averaged 53.4 per cent per annum during 1945 to 1948 and 12.9 per cent from 1949 to 1952, but prices actually fell 2 per cent in 1953).

This was a particular problem for small shopkeepers. One study in 1950 had shown that 80 per cent were involved in some form of fraud, confirming the popular conception of shopkeepers as people of money who paid few taxes (a conclusion which has lived on in many academic accounts).[6] Nevertheless, it is important to remember that the French tax system was extremely complicated (twenty-five different taxes affected the café owner, twenty-four the garage owner); assessing tax liability was difficult.[7] Moreover, many shopkeepers lived on the margins of survival. The statistics must be treated with caution, but it seems that growth in the small shop sector came to an end in 1954, when 3,000 more businesses disappeared than were created. In the previous year 73 per cent of shopkeepers had declared an income below that of the average industrial worker. Even allowing for the greater opportunities to defraud open to the self-employed, it cannot be denied that many, if not most, shopkeepers were genuinely poor; certainly *Paris Match* on 9 April 1955 claimed that 65 per cent of *pâtissiers* at retirement were 'poor'. A further problem was that many tax officials came from Paris, or large towns, and had little understanding of the small, rural shop-keeper, a man who might have no clear distinction between stock and personal belongings, a man who lived out the ideal of the self-sufficient economic man rather than the profit-maximising entrepreneur. This tendency was compounded by the way in which tax officials treated shopkeepers as guilty of fraud unless proven innocent. For many small businessmen on the margin, the taxman was therefore an alien enemy engaged in a battle to the death.

France's fragmented pressure groups seemed unconcerned — or unable — to halt these trends. The CNPF (Conseil National du Patronat Français) had been established in 1946 in theory to represent the interests of all business, but it mainly concerned itself with the needs of the larger firms, many of which were doing well. The interests of small business were more specifically taken care of by several organisations, most notably the CGPME (Confédération Générale des Petites et Moyennes Entreprises), sometimes abbreviated to PME, founded in 1944 and led by Léon Gingembre. However, the CGPME was more representative of small industrialists than of shopkeepers and artisans, and its leader was an educated man who seemed mainly interested in securing the group's acceptability within the system.[8] This might not have mattered if the economic planners and politicians of the Fourth Republic had shown more interest in according intermediary groups an important role. In practice, genuine negotiations were few, and little attention was paid to the interests of small business, especially the damned artisans and small shopkeepers. This was a particularly surprising omission in view of their continued importance within the economy, and in the political sphere as electors. In 1954 there were 2.24 million people employed in commerce alone, 1.25 million of whom were independents. This meant that France had nineteen retail shops per 1,000 inhabitants, compared with ten in the USA and twelve in the UK — figures which planners took as further reasons for hastening the decline of small business rather than negotiating with its representatives. Blocked from the corridors of power, it was hardly surprising that shopkeepers should take to the streets to defend their traditional way of life.

Enter Poujade

In the small town of St. Céré (Lot) on 23 July 1953 small shopkeepers decided to prevent tax inspectors making a series of *contrôles* (official audits). Their technique was to mass outside the shop which was to be assessed, preventing the inspectors from entering; the owner of the shop remained inside, and could therefore not be charged with obstruction. News of the ensuing success of this method of collective action travelled quickly. Travelling salesmen spread the word to even the smallest village; owners of that political centre, the *bistro*, were only too happy to divert the conversation to taxation; even the local press showed an interest in this new phenomenon. By November it had been decided to hold a Constitutive Assembly in Cahors to establish the UDCA, with an annual subscription of three hundred francs; its own journal, *L'Union*, followed shortly afterwards. In November 1954 the UDCA held its first national Congress in Algiers, and announced the creation of a second journal, *Fraternité Française*. In the intervening twelve months many parts of France had witnessed a spectacular increase in the activities of the UDCA, or *'le mouvement Poujade'* as it quickly became known.[9]

The movement's propaganda portrayed Pierre Poujade as a young (he was thirty-three in 1953) apolitical family man, brought into the limelight by the iniquities of the tax system, and by corrupt, uncaring politicians. The truth was rather different. In his teens Poujade had been involved in proto-fascist politics — though his nationalism had been too strong to make him a collaborator — and he had left France, eventually joining the British Air Force. Returning to France after the Liberation, he set up a small stationery shop and wholesaling business in his home town of St. Céré. Thus whilst not wealthy, he was also not quite the *'petit papetier'* of Poujadist myth. However, such mythology was important to Poujade. He was a dynamic man, intensely conscious of the use of language, image and the media in political mobilisation.[10] Portraying himself as the simple man of the people, the *'petit gars'* who spoke in shirtsleeves, he used the vocabulary of the streets (and fields) to rally the oppressed small man. The metamorphosis of the UDCA into the Poujadist movement reflects his success in cultivating this image, as well as his tireless travels spreading the word in the early days of the movement.

Nevertheless, Poujadism was far more than a leader backed by an amorphous and rather troublesome mass. Hoffmann has pointed out that the UDCA's organisation was never well defined, and claimed this was a weakness of the movement.[11] Certainly the UDCA lacked the formal constitution normally associated with a pressure group, but the general structure was clear; moreover, it marked a notable development in the organisation of the traditionally individualist small businessman. The UDCA was based on a central organisation which issued vast quantities of detailed circulars on taxes, social security and other relevant topics, together with making arrangements for Poujade's major rallies. Below this was a series of committees stretching down to the cantonal level. They served in part to supply information, but acted primarily to coordinate self-help against *contrôles*, and to organise demonstrations. By the autumn of 1954 the UDCA was organised in fifty-four departments, mainly in the centre and south.[12] The giant Poujadist rally in Paris during January 1955, which attracted between one and two hundred thousand people in spite of floods and a ban on the use of public transport, unquestionably testifies to the fact that this was much more than a shadow organisation. Indeed, by the summer of 1955 the UDCA was well on the way to being a truly national movement, with 356,000 members, while central reserves stood at 160 million francs (subscriptions having been raised to 1,000 francs in 1954).[13]

In spite of this growing support, by the summer of 1955 the Poujadists had achieved little in policy terms. Raymond Aron and many others have accused the movement of having no serious programme.[14] Certainly a typical early Poujadist pamphlet called 'A Taxpayer's Dictionary' was hardly constructive; it included terms such as 'shopkeeper — vermin to be exterminated' and 'direct taxation, or a direct right to the chin'. The UDCA was defined more by what it was against than by what it was for. It was against Paris, urbanisation, faceless bureaucrats, and most of all the hated tax system. Even so, from 1953 it had an eight point programme, which whilst narrow was far from unreasonable given the nature of the tax system. It called for a series of changes, including simplifying the tax structure, ending certain tax concessions to larger businesses, an amnesty for shopkeepers charged for their part in the Poujadist troubles, and the same social security rights as other groups. From the movement's early days it had called upon Parliament to make reforms, but the Assembly's main response had been the famous Dorey Amendement of 1954 which allowed the imprisonment of anyone opposing *contrôles* (the UDCA was thus given plentiful 'martyrs'). In January 1955 the UDCA tried to pressure Deputies by requesting the parties to make specific replies to its programme. Some changes resulted in the tax administration, and there was an easing of *contrôles*, but by the summer of 1955 Poujade had decided that nothing of significance had been achieved on the policy front. This was an important factor in helping persuade Poujade to create a Poujadist Party, the UFF (*Union et Fraternité Française*).

In the French multi-party system such a party offered the prospect of wielding useful influence. However, Poujade's main goal at this time was not incorporation within the system. This can be seen by his call in 1955 for a new Estates General to hear the will of the people and break the influence of the bureaucrats and politicians. This proposal could be seen as fitting into the French Revolutionary tradition; certainly Poujade's language was replete with allusions to, and metaphors from, France's past. Nevertheless, many have preferred to see its attack on the parliamentary system as part of a growing fascist tendency within the UDCA.[15] In its early days there had been a strong Communist presence in the movement, a reflection of their interest in movements of the poor and of their electoral strength in some central departments. By 1955 Poujade had largely eliminated this PCF influence. Against a background of withdrawal from Indo-China and war in Algeria, he began to develop a strongly nationalist line; and the fact that France had a Jewish Prime Minister at the time, Pierre Mendès-France, reinforced anti-semitic strains in the movement. The creation in 1954–5 of parallel *Unions* for youth and other social groups, notably farmers, reflected a further attempt to broaden the social base of the movement. Even so, it would be a mistake to analyse the appeal of the UFF in the January 1956 parliamentary elections within the framework of fascism.[16]

In these elections the UFF and allied Poujadist lists captured 2,482,406 votes (11.6 per cent), a total which gave them 52 seats. Many commentators have tried to analyse this remarkable vote in terms of a geographical tradition of extremism or protest, an approach which owes much to the works of André Siegfried.[17] In fact, the Poujadists gained as many votes in former left-wing areas as in right-wing ones, and the exact pattern of the Poujadist vote is not only extremely complex but can only be fully understood by detailed local studies. Even so, two broad generalisations can be made about the vote. First, it was made up of *mécontents*, people protesting against the system. In his television broadcast before the election, the UFF peasant leader concluded that this time they would not need the guillotine as a rope was cheaper and faster! Poujade was more conciliatory, but there can be no doubt that the UFF appeared to be the protest party *par excellence*. Its most popular slogan sums this up perfectly — *'Sortez les Sortants'*. More specifically, the UFF appealed to two socio-economic groups, small farmers and especially artisans and small shopkeepers — people who had previously been politically heterogeneous, even non-voters. In most areas artisans and shopkeepers accounted for over half the UFF vote!

Nevertheless, the UFF had far from rallied everyone in this group. One major reason for this was the shopkeeper's dislike of 'politics'. Some felt they needed to be apolitical to retain customers, and many believed that little would come from political action. The UFF's entry into the parliamentary arena was therefore strongly opposed even by many who had joined the UDCA. Subsequent events in no way silenced this growing opposition. Indeed, the UFF group proved largely ineffective, mainly through the lack of any political experience and divisions within its numbers (in spite of an oath to remain loyal on pain of death!). The invalidation of eleven of its Deputies on account of alleged irregularities in their alliances reinforced the anti-parliamentary side of the movement.[18] Paradoxically, parliamentary deals in an attempt to gain influence created the impression that the movement was trying to become part of the 'system'. Poujade countered by trying not to lose sight of the movement's origins. Shopkeepers were still called upon to attack the 'fiscal Bastille' and its 'Gestapo'. The UDCA claimed over 400,000 members in 1956. Chamber of Commerce elections, which had witnessed a UDCA breakthrough in 1955, showed that the movement had continuing support at the professional level. However, when Poujade himself fought a parliamentary by-election in Paris in 1957, the Poujadist vote fell by 42.3 per cent.[19] Even before General de Gaulle's return to power in 1958 it was clear that Poujadism was collapsing as a major electoral force, and the UDCA was increasingly being rent by internal divisions and defections.

Poujade had been elected as a Gaullist *conseiller municipal* in the early 1950s, and was later to claim that de Gaulle and many of his entourage had voted UFF in 1956.[20] After the elections there had undoubtedly been close contacts between leading Gaullists and some in the UFF group. There were also close contacts between the Gaullists in Algeria and the strong Poujadist group there, a group which was to play an important part in the 1958 revolt. It was hinted that Poujade might receive a ministry in de Gaulle's new Government. Poujade was tempted, but eventually concluded that cooperation was only possible if a government adopted the philosophy of the UDCA. Otherwise the UDCA would be compromised like the other parties and groups which engaged in the unseemly scramble for office. This tendency to opposition was reinforced by fears that de Gaulle had little concern for small business, by the belief that the new constitution was a vehicle for de Gaulle's dominance, and by the suspicion that de Gaulle was less than fully committed to the retention of Algeria.[21] This opposition to de Gaulle was not shared by most small shopkeepers, and in the 1958 elections the Poujadists managed to win less than 3 per cent of the vote.

Membership of the UDCA slumped too — from 200,000 in 1958 to under 100,000 in 1959. Poujade became increasingly drawn into conspiratorial politics. In May 1958 General Chassin had invaded the St. Étienne Préfecture, but unsupported by an expected Poujadist uprising he fled for the hills.[22] This should have served as a warning to those in the *Algérie française* movement who saw Poujadism as a mass movement of nationalist hard-liners; most Poujadists in fact had few political interests outside immediate socio-economic ones. Nevertheless, Poujade was brought into the plotting of General Salan and other officers (some of whom feared the implications of technological change in the armed forces, a kind of military Poujadism). Once again Poujade seemed uncertain what course to follow, pulling out at the last minute when he realised that the plotters had no idea what they wanted to do once de Gaulle was deposed.[23]

A major change was also taking place in Poujade's attitude to protest. As he was later to write, 'We learned from experience that problems don't resolve themselves in the street'. Such action was only necessary if governments did not listen to grievances.[24] In 1965 an important meeting took place which confirmed this trend. De Gaulle had been forced into a second ballot in the Presidential election by François Mitterrand. On the first ballot, Poujade had backed the centrist Jean Lecanuet rather than the extreme right-wing Jean-Louis Tixier-Vignancour, who had been closely linked with the UFF in the late 1950s. Between ballots Poujade was approached by a member of Georges Pompidou's *cabinet*. The Prime Minister, whom Poujade knew from his contacts with the Gaullists in the 1950s, promised that in return for supporting de Gaulle, Poujade would become a privileged consultant on matters affecting small business. The UDCA remained only a shadow of its former self, but Pompidou realised that it reflected interests which were not catered for by the CGPME and other groups. Pompidou, realising that de Gaulle's charismatic appeal would die with him, also sought to ensure stability in the transition by the establishment of a more pluralist system. On 13 April 1968, *Le Monde* noted: 'If M. Pierre Poujade is received by M. Georges Pompidou the meeting will mark the culmination of a slow but sure evolution of the Poujadist movement towards the majority'. In fact, a series of meetings had already taken place between representatives of the UDCA and the government; in November 1967 Poujade had even attended the national Congress of the Gaullist party, the UDR, in Lille. During the troubles of May 1968 Poujade strongly supported the Government. He was rewarded by a special meeting between himself and Pompidou at the Hôtel Matignon in early June to discuss the problems of small business.[25]

Small business undoubtedly still faced major problems. In 1970 the UDCA's new manifesto put forward a programme to deal with these troubles. The centrepiece was a *'contrat de progrès'* between the government and groups. The growing importance of the state in economic policy, together with the far stronger Governments of the Fifth Republic, meant that negotiations were far more attractive than they had been in the 1950s. Indeed, the UDCA manifesto specifically stated that without government intervention, the position of small business would continue to deteriorate, and this would be accompanied by 'rebellion' and a 'crisis for the regime'.[26] Poujade and the UDCA were trying to show their supporters that the state was a necessary partner rather than an alien oppressor. The result of these changes was that during Pompidou's presidency Poujade became a regular adviser to the Government on issues affecting small business — an exponent of influence rather than charisma. Symbolically, he now wore suit and tie!

During the May 1974 presidential election campaign, Poujade wrote to Valéry Giscard d'Estaing offering support in the forthcoming second-ballot run-off against Mitterrand if he promised to continue Pompidou's approach at seeking an accommodation and consultations with small business. In spite of reassurances, Poujade soon found himself and the

UDCA excluded from discussions, though members of the CNPF and other groups were still received as honoured representatives. As a result, in September 1976, the National Council of the UFF decided to re-enter politics. The first main result of this was the 'apolitical' UDI (*Union de Défense Interprofessionnelle*) list which was put forward in the 1979 European elections. The list only gained 1.4 per cent of the vote, and by 1979 Poujade had launched a new organisation – the ANUREF (*Association Nationale pour l'Utilisation des Ressources Énergétiques Françaises*). In the 1960s Poujade had brought a hundred hectares at Villefranche Rouergue (Aveyron), which he used as a tourist centre and for farming. Small-farmer Poujade now launched himself into the field of '*biomasse*', the production of alcohol from vegetable products. As early as the 1950s he had been interested in the question of energy, though mainly in the context of Algerian oil. By 1980 it had become his central theme. June 1980 saw the publication of a new Poujadist journal, *Énergies Françaises*, which recounted in full detail the history of artichoke growing, and called on the government to authorise the use of ten per cent alcohol in petrol. In July he organised a well attended *biomasse* colloquium near his home. This was followed by a new tour of France, but most of these meetings only attracted a handful of listeners; gone were the days when Poujade could rally thousands even in a small town![27]

Gone too was the violence of the past campaigns. This reflected a change of tactic more than diminished support. Poujade openly stated that his appeal to artichoke growers was a lever to show that he could still gain the confidence of the little man. He also believed that energy would be central to the next presidential election.[28] Poujade wanted to reopen communication with the government and parties. In June, his new journal stressed the need to keep open all channels of communication, and the *biomasse* colloquium in July was in part designed to bring representatives of the parties to see him. This was achieved, and Poujade duly had his meetings with government representatives. However, in a letter to the President in April 1981 Poujade announced that he would call on his supporters to vote for Mitterrand. He claimed that he had been led from one government department to another, through hours of discussion for nothing.[29] Behind this was the bitterness which had swelled up during his exclusion from the councils of government after 1974. The endorsement of Mitterrand was his revenge. As such, it was a remarkable turn of history. In the 1950s Mitterrand had been one of the major targets of the Poujadists – the Minister of the Interior who had locked up their demonstrators, the slippery career politician. In 1965 and 1974 Poujade had endorsed Mitterrand's presidential opponents. In 1981 Mitterrand received Poujade's blessing as the candidate more likely to pay heed to his new crusade — and to the interests of his old constituency, the artisans and shopkeepers.

II. From Poujade to Nicoud

The rise of CIDUNATI

Poujade's failure to rally small business in the late 1970s with his UDI stemmed in part from the emergence at the end of the 1960s of a new movement which took over the UDCA's mantle — Nicoud's CIDUNATI. The rapid decline of the UDCA in the late 1950s had marked a significant reduction in artisan and small shopkeeper protest. The early 1960s was a period of sporadic outbursts, as these groups lacked both a specific issue to mobilise them and the dynamic leadership which Poujade and his movement had provided. In 1961 the number of small shopkeepers had even begun increasing, a trend which continued until 1967. However, this growth hides notable gains in some areas such as electrical goods and furniture, and losses in groceries and cafés, especially in the more rural areas. Moreover, the 1960s saw the rapid expansion of American-style super- and hypermarkets (and a new wave of *franglais* such as '*le freezer*'). In 1969 their number grew by 20 and 80 per cent respectively.[30] In the previous year, the number of small businesses once more had begun to decline dramatically.

The great protest waves of 1968 and their aftermath further troubled many small businessmen. In total, the commercial sector still accounted for 2.45 million workers, of whom 750,000 were independents.[31] This group had rallied strongly behind de Gaulle in the June 1968 elections. They received few rewards, reinforcing their belief that they were still unloved and ignored. Agricultural workers, who increasingly in the 1960s had proved a troublesome group, found their minimum wage raised by 56 per cent; SMIG (the official minimum wage) was raised by 35 per cent. The Fifth Plan envisaged wages increasing by only about 4 to 6 per cent per annum, but industrial wages in 1968 rose by 11 per cent. At the same time, workers gained concessions over the length of the working week, holidays and the right to negotiate within factories. The students, whose activities had provided the spark in May, were promised reforms; years of negotiations had failed to produce such movement.[32] The lessons were not hard to draw; all that was required was a specific issue and leadership.

Both were to arrive in 1968. In November the Government's austerity programme included increases in VAT, but tax concessions were made to larger businesses in an effort to help dampen home demand and boost exports. VAT was already a contentious issue with small shopkeepers. There were five main rates calculated on returns (thus making the 15 per cent rate in reality 17.65 per cent). More specifically, VAT's application had been extended to all retail sales in 1968, thus involving shopkeepers in much more work and making them *de facto* tax collectors! However, the most immediate issue which concerned small business at this time was the Social Security Law of 1966, which made health insurance obligatory for artisans, small shopkeepers and the liberal professions. Prior to introducing the system the Government had hastily consulted the CGPME and some other business groups (but not the UDCA), and there had been general agreement.[33] But the resulting system was less favourable than the one which covered other groups, and when demands for the first payment (to be made on 1 January 1969) were received, it was found that the premiums were higher than had been anticipated.

Throughout France small groups began to organise in late 1968. Typical of this development was a meeting on 8 December in the small village of La Bâtie-Montgascon (Isère). Among the handful of small shopkeepers present was a 23-year-old café proprietor in the village, Gérard Nicoud. Nicoud, who had been born in Marseille and only recently bought his café, had not previously been active in any sort of organisation, but he launched himself with enthusiasm into the fray. More meetings followed, often covered by the local press. In February 1969 ten thousand small businessmen attended a mass rally in Grenoble. Poujade decided to attend, but he spoke only briefly. He received a rough reception from many delegates. Some claimed that his dealings with the government meant that it was he who was now the '*ensaucissonné*'. Others reproached him for the decline of the UDCA as a mass organisation — Nicoud was later to claim that Poujade could hold a rally of his supporters in a telephone kiosk. No love was to be lost between Poujade and the new organisation.[34]

This organisation adopted the title of CIDCAPL (*Comité d'Information et de Défense des Commerçants, Artisans et Professions Libérales*), and decided to broaden the movement to other departments by collecting a petition against the new social security system. Support poured in, especially from the south-east, south-west and parts of the north-west. This was a rather different geographical pattern to the early expansion of Poujadism, but it reflected support primarily within the same relatively poor, more rural communities (although the home of CIDCAPL was changing rapidly and becoming more prosperous — the Isère had also been a Poujadist stronghold in the 1950s). This growing support was accompanied by widespread troubles among shopkeepers. Roads were blocked, supermarkets attacked and one mayor kidnapped briefly. The

CGPME, anticipating this tide of protest, called its own day of action Many ignored this token. For them the PME were *'Petits Mous Endormis'* ('little sleeping wets'). In April, four hundred artisans and small shop-keepers with a taste for more serious action closed off the town of La Tour-du-Pin, where the CIDCAPL had established its headquarters, and sacked the tax offices. Nicoud threatened to throw the documents in the river unless there were concessions. The police responded by arresting Nicoud, an act which provoked serious troubles between his supporters and the CRS (the national riot police). With de Gaulle's referendum on regional and Senate reform imminent, changes were promised and Nicoud released. In the aftermath of de Gaulle's defeat, a defeat which Nicoud claimed owed much to the small shopkeeper vote, Nicoud called a truce. In spite of the opposition to de Gaulle over his government's lack of concern for the plight of artisans and small shopkeepers, CIDCAPL was keen to retain an apolitical stance to maximise its support.

France's new President, Pompidou, had promised small shopkeepers an important future in a speech before the Assembly of Chambers of Commerce in March 1969. In June he even visited Grenoble and promised changes in the 1966 law and other reforms. Round table talks followed in August, but the delegates were divided and small business was not a major concern of the new Prime Minister, Jacques Chaban-Delmas. He believed that the 'stalemate society' still plagued France, a view shared by many academics.[35] Although Chaban-Delmas talked of a 'new society', involving more consultation and decentralisation, his plans centred on industrial expansion. In the autumn of 1969 Nicoud responded with a new campaign of direct action. Once more hunted by the police, he told his supporters that he had to disappear into the *'maquis'* (Nicoud shared with Poujade a taste for Resistance imagery). Two months later he allowed himself to be caught. In court he told his judges that legality and justice were not always the same thing. They seem to have agreed, for he was given only a six month suspended sentence. A Gallup poll in the same month showed that a surprising number of French people agreed too: 49 per cent sympathised with the small business protest, whereas only 35 per cent disapproved.[36]

These brushes with the law in no way curbed Nicoud's activities, nor did a partial reform of the social security law in January 1970. Nicoud travelled widely, attracting large audiences wherever he went. In March twenty thousand gathered to hear him speak at the Parc des Princes. Immediately afterwards, he requested a meeting with Chaban-Delmas, claiming his movement was now representative. The Prime Minister refused, and Nicoud responded with a call for renewed direct action.

Nicoud openly called himself — with obvious allusions to the students' leaders — a 'revolutionary who worked'. Politicians, bureaucrats and trusts were all damned in terms reminiscent of Poujade. Once again the accusation was made that here was fascism in the making — a charge with little serious foundation, though the movement did attract a certain amount of interest from both the extreme left and the extreme right.[37] An IFOP poll in April showed that 44 per cent disapproved of Nicoud's mounting extremism, whereas only 26 per cent approved.[38] However, by this time Nicoud had again been arrested. This time he was sentenced to six months in prison (two after appeal), a decision which led to further rioting in Grenoble.

Elections in April to the local administrative bodies of the artisans' and shopkeepers' social security organisations indicated that the Government might have been better advised to treat this new group as representative; CIDCAPL gained 24 per cent of the vote. Supporters of another more loosely organised group which had emerged during 1968–9, the UNATI, gained a further 22 per cent. The UDCA received 17 per cent. Over the summer of 1970 these two new groups were to merge, thus forming the CIDUNATI. This new organisation was to have a General Secretary, plus committees at the national, departmental and cantonal level. A relatively high subscription of fifty francs was set, partly to finance the movement's own journal, L'Objectif (other publications followed later). The movement thus took on the more formalised aspect of a pressure group, though as André Bonnet has noted, the public continued to identify it with Nicoud, the CIDUNATI's first General Secretary.[39]

In an interview with L'Express published on 1 June 1970 Nicoud claimed that the next step for the movement was the development of its organisation and policies; the advice of experts was to be sought in a variety of fields. In part such help was clearly to be provided by local groups on specific issues such as taxation and the creation of cooperatives, but it is clear that Nicoud had in mind more general dealings with the Government. He claimed that he had only ordered the violence in 1970 after Chaban-Delmas had refused to hold negotiations. He saw the cause of violence in society as bad organisation, a bureaucratic structure which failed to take notice of people's desires and feelings. He claimed that he had frequently written to de Gaulle about the problem of small shop-keepers, but he had never received a reply. Nicoud concluded by stating that the CIDUNATI would always be ready to negotiate with the Government. The declining popular support for the problems of small business revealed by opinion polls had almost certainly brought home to Nicoud that excessive violence was counterproductive. He was rewarded shortly afterwards when in July for the first time a Government minister officially met members of the CIDUNATI.

These meetings did not produce sufficient concessions, and the CIDUNATI's campaign of demonstrations was renewed. Nicoud again found himself in gaol. The CIDUNATI responded by adopting a more overtly anti-Government stance. At the time of the referendum on the extension of the EEC in April 1972 it recommended abstention to its members. In December 1972 *L'Objectif* was to claim that this was a major factor in the low turnout. The attitude of the left was undoubtedly more important, but the referendum played its part in Pompidou's decision to change the leadership of the Government, a decision reinforced by accusations that Chaban-Delmas had been involved in tax evasion! In July 1972 he was succeeded by Pierre Messmer, while Edgar Faure was created Minister of Social Affairs. The latter had undertaken the delicate task of appeasing the farm lobby after it had recommended abstention against de Gaulle.[40] His new role clearly involved handling the troublesome small businessmen. Yvon Bourges was also appointed to the newly created Ministry of '*Commerce et Artisanat*'. Nicoud was released from gaol, and during August he was received by both Bourges and Faure.

D. L. Hanley has claimed that the CIDUNATI shows that 'a delinquent group is still able to frighten Paris into giving something away'.[41] However, by this time the CIDUNATI had established itself as a serious small business organisation. In 1972 it claimed 210,000 members, compared to 140,000 in 1970. *Le Monde* on 7 March 1972 claimed that the CIDUNATI was well organised at the local level, providing extensive services to its members. Nicoud claimed that a third of these members were old, a third young, and a third women ('*les plus dures*'). The exact composition of membership is hard to assess, but its main strength was undoubtedly among the artisans and small shopkeepers, though like the UDCA it had its larger business members. This can be seen by the programme which it developed during 1970–2. Its first demand was the complete reform of the 1966 social security law. Its second concern was the control of the establishment of new super- and hypermarkets, and the unfair tax concessions allowed to large businesses. Finally, it sought the reform of local taxation, especially *les patentes* – 'a model of incoherence' according to Maurice Roy – and the tax which had risen most rapidly during the Fifth Republic.[42] This unfair system of local taxation meant that poor small shopkeepers helped finance the infrastructure for the new commercial developments on the peripheries of towns and cities, a growth which furthered the decline of inner-urban areas.

Pressure politics and political change: towards incorporation?

By the beginning of 1973 the government had made several concessions on these issues, for example a more generous system of pensions and the introduction of some controls on the establishment of new super- and hypermarkets. However, with parliamentary elections due before the Spring of 1973 it was inevitable that small business groups could extract further concessions. While Nicoud had been in prison during 1972 he had received letters from 129 Deputies, including four from the General Secretary of the Gaullists.[43] The prospect of a more sympathetic Government was undoubtedly a factor in the overwhelming vote against entering the political arena at the CIDUNATI Congress in November 1972. *Le Nouvel Observateur* had earlier reported on 10 January that there were strong rumours that Nicoud was planning to follow Poujade by contesting the forthcoming elections. Nevertheless, this reaffirmation of the CIDUNATI's apolitical stance did not prevent its supporters waging campaigns against individual Deputies whom they disliked. Giscard d'Estaing, the Finance Minister, found himself present at several unruly meetings where CIDUNATI members seemed to remember his role in introducing VAT, and more recent policies which were seen as less than sympathetic to small business. René Pleven, the Minister of Justice, may even have been defeated as a result of a campaign of revenge for his role in imprisoning Nicoud.

By May 1973 tax inspectors were on strike as a result of the lack of prosecutions against those who had opposed *contrôles* or had failed to fill in various tax forms as a result of the CIDUNATI's call for a boycott. The government showed no taste for pursuing such offenders, and in some parts of France tax inspection was paralysed.[44] In the autumn of 1973 the new Minister of Commerce, Jean Royer, made a trip around France to discuss a major concession. Royer had decided to accept one of the major proposals of the CIDUNATI (and Poujade), that of moving the power to approve new supermarkets from the Prefect to a series of commissions, composed partly of small businessmen. France still had only forty-three super- or hypermarkets per million inhabitants compared to fifty-three in West Germany, but the number was growing rapidly. Even public opinion was not entirely happy about this trend. An IFOP poll at the time showed that 78 per cent of French people did not want to see small business ruined.[45] A delighted CIDUNATI warned Deputies that their attitude to the *Loi Royer* would be important when it came to the next elections; even Giscard d'Estaing cancelled a holiday in the Niger to speak in the debate. In the debate Royer claimed: *'Les commerçants, c'est la France'*.

Cynics might have remembered the old cry: '*L'Algérie, c'est la France*'; but many shopkeepers undoubtedly saw the law as heralding a new age in which their interests would be treated more sympathetically. Even Nicoud announced in December 1973 that he would now devote himself more to the philosophy of the movement.[46]

In the 1974 presidential elections Nicoud continued CIDUNATI's non-partisan stance by declining to endorse Royer's candidature. In fact, Royer attracted few votes outside his home fief of Tours. The small shop-keeper vote seems to have been divided, though Giscard d'Estaing received a surprisingly large percentage of the vote in view of his troubles with this group. Chaban-Delmas was if anything even less popular, and there were fears about possible changes if Mitterrand were elected. The general drift of the policy of the *majorité*, especially since 1971, had been one of concessions to artisans and small shopkeepers, and of according them a more respected place in the system. Clearly many hoped that Giscard would continue this trend. Nicoud's election to the presidency of the artisans' and shopkeepers' social security fund in August 1974 was taken as a further sign by many of his accommodation to the system. Nicoud, whose supporters in the March elections to the Chambers of Commerce had won 56 per cent of the votes, seemed on the point of becoming a respected representative of small business. A 1974 study of the changing relations between state and society showed that behind Nicoud, artisans and small shopkeepers were one of the least dissentient groups.[47]

However, some *enragés* within the CIDUNATI were far from happy about these developments; the old suspicion of the state lingered on. Others pointed to Nicoud's new cars, smarter clothes; were these not the proof that he too had become '*ensaucissonné*'? In truth, Nicoud had never fully given up his self-image as the revolutionary. This tendency to renewed pro-test was quickly reinforced by the attitude of the Government. Although the Fifth Republic had seen an increasing tendency to consult groups, even to negotiate with them, old authoritarian tendencies died hard. Govern-ments seemed keen not to increase the power of groups to the extent that they could challenge the strength of the government itself. Moreover, Giscard soon proved that he was less concerned with the interests of artisans and small shopkeepers than his predecessor. The Seventh Plan in 1975 retained a strong commitment to economic growth; Giscard's general vision seemed to be the introduction of a more liberal economy. Groups representing the interests of large business, such as the CNPF, were fre-quently consulted, but some of the smaller groups found themselves once more in the cold. By 1980, not a single work group preparing the Eighth Plan was specifically interested in the problems of domestic commerce.[48]

By the autumn of 1975 Gingembre on behalf of the CGPME wrote to the President saying that small business was again suffering nothing but insults and handicaps; he quickly received 100,000 letters of support.[49] One reason for this was the growing number of tax *contrôles* as part of a campaign to stamp out evasion. A study was subsequently to show that in 1974 evasion among non-salaried independents had in no way decreased over the years. It was estimated that income was under-declared on average by 50 per cent.[50] However, the main beneficiaries of this were undoubtedly the liberal professions and the smaller man represented more by the CIDUNATI was therefore again aroused to protest. A new campaign of direct action began. In June 1978 Nicoud and CIDUNATI activists occupied tax offices in La Rochelle, insulting local tax officers ('the Gestapo'). During the subsequent trial in January 1980, two hundred CIDUNATI supporters blocked roads in the town with flaming tyres. An extraordinary CIDUNATI Congress in Paris later in the month saw seven hundred delegates gather to discuss the new term of imprisonment imposed on Nicoud. The result was a remarkably restrained meeting; behind the occasional outbursts of violent language there was a clear desire to present the image of a respectable pressure group rather than a bunch of *mécontents*.[51] This preference for negotiations can further be seen in the continuing troubles over the social security system. The CIDUNATI claimed that a change had been made in the retirement scheme for artisans without sufficient consultations. A meeting was demanded with the Government. After talks had failed to materialise, one hundred and fifty CIDUNATI members in February 1981 raided the Paris headquarters of the retirement fund and made off with three tons of documents. Still denied round-table discussions, the CIDUNATI decided to dump the documents in the Seine at the beginning of March.[52]

Even Government policies which it might have been thought would please small businessmen tended to be viewed at best with suspicion by many of the CIDUNATI's supporters. The extension of price controls as part of the anti-inflation programme had been another contentious issue in the mid 1970s. When Prime Minister Raymond Barre in 1977 announced maximum prices on some products, notably bread and drinks, *boulangeries* and cafés throughout France closed in protest. However, when the Government after the 1978 elections began a relaxation of price controls, some shopkeepers began to have second thoughts. In particular, a price war broke out over that every-day staple, the *baguette* (the standard bread stick). This reinforced fears that Giscard was trying to maximise economic growth through a freer market structure; and many small shopkeepers were at last learning that the free market had particular dangers for them.

Meanwhile, as unemployment rose in the late 1970s, Giscard and Barre rediscovered some of the virtues of small business. The Minister of Commerce in October 1978 expressed the view that the best hope of creating new jobs lay in small business; but in spite of a 12.5 per cent increase in the budget of this ministry, its expenditure remained one of the lowest of any government department.[53] Moreover, many of the specific measures introduced during 1978–81 helped the PME-type firm, or artisans, rather than the small shopkeeper.

The final nail in the coffin of the Government for Nicoud and many in the CIDUNATI came in 1980 when the *Procureur de la République* (public prosecutor) in Bourgoin-Jallieu sought to debar Nicoud from his position as General Secretary of the CIDUNATI under a section of the Code of Work which stated that leading members of unions must not have been condemned to more than three months in prison.[54] Nicoud announced sarcastically that he would be applying for nationality of the Central African Republic (Giscard must have been ruing the day he accepted a 'small' gift of diamonds from the Republic's Emperor). He added that he was tearing up his voter's card. CIDUNATI supporters responded by blocking the Paris-Annecy rail link, and increasing verbal attacks on the Government's treatment of them. (It was even claimed that government *agents provocateurs* were behind some of the alleged activities by CIDUNATI '*casseurs*').

This episode attracted considerable attention, not least from the Socialist Party, which had been taking an increasing interest in small business. In the late 1960s Nicoud's advocate had been Robert Badinter (now Minister of Justice), who found himself criticised by many left-wing colleagues for defending this 'fascist'. By the late 1970s times had changed. When in 1978 a CIDUNATI official was taken to court for publishing a pamphlet abusing tax inspectors, he was able to produce at his trial a letter from the leading Socialist Michel Rocard, claiming that the French tax system was one of the most archaic and unjust in Europe! Even Mitterrand allowed himself to be photographed with Nicoud. With 2.5 million people working in commerce in 1981, 580,000 of whom were independents, this was a group well worth courting electorally, especially as opinion polls showed a continuing popular desire not to see small business destroyed. The Socialists were also increasingly becoming aware of the importance of small business in terms of creating new employment. For example, in spite of rising unemployment, the number of artisans had actually risen since 1972, halting a long period of decline.[55]

In January 1981 the well-known professional clown Coluche, whose presidential candidacy had just received Nicoud's endorsement, claimed that he would easily acquire the five hundred signatures needed from 'among the three thousand mayors' who were members of the CIDUNATI.[56] However, there had been growing opposition to Nicoud over his continuing violent activities, and many CIDUNATI members seem to have been reluctant to follow the advice to vote for *'le plus con'*. Small businessmen, like the farmers before them, were learning to use the vote as a tactical weapon, eschewing the more charismatic and spectacular leadership for the politics of influence. The tendency was further encouraged by the Socialist programme. Mitterrand's election address in April specifically promised to introduce a fairer social security system for artisans and small shopkeepers. Other specific campaign promises to small business included a moratorium on further hypermarket construction. The more general commitment to a fairer tax system also had its appeal. So did the balance between the emphasis on new state activity, together with greater individual freedoms. (The latter was an important theme to the Socialists for it helped counter the myth that socialism equalled statism and bureaucracy.) More generally, the Socialists' vocabulary reflected a new social vision more in keeping with that of many small businessmen; references to the working class, to development, progress and organisation were fewer than in the past. Their slogan, *La Force Tranquille*, and the poster which showed Mitterrand in front of a small village bathed in warm sunlight, encapsulated this new appeal.

It would be wrong to conclude that there was a unified small business vote in 1981, either in the presidential or subsequent parliamentary elections. A poll published in *Le Nouvel Observateur* on 4 July 1981 showed that in June the Socialists had attracted 35 per cent of the artisan and small shopkeeper vote, the Gaullists gained 31 per cent, and the supporters of Giscard 19 per cent. Nevertheless, this represented a notable change compared to elections from 1965 until 1978 when the parties of the previous *majorité* had enjoyed the support of most of this group. Moreover, the general motivation behind the small shopkeeper vote had changed dramatically since the 1950s. In 1956 many had voted for the UFF to destroy the system rather than to reform it. In 1981 a vote for Mitterrand and the Socialists was more a vote for a change of policy than a negative protest, a desire for renewed contacts with the Government on a variety of issues. Poujade's endorsement of Mitterrand in 1981 thus symbolises a quite remarkable change in small business politics during the preceeding generation: the movement from revolt to reconciliation.

Conclusion

It would be foolish to predict that the new Socialist Administration will achieve a permanent accommodation with small business. Although some parts of small business are buoyant, the general economic situation is uncertain, and small business protest in the past has been strongly correlated with economic factors. However, both small businessmen and the new Government seem to have learned many lessons from the past. Small business has increasingly become aware of the need for government aid, using protest for specific purposes rather than in a blind attack on the whole system. The Socialists have come to terms with small business as an important group both economically and electorally. The accommodation which has taken place is therefore not quite the classic institutionalisation/goal-displacement model. Small business groups have modified their organisation and values, but so too has the system. *Le Figaro* on 2 and 3 May 1981 claimed that some small business groups believed that the Socialists' promises to small business were incompatible with their more general commitment to growth, nationalisation and state control. Clearly, this question raises complex economic and political issues. However, small business is now far less afraid of state intervention than it was a generation ago and both the UDCA and CIDUNATI have since the 1950s tried to stress the importance of the state in many activities. Moreover, the Socialists' commitments to small business should not be seen as purely cynical. There is now a more general agreement about the importance of small business in creating employment, especially in a country like France where small business has in many ways remained remarkably resilient. More generally, the Socialists' interest in small business provides a useful counter to their statist tendencies; they are showing a greater sophistication about the exact nature and extent of governmental activity. A commitment to economic growth and concentration will undoubtedly remain the reality in the foreseeable future, but after a generation of neglect France is rediscovering the myth of the small man as the reification of Liberty, Equality and Fraternity. This trend will undoubtedly be accompanied by more peaceful relations between the state and the once frequently troublesome artisans and small shopkeepers.

Notes

1 S. Hoffmann, 'Protest in Modern France' in M. A. Kaplan (ed.), *The Revolution in World Politics* (New York: John Wiley and Sons, 1962), pp. 74–5.
2 D. Thomson, *Democracy in France since 1870* (Oxford: Oxford University Press, 1969 edn.), p. 42.

3 The best general account of French society and politics in this period is T. Zeldin, *France, 1848-1945*, 2 volumes (Oxford: Oxford University Press, 1973 and 1977).

4 The best general account of the politics of the Fourth Republic can be found in P. M. Williams, *Crisis and Compromise* (London: Longmans, 1964).

5 The most convenient source of statistics is B. R. Mitchell, *European Historical Statistics, 1750-1975* (London: Macmillan, 1980). Unless otherwise acknowledged, more detailed statistics in this chapter come from INSEE, *Annuaire statistique de la France*, 1950-1980 (Paris: Presses Universitaires de France, published annually).

6 For example, B. E. Brown, 'Pressure Group Politics in France', *Journal of Politics*, vol. 20, no. 4 (November, 1958), p. 705.

7 For an account of the development of the French tax system see G. Ardant, *Histoire de l'impôt*, vol. 2 (Paris: Fayard, 1972).

8 The best general account of business groups at this time is H. W. Ehrmann, *Organized Business in France* (Princeton, N.J.: Princeton University Press, 1957). See also G. E. Lavau, 'La Confédération Générale des Petites et Moyennes Entreprises', *Revue Française de Science Politique*, vol. 5, no. 3 (June, 1955).

9 The best account of the rise of the UDCA may be found in S. Hoffmann, *Le Mouvement Poujade* (Paris: Colin, 1956). Cf. D. Borne, *Petits bourgeois en révolte? le mouvement Poujade* (Paris: Flammarion, 1977). Poujade's own account may be found in *J'ai choisi le combat* (St Céré: Société Générale des Editions et des Publications, 1955).

10 C. Guy, *Le cas Poujade* (Givors: André Martel, 1955), esp. p. 58; Guy was a journalist from *Paris-Presse* who for a time was swept away by Poujade's charms.

11 Hoffmann, *Le Mouvement Poujade*, op. cit., esp. pp. 412-13.

12 *L'Union*, August-September 1954.

13 H. Bonnaud, *L'aventure Poujade* (Montpellier: Cl. Brunel, 1955), pp. 107-10; Bonnaud had been Treasurer of the UDCA.

14 R. Aron, *France: Steadfast and Changing* (Cambridge, Mass.: Harvard University Press, 1960), p. 36.

15 For example, S. M. Lipset, *Political Man* (London: Heinemann, 1976 edn.), esp. pp. 154-63.

16 For an account of the UFF in the context of the elections see M. Duverger, *et al.*, *Les élections du 2 janvier 1956* (Paris: Colin, 1957).

17 See for example, A. Siegfried, *De la IVe à la Ve République* (Paris: Grasset, 1958), pp. 233-6.

18 The Fourth Republic system of *apparentements* (loose coalitions of electoral *lists* in the proportional representation) had been introduced mainly to help the moderate parties gain at the expense of the PCF and the new Gaullist RPF in the late 1940s; it was ironic that the UFF should have used the system rather too well against the established parties in 1956.

19 See L. Bodin and J. Touchard, 'L'élection partielle de la première circonscription de la Seine', *Revue Française de Science Politique*, vol. 7, no. 2 (April, 1957).

20 P. Poujade, *A l'heure de la colère* (Paris: Albin Michel, 1977), p. 186.

21 Ibid., esp. p. 217.

22 J. S. Ambler, *The French Army in Politics, 1945-1962* (Columbus, Ohio: Ohio State University Press, 1966), p. 267.

23 Poujade, *A l'heure de la colère*, op. cit., especially pp. 226-8.

24 Ibid., p. 247.

25 *Le Monde*, 9-10 June 1968.

26 UDCA manifesto, p. 4: supplement to *Fraternité Française*, 13 June 1970.

27 For example, see *Ouest-France*, 28 October 1980.

28 *Midi Libre*, 1-3 April 1980.

29 Full text kindly supplied to me by M. Poujade.
30 *Association Française de Recherches et Etudes Statistiques Commerciales*, no. 172 (May, 1970).
31 R. Vouette, 'Le commerce et les services commerciaux', in J. P. Page *et al., Profil économique de la France* (Paris: La Documentation Française, 1975), p. 169.
32 For details of the changes in 1968 see M. Cohen, *et al., Le bilan social de l'année 1968* (Paris: Revue Pratique de Droit Social, 1969).
33 R. Millot, 'La position des travailleurs indépendants face aux problèmes de l'assurance-maladie avant l'adoption de la Loi du 12 juillet 1966', *Droit Social*, no. 3 (1970).
34 For Nicoud's own account of these events see his *Les dernières libertés* (Paris: Denoël, 1973).
35 See J. E. S. Hayward, 'State Intervention in France: The Changing Style of Government–Industry Relations', *Political Studies*, vol. 20, no. 3 (September, 1972).
36 G. H. Gallup, ed., *The Gallup International Public Opinion Polls: France, 1939, 1944–1975*, 2 vols. (New York: Random House, 1976), p. 722.
37 For an example of this charge see J. Ardagh, *The New France* (Harmondsworth: Penguin Books, 1973 edn.), p. 169.
38 *L'Express*, 20 April 1970.
39 A. Bonnet, 'Un nouveau groupe de pression: le CID-UNATI', *Revue Politique et Parlementaire* (June–July, 1973), p. 47.
40 See Y. Tavernier, 'Le syndicalisme paysan et la Cinquième République', *Revue Française de Science Politique*, vol. 1, no. 5 (1966).
41 D. L. Hanley, A. P. Kerr and N. Waites, *Contemporary France: Politics and Society since 1945* (London: Routledge and Kegan Paul, 1979), pp. 181–2.
42 M. Roy, *Les commerçants entre la révolte et la modernisation* (Paris: Seuil, 1971), pp. 75 and 89.
43 *L'Express*, 28 August 1972.
44 'Confession d'un percepteur', *L'Expansion* (February, 1973).
45 *L'Express*, 8 October 1973.
46 *Le Nouvel Observateur*, 31 December 1973.
47 See chapter 1, p. 4.
48 *Le Figaro*, 11 February 1981.
49 *Le Point*, 26 April 1976.
50 Centre d'Études des Revenus et des Coûts, *Les revenus des non-salariés* (Paris: CERC, 1980).
51 *Le Monde*, 22 January 1980.
52 *Le Figaro*, 3 March 1981.
53 *Le Monde*, 28 October 1978.
54 *Le Monde*, 5 April 1980.
55 M. Durand and J.-P. Frémont, *L'artisanat en France* (Paris: Presses Universitaires de France, 1979), p. 46.
56 *Le Monde*, 21 January 1981.

I should like to thank the British Academy for funding my research in France.
I should also like to thank Judith Evans for her draft reading of this chapter and her stylistic suggestions.

5   Non-Terrorism and the Politics of Repressive Tolerance

PHIL CERNY
Lecturer in Politics
University of York

Terrorism as a political phenomenon lies at the margin of the modern social order. Defined by the norms of the liberal–democratic state, it appears as a form of deviance, an extreme form of political pressure that threatens to subvert the fragile balance of cross-cutting interests upon which the stability of politics in a pluralist society rests. Seen thus in a pathological perspective, it is treated by the state as a 'law-and-order problem' — and the methods of law and order, always problematic in a liberal–democratic context, inevitably mean the recourse to measures of a repressive nature. However, the widely internalised pathological image, far from evoking a mass outcry or protest, not only carries public opinion along with greater repression but also creates public — 'democratic' — pressure for tougher measures still. For terrorism, as communicated by contemporary mass media, has become the eschatological myth of capitalist society, evoking an existential dread, the fear of the collapse of the social order itself.

The reason for this is not simply the 'revolutionary' ideology of certain terrorist groups. Rather, it is their own self-definition of their position as outside, rather than inside, the social order itself, and the definition of their stance as that of war. Far from seeking 'legitimate' ends within the political bounds of pluralism, they threaten the social contract with a new state of nature by attempting to force the authorities to break their own contract, to reveal the underlying authoritarianism of the political bond, and thereby to demystify 'democratic' capitalist society and catalyse a popular search for alternatives. The potential power of these groups seems to lie not in their threat to overthrow society by force of arms *per se*, but in their ability to symbolise the fragility and vulnerability of the social order and to force that order to subvert itself by eroding the liberal and democratic values upon which its own legitimacy is based.

The evidence of the 1970s suggests that such a confrontation leads to a twofold trap. In the first place, the terrorist groups themselves are caught in a trap of escalation. Although their symbolic threat is felt as a deadly broadside by the guardians of society, the material resources of such groups in money, arms and troops are circumscribed and vulnerable. In a pitched battle with the army and the police, they will succumb, unless they have a territorial base (as nationalist or ethnic guerrilla groups sometimes have) that is relatively defensible. Only where the old social order is so unjust and inherently unpopular that to speak of 'terrorists' is wholly misleading (and may more aptly be applied to the authorities themselves), and where a true guerrilla movement can take root, do 'terrorist' methods really threaten society — and only then as part of a larger strategic picture. In contrast, terrorist methods employed in a society where systemic norms are widely internalised will lead to strong popular support for increased repression. Terrorism is thus firstly a trap for the terrorists themselves.

The second trap, however, is set for the social order. For while the terrorists may fail to spark a popular insurrection, the reaction to their threat does put the value of liberal democracy at risk, all the more because public opinion has been anaesthetised by the fear of the collapse of society itself. Repression in this context takes many forms. On the one hand, censorship, increased police and military coerciveness, the erosion of the rights of defendants, psychological torture and the political manipulation of the judicial process all affect the individual in his relationship with the state. On the other hand, the identification of 'sympathisers', the association of terrorism with radicalism of any kind, the generalisation of the notion of 'violence' to include political demonstrations, the blacklisting of groups and individuals, and the like, threaten the rationale of the pluralist state itself by interfering with the interaction of groups and are often aimed at the suppression of free political and ideological opposition. When both of these forms of repression are used *in tandem*, as in the Federal Republic of Germany today, society falls headlong into the trap set by the terrorists, although the terrorists themselves are in no position to exploit the situation (if they still exist at all).[1]

In this context, terrorism itself becomes a myth that can be used for purposes of social control. It becomes embedded in the catch-phrases of the media and the rhetoric of politicians. In an age of limited wars in faraway places, it fulfils the function of a war-in-microcosm, increasing social solidarity. In this era of international communications and the increasingly interlocking interests of the developed capitalist countries, it does not merely evoke the image of defending a nation, but raises the spectre of a threat to Western civilisation not seen since 'international Communism' was deactivated by polycentrism and peaceful coexistence. But it goes even deeper into the heart of social mores, providing visible and frightening bogeymen and pirates to reawaken the dark and mystical fears that still lie latent in a culture that demands a modern and empirically verifiable veneer for its supersitions.

The political significance of terrorism, then, lies less in its organisational or violent manifestations than in its interaction with the social formation and political system in which it occurs. If a strong authoritarian potential is latent in a society with a liberal–democratic political order, then the danger to liberal democracy is that it will be subverted through its own forms and institutions as the objective of social survival takes priority. This danger exists most strongly where the process of modernisation has been controlled, overtly or covertly, by a coherent set of elite groups whose position derived originally from a pre-modern — feudal or dynastic — social order, but who have been able to transform and reinforce that position in the context of industrial capitalism. In contrast, if the democratic political revolution, based on social pluralism and the peaceful competition of elites, antedates the economic modernisation process, and if the idea of progress is culturally associated more strongly with the former, then the threat of terrorism — like the threat of foreign war — is less likely to subvert liberal democracy. Indeed, it might by hypothesised that terrorism is less likely to occur, less likely to lead to public paranoia where it does occur and less likely to provoke systematic repression from a state that not only fears the undermining of its democratic legitimacy but may also contain within itself countervailing elites who will resist the temptation to fall into the trap.

To all appearances, France fits the second stereotype fairly well. She has not experienced the appearance of an archetypal terrorist organisation comparable to the Red Army Faction in Germany or the Red Brigades in Italy. There has certainly been no full-scale urban guerrilla movement comparable to the Tupamaros in Uruguay, nor any guerrilla-cum-terrorist group with a strong territorial base like the Provisional Irish Republican Army or the various Palestinian guerrilla organisations. Although violence has become an issue in France, its ideological overtones have always been overt rather than covert, and the plurality not only of French political parties and groups but also of the French press has kept it in perspective. And the state, while making minor symbolic moves, has relied primarily upon ordinary criminal law and enforcement methods and has eschewed emergency measures and extraordinary powers. The democratic tradition appears to have stood firm. However, the picture is far more complex than this favourable generalisation admits, and an analysis is required of the tangled skein of French political culture, the development of the French state and the French experience of terrorism if we are to explain the balance of non-terrorism and repressive tolerance that characterises French society today.

I. Terrorism and Non-Terrorism: The French Experience

Terrorism and the French political tradition

The concept of terrorism is deeply embedded in French culture — but it is a different form of terror from that with which the world has become familiar in the 1970s. To the French, the state terror of Robespierre and the Jacobins in the wake of the French Revolution remains the touchstone of terrorism, whether carried out by the state or by a self-appointed revolutionary 'counter-state'.[2] Just as the Revolution of 1789 is still seen by all groups in French society — whether approvingly or pejoratively — as the first truly modern revolution, foreshadowing the collapse of feudalism and absolutism everywhere, so the three periods of terror between August 1792 and the *Grande Terreur* of 1794 (culminating in the fall of Robespierre) are seen as the forerunners of the modern terrorist state (culminating in Stalin's Russia and Hitler's Germany but ever-present in Chile, Argentina, Pol Pot's Kampuchea and many other places) and of the small groups of revolutionary terrorists whose victory, it is feared, will simply transform anti-system terror into new manifestations of state terror.

Paradoxically, however, this entrenched concern with terror and terrorism, rather than exacerbating public reactions to contemporary terrorism, demystifies it, making it somehow less terrifying. At the same time, it provides a form of expiation, reflecting as it does the most extreme excesses of that most revered of traditions, the Revolution, and thus appearing as a form of catharsis, a purging of the guilt for those excesses, symbolised in the death of Robespierre himself. Seen as a ritual bloodletting, an anachronism yet hallowed in tradition, terror still frightens, it still evokes outrage and protest, but it ceases to strike so deeply into the heart; it has a certain air of *déjà vu*. At another level, though, the romanticism of the revolutionary tradition, so strong even among some conservative groups in France, creates a certain emotional sympathy with the aims, if not the mehtods, of many so-called 'terrorist' groups, whether ideological revolutionaries or national irredentists. After all, France was the crucible of revolutionary nationalism of the left; it was only towards the end of the nineteenth century that the right donned the mantle of French nationalism. Indeed, it is sometimes asked, what was the French resistance during the Second World War if not a form of terrorism? Thus the revolutionary (and nationalist) tradition provides a frame of reference that explains terrorism in a manner that mutes its pathological connotations and thus mitigates the cultural perception of its potential threat.

At the same time, the democratic tradition in France, rooted in other revolutionary values — especially the Declaration of the Rights of Man and Citizen — and experienced in the various forms of liberal–democratic constitution that have been dominant since 1870, has established a greater confidence in democratic political processes *per se*, which are valued for their moral qualities and not merely as a means to material prosperity. (In contrast, Almond and Verba suggest that cultural support for democratic institutions in West Germany is derived from their coincidence with postwar prosperity and might be undermined if prosperity collapsed.[3]) However, it is not merely the forms and institutions of French democracy that give it its resilience; indeed, governmental instability and political immobilism have until quite recently been its most salient and visible characteristics, and much ink has been spilled in describing its flaws.[4] Rather, it has been the deep social roots of defensive pluralism — a distrust of others and of the state itself, combined with a recognition that no one group is strong enough to dominate, leading to social and political strategies based not on dominating but on preventing others from dominating — that has given the democratic tradition in France its stubborn durability.[5]

This resilience is found at many levels. It has been seen in the forms of political leadership characteristic of France — a weak, shifting form of routine authority, dependent upon the grudging acquiescence of coalition partners and vulnerable to the appearance of new problems, tempered by the occasional resort to an exceptional form of crisis authority, based on a specifically delegated set of tasks and limited to their successful discharge.[6] It has characterised the political party system, wherein old 'families' or 'tendencies' continually reappear in new guises,[7] readjusting their blocking strategies to new circumstances and constraints.[8] It is found in the particular forms of French bureaucracy and administration, where the fear of face-to-face relations and the compartmentalisation of offices creates strong internal vested interests and poor communication except on a highly formalised routine basis of rituals and red tape, short-circuited only by the old-boy network of the *grandes écoles*.[9] And it forms the sociological basis of political behaviour itself, as class and religion intersect to form distinct subcultures in permanent but uneasy coexistence and competition.[10] Therefore, despite the modernisation of French capitalism since 1945[11] or that of French political institutions since 1958,[12] the structures that underlie French political culture reflect the specifically French process of political development over a much longer historical period.[13]

The significance of the French democratic tradition for the development (or non-development) of terrorism is two-fold. The first consequence is that France has never developed a pure authoritarian tradition comparable to fascist or totalitarian regimes in other parts of Europe. Even Napoleon sought to spread the French ideals of *liberté, égalité, fraternité* in a Europe still dominated by dynastic regimes. The July Monarchy nursed the development of a liberal bourgeoisie. And the Second Empire sought to establish a supervised form of democratic process in the 1860s. In the 1930s, fascism never progressed beyond the organised street-gang stage underpinned by a conservative vision of the social order represented by Maurras and the *Action française*, while even under the German tutelage of 1940–45 the Vichy regime concerned itself primarily with strengthening the traditional values of *travail, famille, patrie* (work, family, country) through social conservatism and a mild form of corporatist economic decision-making that actually had a decentralising effect.[14] Maurice Duverger has written that France would not have turned to a leader like Hitler, as this was not in her political temperament;[15] and de Gaulle, the closest France has come to a dictator, had no desire to be one even when, in 1945, it was within his grasp.[16]

Without such an authoritarian tradition, the various groups in French society have seen fascism as an external phenomenon, foreign to the nature of France. It is significant in this context that some of the most virulent revolutionary terrorist groups in the 1970s have developed in societies characterised prior to 1945 by various forms of fascism — Germany, Italy and Japan — where the twofold issue of whether 'fascism', as a form of socio-economic structure (as distinct from its façade of political authoritarianism), was ever really defeated from within after the Second World War, and of whether new forms of fascism are taking over the façade of the liberal–democratic state today, will always be at the back of people's minds both at home and abroad. In France, in contrast, the enemy is kept at arm's length. Each group has its stake in the maintenance of the equilibrium, and thus fascism faces a huge credibility gap. In this context, the resort to terrorism appears to be out of proportion, a distorted form of political response in a society that provides many other channels for political opposition, even revolutionary opposition — which retains its own rather abstract, intellectual romanticism in a culture that has traditionally prized critical intellectualism.

The second consequence, then, is the reverse of the token — the continual effervescence and ferment of French politics itself. In a society with as diverse a political culture as that of France, despite the appearances of a developing dominant 'consensus',[17] opportunities for ideological assertion and political activity are widespread. Furthermore, such activities are usually regarded, even by conservative circles, as creative and culturally legitimate. The vacillation of large sections of the bourgeoisie during the complex and intense events of May 1968, with even the centre-left and sections of the liberal right being swept along in the revolutionary tide for a time, is merely an extreme manifestation of this ambivalence. Trotskyists stand for the presidency and get their share of free television time. A large section of French trade unionism retains its nostalgia for syndicalism. The Socialist Party ceaselessly debates the more abstruse aspects of defining and achieving the *rupture* with capitalism, and the Communist Party vacillates between a social-democratic Eurocommunism, obeisance to its Leninist (some would say Stalinist) traditions and a kind of nationalist worker populism. The party of the former President, Giscard d'Estaing, is a hotch-potch of liberals, conservatives, social christians and progressives in an uneasy alliance, and the Gaullist party, the most authoritarian party of them all, is committed to a welfare state and economic planning.[18] Defining one's political stance in such a way as to inject a dose of originality, and expressing that stance in a polished and intellectualised rhetorical form, is a key element in the hallowed political ritual of the Republic. And the debates and discussions — and polemics — that take place within and between the multifarious intellectual groups and ideological factions provide a kaleidoscopic backcloth for political activity, especially in the centre around which much of that activity revolves, Paris.

An admirer of French political life might say that these legitimate forms of activity provide sufficient variety and choice to accommodate almost the entire spectrum of political taste and opinion, ostracising none and offering opportunities to all to pursue their own viewpoints. A sceptic would argue that they provide a safety valve through which potentially dysfunctional activity can discharge itself harmlessly. In either case, opposition groups are not forced to choose between tame consensual politics and extra-systemic opposition, even though, in the long run, radical groups may not have a very great impact upon macropolitical processes. Nonetheless, the impact of regional and ecological pressure groups, along with the more innovative sections of the trade union movement such as the French Democratic Confederation of Labour (CFDT), have been identified as the source of political innovation in the Fifth Republic (see chapter 1), and the political will of the Communist Party to innovate in local politics has been the source of a variety of significant concrete initiatives in public policy.[19] Thus the direct frustrations that often lead to revolutionary terrorism in other societies are less salient in

France, and a variety of more or less efficacious forms of substitute political behaviour exists for radical activists.

Reactionary terrorism in the twentieth century: the OAS

Favourable conditions for the development of classic revolutionary terrorism are thus significantly lacking in the French scene. But this does not mean that terrorism has been totally absent from France. In the course of the twentieth century, however, indigenous terrorism has been primarily a reactionary terrorism of the right and not a revolutionary terrorism of the left. In the late 1930s, after the dissolution of the quasi-fascist leagues and the electoral victory of the Popular Front coalition of Radicals, Socialists and Communists, some of the more extreme ex-members of the leagues allied with some of the more reactionary middle-ranking officers within the army (supposedly with the approval of certain senior officers and, it was claimed, the tacit indulgence of Marshal Pétain) to form a secret society known as the 'Cagoule' (a hooded robe or cloak, copied from the Ku Klux Klan). They set up a clandestine organisation, collected arms and made plans to take over the state in the event of an attack from the Communists. They even attempted to trick army leaders into a preventive coup d'état in October–November 1937. Their time, however, did not come.

In the period after the Second World War, certain right-wing elements, some with connections with the Cagoule or the Vichy regime, attached themselves to General de Gaulle, whom they saw as the best hope for a right-wing authoritarian regime. They, too, organised clandestine networks, and in the period following de Gaulle's resignation in January 1946 until his return to power in 1958 they were ostensibly prepared to attempt a coup, especially during the depths of the Cold War, when the Communist Party, having accepted the Cominform line in 1947, was ousted from the Government in the summer of that year and thereafter attempted to exert extra-parliamentary pressure, especially by means of a series of damaging strikes in the winter of 1947–8. De Gaulle, however, merely made use of this group for political intelligence, keeping order at the meetings of the Gaullist party (the RPF) and occasional strong-arm tactics and 'dirty tricks' during election campaigns and so on; he never gave the call for an uprising. The '*barbouzes*' (bearded ones), as they were called, did, however, play an important clandestine role in the internecine right-wing terrorist battle between the Gaullists and the OAS – the Secret Army Organisation.[20]

The OAS was the closest one can come in the history of twentieth-century France to identifying a genuine terrorist movement. Yet, unlike the somewhat more hypothetical terrorists of the Cagoule or the *barbouzes*, the alliance of hard-line French settlers in Algeria, right-wing groups within the army and certain reactionary elements within France that comprised the OAS engaged in a real terrorist war lasting nearly two years. The background to their campaign was, of course, the bloody and traumatic Algerian War. With one-tenth of Algeria's population of European origin, some of several generations' standing, this was no ordinary colonial war. Regarding themselves as French Algerians rather than as colonial occupiers, the *pieds-noirs* opposed any move to loosen ties with the mainland or to give greater rights to the native Muslim population — other than those who had been assimilated into the dominant French culture and socio-economic system. The uprising by the Algerian National Liberation Front (FLNA), which broke out in 1954 and which in its guerrilla campaign employed terrorist methods, was seen even by high-ranking members of the French Government, such as the then Minister of the Interior, François Mitterrand, as an attack upon the integrity of France herself. Successive Governors-General, the Socialist Robert Lacoste and the Gaullist Jacques Soustelle, had been sent to Algeria to promote incremental reforms, but had been converted to the hard-line stance of the colonists. The Socialist Prime Minister, Guy Mollet, also adopted a tough stance towards the FLNA, refusing to open negotiations before the declaration of a cease-fire.

The French army's role in this situation was crucial. Torn apart by the conflict between de Gaulle's Free French and the Vichy regime during the Second World War, its traditional acceptance of subordination to the civil power had come into question. After a long, losing struggle with the Viet Minh in Indochina, a defeat that was attributed to Mao's and Giap's doctrines of guerrilla warfare, the officer corps was more than ever loath to be defeated again. They developed the first coherent experiment in counter-insurgency, using irregular groups, hostage-taking, torture and the like, in their attempt to prevent the FLNA fish from swimming in the water of the Muslim population; they even claimed, by 1960, to have defeated the guerrillas. But along with new methods came new attitudes. The war against the FLNA was seen as a holy war for Western civilisation against the communistic barbarians, and the cause of the colonists themselves was espoused with missionary fervour. In 1958, a coup in Algiers led by the army commander there, General Raoul Salan, threatened Paris with an airborne invasion if a government were elected there that was not hard-line enough on Algeria; it was by manipulating the conditions created by this uprising that de Gaulle himself returned to power, and for a time he was thus at least partially dependent upon the forces of *Algérie française* (French Algeria), led by the high-ranking Gaullist Jacques Soustelle.

In 1959, however, de Gaulle began to change his line on Algeria, calling for a greater degree of self-determination and proposing a referendum in Algeria itself to choose between three options — integration with France, independence, and a form of association the details of which were never laid out. In January 1960, hard-line elements in Algeria, at first with some tacit support from the army, set up barricades and tried to take over government offices, in order to force de Gaulle to ensure the victory of the first alternative. De Gaulle, having ensured the purging of his party, the Union for the New Republic (JNR), of the most hardline supporters of *Algérie française* during 1959, did not budge, and the army did not rebel — this time. A year later, in place of the local referendum, came a national one, proposing self-determination for Algeria and a provisional Government for an eventual Algerian Republic. This received the support of 75 per cent of those who voted, but it also brought to a head the crisis in the army; three months later, in April 1961, four high-ranking generals, Challe, Salan, Jouhaud and Zeller, staged a putsch in Algiers, which failed because the authorities in Paris did not crumble and because the largely conscript ranks, ordered by de Gaulle over the radio not to follow the orders of rebellious officers, were listening in on their transistor sets. From the failure of the 'generals' putsch' came the birth of the OAS.[21]

The aim of the OAS was to ensure French control of Algeria despite the 'abandonment' of the country by the French Government. Its members terrorised Muslim neighbourhoods, assassinated Muslim leaders, bombed public places and threatened French officials who were too compliant with their Government's policy. Growing out of earlier *Algérie française* movements, such as the *Front National Français*, it was led by the retired General Salan, who had been in exile in Madrid since 1960, and the official headquarters were set up there. The operational leadership came mainly from Jean-Jacques Susini, an Algiers student leader who had succeeded Pierre Lagaillarde, the leader of the 1960 barricades revolt, as leader of the student movement that had provided the organisational underpinning for the early *Algérie française* protests. Many in the army were sympathetic to the OAS, as was much of the administration within Algeria; sympathy was, of course, also widespread in metropolitan France. The violence of the FLNA,[22] which had been raging for more than six years, matched by the counter-terror of the army, had inured the conflicting groups in the province to violence, and a peaceful solution did not appear to be viable to any of the participants. Only the French Government, with a realism that, with hindsight, appears all the more remarkable in view of the pressure it encountered within the French right as well as within the intensely committed Algerian crucible, was able to sever the Gordian knot. Unlike the British Government after the First World War, which in comparable circumstances surrendered to the blackmail of the Ulster Volunteer Force and partitioned Ireland (partition was considered as an alternative in Algeria too), de Gaulle realised that anything less than complete independence would do nothing more than create a permanent sore that would plague French and Algerian politics for many decades to come. So negotiations with the FLNA continued, despite disputes, delays and adjournments, and on 19 March 1962 a cease-fire agreement was signed at Evian along with agreements setting out the terms of Algerian independence.[23]

In the meantime, the OAS had been active. Its original programme, which appealed to Christian, corporatist and anti-parliamentary values, revealed shades of the Cagoule and of Vichy. But it was far too disparate an organisation for its programme to do more than reflect a mood within a particular context of action. That action context was the dedication to keeping the French presence in Algeria, and, if that failed, to maintaining European control by force within Algeria itself, even if this meant merely the coastal enclaves around the major cities where the vast majority of the European population lived. In 1960, with the tacit support of much of the army, with the FLNA hard-pressed militarily in much of the country, and with much sympathy within official circles, the objectives of the OAS seemed credible. Its downfall was due to three factors: the determination of the French Government, both legally and clandestinely, to prevail; the long-term position of strength of the FLNA; and the political and military weaknesses of the OAS itself.

De Gaulle had seen the writing on the wall for Algeria well before his return to power, but the manner of his ascendancy — on the back of the army revolt in Algiers in May 1958, and seemingly at the behest of General Salan himself, the leader of that revolt — forced him to dissimulate his intentions until he was firmly enough in the saddle to control opposition to his plans.[24] The purging of the UNR, the policy switch from a referendum on three options (one of which — integration — would have satisfied the hard-liners) to a vote simply on self-determination and the setting up of a provisional government, the barricades trial of a cross-section of civilian and military participants, and the dogged pursuit of negotiations with the FLNA, were mere prelude. The attempted 'generals' putsch' provided the basis for more severe action. For the only time in the history of the Fifth Republic, the President invoked the emergency powers provided in Article 16 of the constitution, reasserting control of the army and the administration and establishing special military tribunals to try the rebels. He also unleashed the *barbouzes*, who fought the OAS in a war of clandestine terror and counter-terror, infiltrating its networks and eliminating its activists. In the meantime it became obvious that the FLNA had not been pushed out of its positions of strength, whether in the countryside or in the Muslim quarters of the European-dominated cities. Furthermore, its political strength was continually increasing because of recognition from abroad (the late 1950s and early 1960s were the great era of anti-colonial victories in terms of both the rate of colonies becoming independent and the influence that these 'new states' were coming to wield internationally, in the UN, for example) as well as *de facto* recognition by the French Government itself, which insisted on bargaining solely with the FLNA as the representatives of the Algerian people.

The OAS itself, despite its network of sympathisers and its position of strength within the European quarters of Algerian cities, was in no position to hold out in these conditions. Its ability to acquire arms did not compensate for its lack of organisation and the enormity of its task. In the first place, the official headquarters were in Madrid, and although Salan and Susini were able to enter and leave Algiers relatively easily, communications between the leadership and the ranks were weak and intermittent. The relative isolation of the leadership, who, even when in Algeria, had to communicate orders and receive information through a tortuous clandestine structure, led them to envisage plans far beyond the material and human resources, not to mention the possibilities of coordination, of the organisation itself. Most of the action undertaken by the OAS, then, was envisaged and carried out by fairly isolated operatives in the field, and consisted mainly of attacks on local Communist Party offices and FLNA networks. In the second place, the OAS had to fight on two fronts if it was to succeed – in Algeria itself and in metropolitan France. Whereas in Algeria it represented a strongly committed section of the population – the mass of Europeans – in France it faced the hostility of the great majority, symbolised in the huge referendum majorities for de Gaulle's proposals in January 1961 and April 1962 (ratification of the Evian Agreements, which gained a 'yes' vote of over 90 per cent!), as well as a much more closely controlled police and legal system – not to mention the *barbouzes*.

But the problems of Algeria did not penetrate the surface of life in the *métropole*, concerned with economic prosperity, the political competition of the new Fifth Republic, the Cold War, and the like. Even the referendums on Algeria were seen more as tests of confidence in de Gaulle's overall political leadership than in terms of the detailed policy questions involved. And the state broadcasting monopoly, the ORTF, presented only the Government's line; television was not yet ready to play the role that it was later to do in Vietnam at the height of American involvement. In any case, most of the attacks in metropolitan France were the work of unconnected *groupuscules* using the OAS label. Hard as it might try, the OAS was never able to rally and control these movements; and competition between Madrid and Algiers exacerbated matters. Most operations were diversionary tactics, and the attacks on the Communist Party failed to achieve their aims of exacerbating the contradictions of the French party system.[25] The most spectacular operations were the various attempts on de Gaulle's life — their number is estimated at thirty-one, some of which failed only because of the most extraordinarily lucky escapes for the President[26] — but these were usually the work of isolated individuals and groups, occasionally acting against OAS policy. And after the signing of the Evian Agreements and the eventual transfer of power to the new government of the Republic of Algeria, the massive exodus of the European population to France destroyed the last foundation for the OAS. General Jouhaud had been arrested in March 1962 and Salan in April; Jouhaud was to be sentenced to death, Salan merely to life imprisonment (after which de Gaulle, in disgust, dissolved the High Military Tribunal). However, Jouhaud was later reprieved on the intercession of the Prime Minister, Pompidou, and both were released in the amnesty declared during the election campaign of 1968, after the Events of May. Susini went underground, later appearing briefly in bank raids and in an attack on the former treasurer of the OAS.

But as the Algerian War faded into French history, it became clearer that the OAS represented the exception that proved the rule. As Alfred Grosser has pointed out, France was the only major Western country in the postwar period to experience both of the great international conflicts of the age directly in her domestic politics — the opposition between Communism and anti-Communism and the mammoth task of decolonisation.[27] The army, the colonial administration and the European population of Algeria saw these conflicts in a different light than did the inhabitants of the *métropole*. The anti-Communist fanaticism of the officers, disillusioned by 1940 and by Dienbienphu, and determined to compensate for those failures despite lukewarm support from the French Government, allied with a desperate settler population faced with the loss of its recognised world. Although the long-term causes of the problem lay with French colonial policies in the nineteenth century and with the failure of the French Empire and the French Union in the twentieth, the Algerian War was a parenthesis in the development of postwar French politics and society, and the futility of the desperate rearguard actions of the OAS neither reflected the situation in France nor affected it in any profound way — except possibly further to isolate and immunise French society against the recrudescence of terrorism in the world of the 1970s.

The problem of terrorism

I have already observed that in the 1970s France was relatively free from the kind of classic terrorism that dominated the headlines in that decade. But the analyst is once again caught in the dilemma of definitions. The first of these is the definition of terrorism itself. 'Terrorism' is first and foremost a pejorative term. It denotes something evil and dangerous. Any conscientious anti-fascist will have little trouble in identifying the Cagoule, the OAS and even the *barbouzes* (although the last may have been on the 'right side' in historical perspective) as terrorists or proto-terrorists. It is not even very hard to denounce the Red Army Faction in Germany, the Red Army in Japan and the Red Brigades in Italy as essentially 'terrorist', possibly even in their own definition — despite a permissible sympathy with the underlying *cri du coeur* that motivated them and a distaste for the repressive measures taken as a result of the reaction to their activities. National irredentist movements with an anti-colonial rationale, like the Palestinians or the Provisional IRA, are some-what more problematic, although the random threat to non-combatants offends both political and moral sensibilities; however, one can approve their aims and denounce their methods as terroristic. In contrast, to denounce as 'terrorists' a full-scale national liberation movement fighting a guerrilla war against colonial or authoritarian settler repression — as in Southern Africa or Southeast Asia — or to apply the term to broadly based revolutionary movements fighting against the state terrorism of cruel dictatorships — as in pre-revolutionary Cuba or Nicaragua, El Salvador, Argentina or Chile — implies that the speaker is committed strongly to supporting the forces of repression in those places — even if, in a technical sense, 'terror tactics' are used as part of a wider guerrilla strategy.

This problem also appears on another, interdependent level — a level that is particularly significant to a study of the situation in France. This is the scope of the concept of terrorism. If we see pure terror tactics — anonymous attacks by clandestine groups on either symbolic or random individual targets with the intention of spreading a generalised and abstract fear and anomie among the mass of the target population — as a core of the concept of terrorism, then how far can we move towards the periphery of the notion before it becomes analytically absurd? (Of course, to use such a term in an analytically absurd way implies either an unintentional misuse of the term or an intentional distortion for specific political motives.) Other terms that are often associated in journalistic, political and everyday speech with terrorism include violence, subversion and extremism. Furthermore, if the notion of 'sympathising' is added to the brew, then anybody who dissents from the social order or who frightens 'peaceful, law-abiding citizens' can be ostracised by association with terrorism. Are left-wing political movements somehow essentially terroristic? Are political demonstrations or trade union picketing somehow part of this wider phenomenon? What about juvenile delinquency and football hooliganism? Throw in a reference to terrorism, and the image is reinforced of a world seized by a contagion of violence, with civilisation in danger of collapsing, and with all dissenters from this view categorised as either active or passive sympathisers with the apocalypse.[28]

This mixture is especially potent in a world where terrorism makes the most effective media impact of almost any event short of war. An airplane hijacking or the taking of a hostage, even where no one is killed or there is no intention of killing anyone, is the ultimate media event. A drama of fictional intensity is played out in full view of the public, with the event stretching over hours or days, and with all of the suspense provided by a dramatic, visible yet unpredictable outcome. The pain of the non-combatant civilians such as airplane, train or bus passengers, or the isolation and humiliation of individual hostages, is intensely felt by the audience, and so a limited threat is perceived as a mass threat. The normal credibility gap faced by car accident or lung cancer statistics, not to mention the shadowy outlines of real but distant small wars — the feeling that 'it can't happen to me' — is eliminated. The experience is felt as real and imminent.[29] Therefore the power to tar groups and ideas with the brush of terrorism is one of the most potent symbolic weapons in the armoury of contemporary politics.

Terrorist activity in contemporary France

Although France escaped the direct impact of a domestic terrorist movement in the 1970s, terrorism as a phenomenon nonetheless had a strong impact in terms of these wider questions I have been posing. Four sorts of phenomena were associated, in a more or less relevant way, with terrorism, and an examination of these will highlight the problematic nature of the notion of terrorism today, in ways both specific to France and more widely applicable across national frontiers.

The first category is the most directly linked with terrorism in the broader contemporary sense, and consists of the various ways in which foreign terrorist groups have used France either as a base or as a battle-ground. The tradition of France as a *terre d'asile*, a country that freely accepts political refugees and exiles from abroad, has meant not only that the intellectual life of the country has been continuously leavened by international contacts and ideas, but also that clandestine political activity among foreign groups based in France is not infrequent (refraining from political activity is a normal condition of asylum, but it is hard to enforce).[30] *Sunday Telegraph* journalists Christopher Dobson and Ronald Payne have claimed that 'Paris has become the world capital of terrorism':

> It is ideally placed by geography and circumstances to fulfil this role. It has excellent rail, road and air communications with the rest of Europe and the Middle East; it connects with five land frontiers, which, because of the volume of traffic crossing them, are difficult to police; it is, moreover, traditionally a haven for political refugees and a magnet for young people, still full of romantic notions about its charms.

The Japanese Red Army submerged itself in the 'most numerous colony of Japanese students in Europe'; the members of the Red Army Faction spent long periods there; and the Palestinians swam in the sea of Paris's Arab population of half a million, the legacy of France's lost North African and Near Eastern colonies. Paris provided the base for the establishment of the international terrorist network led by Ilich Ramirez Sanchez, nicknamed Carlos, until his cover was blown in June 1975 and he fled to Algiers and later to Libya.[31] The hard-line Minister of the Interior, Raymond Marcellin, claimed in an article in *Le Figaro* in August 1978[32] that ten years earlier the French police had listed forty-four terrorist organisations in the world, of which twenty included elements living in France, but that present legal provisions, combined with the lack of a preventive capability on the part of the police, stymied any attempt to counteract this menace. Indeed, between April 1973 and July 1977, a leader of the Popular Front for the Liberation of Palestine (PFLP), Basil Al Kubaisi, was shot; Mohamed Boudia, a Fatah activist (and predecessor to Carlos), was blown up by a car bomb; a Chadian opposition leader was shot; five Saudis were taken hostage in the Saudi Arabian embassy by the Palestinian Liberation Organisation (PLO) and flown to Kuwait; the Uruguayan military attaché was assassinated; the Spanish deputy military attaché was seriously wounded; the Turkish ambassador was shot dead; the Bolivian ambassador was shot dead; the former PLO representative in Paris, Mahmoud Ould Saleh, who ran an Arab bookshop there, was shot dead; and the Mauritanian ambassador was seriously wounded.[33]

A more serious incident occurred at the Iraqi embassy on 31 July 1978, when a terrorist (thought at the time to be the brother of Saïd Hammami –

the PLO representative in London who had recently been assassinated),
having taken hostages at the embassy but later surrendered to the French
police, was shot by snipers within the embassy as he was being taken to
a police wagon. In the fusillade, a policeman was also killed, and the
police claimed that at least fifteen snipers were shooting from the embassy
windows at the man who had taken the hostages. The police demonstrated
in protest against the lack of recourse against the snipers, who had
diplomatic immunity, although three Iraqi 'diplomats' were expelled by
the French Government for carrying arms.[34] The war between the PLO
and the Iraqi hard-liners of the Rejection Front did not spare Paris.
Indeed, three terrorists who had planned to massacre passengers (not
hijack an airliner) were killed in an Orly Airport lounge. The operation
was claimed by a group (unknown to the PLO and presumably linked with
the Rejection Front) that called itself the 'Sons of South Lebanon',
presumably in reference to the French presence among United Nations
forces patrolling the supposed buffer zone in that country torn by civil
war and foreign interventions; it had already threatened a series of attacks
in France to protest against French neo-colonialism in the Middle East and
Africa (Zaïre, Chad). The group was thought to be an offshoot of the
PFLP. In addition to the three terrorists killed, a brigadier of the French
CRS riot police also died, and six people were wounded.[35] The Orly
attack brought back memories of earlier attacks at Orly: in October 1972,
when a bomb near the El Al desk was defused; and the two attacks in
January 1975, attributed to Carlos, involving a rocket attack on a full
El Al plane (it missed and hit an empty Yugoslav plane) and another
attempt to blow up an El Al plane, which also failed but led to an attack
on passengers in a departure lounge, the taking of hostages, and a negotiated
escape flight.[36] Indeed, the attacks by supporters of the Rejection Front
continue unabated. In March 1979 a Jewish student restaurant in the
rue de Médicis, catering in fact for a mixed clientele with even some
Muslim students frequenting it, was hit by a large bomb during the lunch
hour on the day following the signing of the Egyptian–Israeli peace
treaty.[37] And another PLO representative was assassinated at the beginning
of August.[38] Of course, Palestinians have been included among the groups
suspected of the rue Copernic bombing in 1980 (considered in chapter 7,
infra).

It is not only the Palestinians who choose France as a haven or a battle-
ground. The Red Army Faction held the German industrialist Hans-Martin
Schleyer hostage somewhere in France, and his body was found in Mulhouse on 16 October 1977. The Basque organisation ETA had an extensive
network in France, which was left alone so long as Franco was in power;

however, in January 1979 the French Government removed the status of political refugee from the Basques, ostensibly because Spain had become a democratic state (including adhering to the Geneva Convention, declaring a general amnesty and introducing a new democratic constitution).[39] Seventeen Basques were removed to forced residence in the Alpes-de-Haute-Provence in February 1979, and seven were expelled from the country and returned to Spain at the beginning of March.[40] A Croat nationalist leader, Bruno Busic, was assassinated in Paris in October 1978.[41] In May 1978 Henri Curiel, the founder of the Egyptian Communist Party and falsely accused by many — including the weekly news magazine *Le Point* and Dobson and Payne — of being the centre of an international terrorist network (in fact, he was a retiring — and retired — radical intellectual), was assassinated by an unknown right-wing group that took the name the Delta Organisation, referring to an affiliate of the OAS that undertook various assassinations, including attempts on de Gaulle, in 1960–62.[42] And in addition, Professor Antonio Negri, accused by the Italian police of being the 'brains' behind the Red Brigades, was said to have directed the kidnapping of Aldo Moro while giving a course of lectures in Paris.

This sporadic terrorist activity on French soil by foreign-based groups does not contain much to strike terror into the heart of the average Frenchman. Of the mere eleven deaths from terrorist incidents in the five years 1972–77, eight were those of foreigners and only three of French citizens.[43] Calls for tougher measures by hard-liners like Marcellin fall on deaf ears. The evidence would seem to indicate that indigenous violence has been even less menacing. However, it is the domestic brand of violence — especially when labelled 'terrorism' — that arouses the political passions, and the other three categories we are considering here are all varieties of this sort. They are, first, the violence pursued by single-issue pressure groups; second, violence that occurs in the course of political conflict and the vague sense of political and social malaise; and, third, attempts to establish straightforward terrorist groups.

Of these, the most violent activity occurs in the first category, carried out particularly by the regional autonomist movements led by those in Brittany and Corsica. The Breton Liberation Front (FLB), sometimes supplemented by the Breton Revolutionary Army (ARB), is merely the most recent of a number of movements that fall somewhere between the IRA and ETA, on the one hand, and a nationalist party on the other. With no territorial hinterland in which to hide and organise, and with the efficient and centralised French state always close behind, the Breton nationalists generally stick to highly symbolic targets for their small bombs. Symbols of central domination such as small gendarmerie head-quarters, telephone exchanges and television transmitters tend to be attacked in the middle of the night, when there is no one around to be injured.[44] Attacks in 1975 and again in January 1979 on the Brennilis nuclear power station actually earned the FLB the fury of Breton environmental and anti-nuclear groups, because it allowed the French Electricity Board (EDF) to claim that anti-nuclear groups were terrorists![45] Occasionally a more spectacular target is chosen, such as the Versailles Palace in June 1978. The two bombers wanted to leave their package in the Hall of Mirrors, but they could not find a hiding place; their six kilogramme bomb was eventually left in recently renovated rooms from the Napoleonic period, and mainly destroyed large canvasses showing Napoleon's victories.[46] All was repairable. But the cost of the FLB was high, as the police response hit the organisation hard and the movement was divided over the action. Nonetheless, the eight charged with the offence admitted twenty-six attacks on television stations, the prefecture at Rennes, the rector's office of the Academy in Brittany, tax offices, an officers' mess, EDF offices, banks, Shell offices, customs offices, etc. Indeed, the FLB/ARB was credited with 206 attacks over the three years prior to the Versailles bombing.[47] In 1981, however, the Breton movement achieved a new stage of development, achieving widespread acceptance and support, and attempting to reconcile its demands with the left at national level. Five demands were presented to President Mitterrand in June, during a truce declared in the light of his decentralisation proposals, along with a request that he come to Brittany to see for himself how 'reasonable' these demands were![48]

Corsican nationalist groups have been busy, too, but the combination of the geographical isolation of the island from mainland France and the intricate socio-political structure of the area has meant that the autonomist groups are as concerned with defending their separate vested interests within Corsica as they are with attacking the central Government. Family feuds, banditry, opposition to the influx of *pieds-noirs* into the island economy and the maintenance of Mafia-like business activities and political patronage are as important in understanding the politics of Corsican nationalism as is the defiance of central authority.[49] But the growing maturity of Corsican groups is evidenced by the truce which they declared just prior to the 1981 presidential election, in which they strongly supported Mitterrand and his regionalisation proposals, which are to include a unique 'special status' for Corsica; thus a 'terroristic' protest group has rather rapidly turned itself into a 'legitimate' pressure group, consulting closely with the new Government.[50] The example of the clandestine regionalist groups has spread to other parts of the country as well. In the Clermont-Ferrand area, a group calling itself the Inter-urban Narcissist Intervention Group (GINI) claimed responsibility for three attacks in 1978 and threatened to bomb mail planes. A Lyon Self-Defence Group threw two Molotov cocktails against the doors of Lyon city hall in September 1978 as 'a warning to all the services of state coercion. This is a response to the only kind of violence we recognise — that of the state.'[51] And a Savoy Nationalist Front bombed a cable-car station of the Aiguille du Midi at Chamonix, symbol of the tourist development of the region.[52]

The low-level symbolic violence of the nationalist groups is probably the closest approximation to indigenous 'terrorism' in France, but there is little terroristic or terrifying about it. In the context of contemporary society, however, some of the mud is bound to stick. The fact that some small ecological groups have been known to attack motorway toll stations, holiday centres, construction sites and even beach-cleaning machines in Brittany[53] has meant that the ecological movement as a whole, especially when gathered in large demonstrations (such as the attempt to prevent the army from extending its practice ranges at Larzac or the anti-nuclear demonstration on the site of the proposed nuclear power station at Créys-Malville in 1977), is regarded as a potentially terroristic element and treated as such, and the public association of environmentalism with regionalism further confuses the issue. Again, however, the Mitterrand Government's cancellation of the Plogoff nuclear power station has reinforced the new-found 'legitimacy' of these groups.

Broader social and political violence, our next category, seems to draw the most fire from Government and police. We can briefly identify three sub-types. The first arises out of the confrontation of the more radical political parties and trade unions with the police during demonstrations and strikes. The fear of another May 1968 is strong among the forces of order in France, and the French police are not known to be gentle. Recently, however, a new phenomenon has exacerbated the situation — the appearance of the 'autonomists'. Not to be confused with the movements for regional autonomy, these are anarchists with new and devastating tactics. Wearing helmets and scarves over their faces, they wait in the wings until a major political rally or demonstration (such as the annual May Day march of trade unionists and leftist parties and groups from the Place de la République to the Place de la Bastille) has very nearly passed off peacefully. As the tail end of the march is about to enter the area where it is due to disband, and where many marchers and bystanders are milling around under the watchful eye of the police, they appear. They start breaking shop windows and building fires in the street. They half-loot some shops, throwing the goods around in the street rather than claiming them for themselves. They throw missiles at the police.

The police in France have still not worked out effective tactics to deal with this sort of attack. Socialised to fear all 'extremists', their first reaction, after a period of vacillation, is to attempt to clear the streets. They bring out the tear gas, and charge marchers, bystanders and autonomists alike. During the demonstration of 23 March 1979, called by the trade unions and parties of the left to protest against the Government's rationalisation plan for the steel industry and against unemployment in general, the police were accused of provoking violence themselves; the arrest and swift conviction of boys claiming to be bystanders was denounced by the left as a 'new Dreyfus Affair'. Photographs taken during the 1979 May Day demonstration show the police attacking the march stewards.[54] Meanwhile, the autonomists, having caused their confusion and destruction, fade away. The result, however, is an embittered atmosphere between the authorities and the political opposition groups, an atmosphere that is exacerbated by the comparison of this sort of violence with terrorism, and the guilt by association that the authorities heap upon the demonstrators themselves.

Second, there is a continuing background of warfare between various groups on the right and left. Attacks on Communist Party headquarters by right-wing groups, the killing of a left-wing picket in Reims in June 1977 by members of the French Confederation of Labour (CFT) — a right-wing 'union' comprising a number of ex-*barbouzes* — bombings of left-wing bookshops, etc., by quasi-fascist or anti-semitic groups, these and other fairly isolated incidents indicate the tension that exists across the political spectrum. This sort of violence, of course, can easily erupt *within* groups. The 1981 Socialist victory created a new threat to the old *barbouze* network centred on the Gaullist *service d'ordre*, the SAC (*Service d'Action Civique*); in an attempt to protect secret records, the entire family of a disaffected local commander was murdered in Marseilles.[55] And third, there is in France, as in all Western societies today, a mood of fear about violence and crime in general. Increased police patrols seek out vandals in the Métro. Unemployed youths and secondary school students imitate the autonomists.[56] And a Government report, solemnly issued in 1977, waffles on about the social causes of violence; its only concrete proposals call for an increase in the numbers of police and the efficiency of the courts.[57] In both of these types of violence the image of terrorism comes quickly to mind, but to ask whether or not there is a causal connection between the incidence of terrorism and the incidence of these more sporadic forms of low-level violence cannot be proved.

Finally, our last category of contemporary pseudo-terrorism in France is just that — the appearance and disappearance of small groups with revolutionary names that flare up and then die out. In September 1978, three youths claiming to be members of the Armed Revolutionary and Anarchist Terrorist Movement admitted having carried out twenty bomb attacks in Lorraine in the previous year. They denied having political motives; they merely wanted 'to be talked about'.[58] More serious were the Armed Nuclei for Proletarian Autonomy (NAPAP) and the International Revolutionary Action Group (GARI), which carried out a number of attacks in the mid-1970s. They were said to have close contacts with the Red Army Faction, and GARI, which was located mainly in the Southwest, was said to have links with Spanish terrorist groups. NAPAP bombed the front door of the Justice Minister in 1977; killed a former Renault night watchman who had himself killed the Maoist militant Pierre Overney in 1973; bombed the CFT headquarters; was involved in the wounding of the Spanish military attaché in 1975 and the killing of the Bolivian ambassador in 1976; and kidnapped a Renault executive in 1972.[59] GARI kidnapped the director of the French branch of the Banco de Bilbao in 1974 and may have been attempting to bomb the then Interior Minister, Michel Poniatowski, in Toulouse in 1976 when the bomb went off prematurely, killing two militants.[60] But both groups were said to lack the motivation for cold-blooded murder and to be hierarchically weak.[61]

In general, however, the *gauchiste* leaders of 1968 and the organisations that grew out of that period and lasted into the 1970s rejected terrorist methods.[62] But while France has not developed an indigenous terrorist threat, other, less intense forms of political violence have been widespread, mirroring the political conflicts that have not found ready expression in the interplay of the official party system. In this, the pattern of violence reflects the intensity and the plurality of French political culture and the intertwining of the revolutionary and democratic traditions. Indeed, the seemingly rather rapid success of the Socialist Government in incorporating some of the more persistently violent groups into a process of consultation and reform indicates that, rather than being terrorists, they are simply pressure groups who had previously been forced to carry on their protests by 'other means'. However, the images of contemporary terrorism have not for all that been kept out by some sort of cultural *cordon sanitaire*. And the state has not lacked instruments to counteract the perceived threat, although it has not had to resort to the extensive measures that have characterised many other countries especially in Europe.

II. Repressive Tolerance: The Reaction of the French State

The French political system has not reacted to the terrorist threat in a paranoid fashion. It is not thought that the social order is in danger, and the demand for special measures has in the main been resisted. In the words of the former Justice Minister Alain Peyrefitte, 'It is not possible to reply to terrorism by a state terrorism which would draw us into a spiral of terrorism.'[63] However, two facts stand out. First, the French state is in a powerful position in any case, for reasons linked with the nature of French bureaucracy and executive power. And second, the special measures that have been taken by the Government, while modifying the relationship between the state and the citizen only incrementally, have nonetheless eroded the latter's rights in certain ways.

A striking feature of the position of the French state is the discretion the Government can exercise in matters relevant to terrorism and violence. This is not merely a matter of specific legal dispositions, but derives partly from the strengthening of the executive power under the leadership of a strong President in the Fifth Republic. The President, who holds office for a term of seven years, has certain *de facto* and *de jure* powers, in terms of both administrative decisions and emergency legitimacy, that ensure that coordinated action is the norm rather than the exception. His ability to control the nomination (and resignation) of the Prime Minister and of the members of the Government means that politically delicate questions are usually decided in accordance with his preferences. In a more direct way, the ability of the President to decide alone (after only formal consultations) whether or not to apply Article 16 in an emergency gives him the ultimate authority if the security of the state is threatened. The use by de Gaulle of Article 16 in 1961, at the height of the OAS threat, provided a precedent that has not required repeating since that time. And given the centralisation of the French administration generally, particularly control over the police and the defence structure, decisions relevant to terrorism usually escape parliamentary or public scrutiny. These decisions can be placed in two categories: those concerning the maintenance of domestic law and order; and those involving other countries of foreign nationals.

On the domestic plane, control of any sort of violence or potentially violent political activity can involve prevention and administrative action, on the one hand, or *ex post facto* repression and judicial action on the other. In terms of preventive action, the Government has, for example, the power to declare a 'state of siege' (Article 36 of the constitution) as well as a state of emergency under Article 16. In a state of siege, the military takes over essential police powers. Furthermore, the Council of Ministers, under the Law of 3 April 1955, can declare a state of 'urgency', in which case the powers of the police are extended considerably.[64] In a more prosaic sense, the government has the power, exercised through the Prefect, Sub-prefect or Mayor, to ban demonstrations or marches on the public highway (decree-law of 23 October 1935).[65] But a more important provision is the Law of 10 January 1936, which allows the Government to dissolve associations or *de facto* groupings 'whose aim is to attack by force the republican form of government or whose activity will prevent the carrying out of measures concerning the re-establishment of republican legality'. In terms of administrative resources, a liaison bureau in the Interior Ministry and in each region links all police forces and coordinates the information available to the police; files of suspects are set up and distributed nationally.[66] 'Special Intervention Units', composed of anti-commando brigades responsible to the Interior Ministry and two gendarmerie units responsible to the Defence Ministry, were established in 1972–4. Also, a parachute regiment and the Foreign Legion are held in reserve.[67]

Judicial action also provides the Government with certain powers. First, special procedures or courts can be chosen. For example, there is the special procedure of *flagrant délit* (which literally means 'caught in the act'), which both gives the judicial police exceptional powers if a crime is in the process of being carried out (and limited to the period of time in which the crime is in progress) and provides for a rapid judicial procedure. This process was greeted with protest and scepticism when applied to the alleged autonomists arrested during the demonstration of 23 March 1979, as it prevented a full defence from being presented. But the most dramatic procedure was provided by the existence of the State Security Court, set up in 1963 as the successor to the special military tribunals established to try OAS leaders in the preceding two years. All offences involving state security in times of peace could be tried by this court, on which military and civilian judges sat together (if the crime is related to national defence, the military judges were in a majority). Its jurisdiction covered the entire country (no territorial limits to the examining magistrate's powers of investigation), but it sat in a military precinct in Paris to which access is difficult, even for lawyers. The public prosecutor cannot decide whether or not the prosecution may go ahead; that decision must be made on the written order of the Justice Minister. The period of time a prisoner can be held without going before a magistrate is extended from forty-eight hours to six days, and twelve days in cases of urgency. Certain restrictions on searches and seizures are lifted, and there is no limit to the period of remand. Appeals are limited more strictly than in ordinary courts, and the instruction procedure is controlled only by written documents. Reasons for decisions are not given unless damages are awarded. And defence lawyers are subject to more stringent controls. However, the Socialist Government elected in 1981 has suppressed the State Security Court altogether and returned all cases to the ordinary courts; many prisoners on remand there have already benefited, in addition, from the new President's post-electoral amnesty.[68]

Second, the government can apply the *loi anticasseurs* of 1970, which can make individual organisers and participants responsible for the results of violent acts or assaults carried out as the consequence of 'a concerted action by a group using direct force'. Aimed directly at violent demonstrations, the law has always been something of a political hot potato; according to *Le Figaro*, it has been applied with prudence, taking into account the common defence that the defendants were mere pawns. Magistrates are said to be hesitant to make defendants pay for damages (other means exist of providing for these), although this would seem to have been one of the main aims of the law.[69] Attempts to pass other special laws have not been so successful, however. In 1976, a bill attempting to make the registration of associations subject to the approval of the Prefect was withdrawn from parliament, and another bill permitting the generalised searching of cars was struck down by the Constitutional Council. However, a stretching of the *flagrant délit* procedure was used to justify the systematic searching of cars at the time of the kidnapping of the Belgian industrialist Baron Empain in January 1978.[70] Indeed, the police were regularly accused of abusing their files of suspects and their limited powers of search, especially at times like the Schleyer kidnapping, when they felt that they had to prove to the Germans that they could mount efficient operations too.[71] The various intelligence services — the DST charged with preventing subversion from abroad, and the Renseignements Généraux in the Interior Ministry — also played an important clandestine role in Government attempts to deal with potential terrorism. But the only special law dealing with a specific terrorist offence is a law of 1971 that sets out specific penalties for hostage-taking: life imprisonment if the hostage is kept for more than a month; 10–20 years if less than a month; and 2–5 years if the victim has been 'voluntarily' freed in less than five days.[72] It must also be remembered that the death penalty still exists in France existed until September 1981, although this and various other provisions have been reformed by the new Socialist Government.

The Government's discretion in the matter of foreign nationals is great indeed. In the first place, whatever the other rules in force, the Ordinance of 2 November 1945 gives the Government power to decide where a foreign national is allowed to reside — and even to expel him summarily — if the Interior Minister judges his presence to be a menace to 'public order or public credit'.[73] The preamble to the 1946 Constitution — still in effect, as it was adopted unchanged in the 1958 Constitution — states: 'Any person persecuted because of his action in favour of liberty has the right of asylum on the terroritories of the Republic.' The Geneva Convention of 1951, extended to cover all countries by the Bellagio Protocol of 1967, applies in France, and asylum is usually granted automatically when a refugee has set foot on French soil. Sometimes the clause in the Convention that states that a refugee must have justifiable cause to believe that he would be persecuted in his own country is interpreted widely — as when members of Salazar's secret police were admitted in 1975. But the combination of this clause and the constitutional requirement that the refugee must be persecuted for his action in favour of liberty are occasionally strictly interpreted. As we have already seen, seven Basque activists were returned to Spain in 1979 although they had previously enjoyed political asylum; and the extradition of Klaus Croissant, one of the lawyers of the Red Army Faction, to Germany in 1977 was justified by the Justice Minister, Peyrefitte, on exactly these grounds.[74] Furthermore, asylum is not unconditional. A circular of 2 July 1974 requires the refugee: (1) not to interfere with the domestic politics of the host country; (2) not to bring the political quarrels of his own country on to the national territory in a violent manner; and (3) not to endanger the internal or external security of the host country nor to endanger its diplomatic relations.[75] During the first ten months of 1976, France expelled 3595 foreigners,[76] but during the entire year only 161 were actually extradited.[77] This latter figure, indeed, represents a normal year.

The European Convention on the Suppression of Terrorism was adopted in Strasbourg in November 1976 and signed in January 1977. It greatly restricts the notion of political crimes, although it includes a safeguard clause that either is meaningless or vitiates the text of its usefulness. A great deal of opposition to this text developed in France, as it was seen as a serious threat to the cherished concept of France as a land of asylum. A young law lecturer wrote in *Le Monde:*

If suffices to think that if such a treaty had existed in another epoch, France would have been obliged to extradite Santiago Carrillo to Franco's Spain and Mario Soares to Salazar's Portugal, not to mention General de Gaulle, a terrorist *par excellence* in the terms of the text, whom the British government would have had to send back to Vichy in 1940![78]

Of course, that was in another era, and the signatories were all liberal democracies now. But the case of Klaus Croissant came to be a symbol of the deficiencies of the new approach; indeed, the Socialist Government has now permitted Croissant's return to France (having served his sentence in Germany) to practice law.[79] The opposition stretched across the left and left–centre of the political spectrum, and strongly present was the League of the Rights of Man. Although it was intended to present the Convention to parliament for ratification in the spring session of 1978, it has still not yet been presented. Giscard d'Estaing's further proposal of a 'common judicial area' would seem, in these circumstances, to have been stillborn.

In more limited areas, France did sign and ratify the Hague Convention of 1970 on air piracy, but did not even sign the subsequent Montreal Convention of 1971.[80]

Essentially, however, the French Government retains a great deal of discretion over political refugees in its territory. The tradition of granting political asylum on a large scale has been maintained and is even being extended by the Socialist Government, especially to the Basques, on a case-by-case basis;[81] the flexibility of this system is evidenced by the case with which President Bani-Sadr of Iran is currently constructing an opposition-in-exile (with the support of the 'terrorist' Mojahadin-el-Khalq) despite strong demands for his extradition. In the domestic arena, ordinary criminal law is still the basis for dealing with violence and terrorism, although the existing structure of that law and of the administrative weapons in the hands of the executive means in effect that further special legislation would not be necessary. In any case, the vigilance of radical intellectuals, left-wing groups and even old-fashioned liberals has made a paranoid over-reaction less credible in the French context, while this liberal tradition has taken on a new vitality with the victory of the Socialists.

Conclusion

The terrorist threat thrives on evoking the existential dread of the social order, which it hopes to force to undermine its own legitimacy. France, however, has been fairly immune from this pressure. In fact, the concept of terrorism itself is a complex one to apply in the context of contemporary French society and politics. The analyst is caught between the narrow definition of terrorism — in which case France is characterised by non-terrorism rather than terrorism — and the very broad definition — in which case all anti-system groups, whether revolutionary or merely dissenting, violent or non-violent, ideological or sectional, active or merely sympathising, come to be seen as potentially subversive and thus become vulnerable to greater repression. This is no mere technical dilemma in the age of modern communications, where media shorthand and the aims of 'terrorist' groups combine symbiotically in a ritual threat of social breakdown, symbolically leading mass publics to internalise the fear felt by the participants in the in fact highly circumscribed 'incidents' that are the raw material of effective news coverage.

That the image of terrorism is diffuse in France is the consequence of two major factors. The first is the lack, fortuitous or otherwise, of an active, visible, coherent indigenous terrorist organisation. Thus terrorism appears as a foreign phenomenon, and linkages with the domestic social order must be by way of analogy rather than through self-evident factual demonstration. An anti-terrorist consensus remains a somewhat abstract formula and is unlikely to lead to policy decisions, pressures for immediate action or the suspension of disbelief in the benefits of bureaucratic repression that is necessary for the acceptance of special legislation and emergency measures. The second, which is inextricably intertwined with the first, is France's political culture, with its unique mixture of revolutionary, liberal-democratic and paternalist–administrative elements, where the label 'left' is often adopted by right-wing groups, where the Declaration of the Rights of Man and Citizen is re-proclaimed in the preamble to every constitution, and where the effervescence of intellectual radicalism is regarded as a political and cultural resource underlying France's humane and civilising mission in the world. Despite the low-level political violence that does exist and despite the short-term erosion in the earlier years of the Fifth Republic of social, economic and political pluralism that nurtured the French political tradition, its cultural power is still paramount.

In a world in which terrorism seems to be in decline, France has done better than many others in maintaining its commitment to those values that must underlie a genuine democratic pluralism, and those values have recently been unmistakeably reaffirmed.

Notes and References

1 See S. Cobler, *Law, Order and Politics in West Germany* (Harmondsworth: Penguin, 1978); 'L'Europe de la répression, ou l'insécurité d'état', *Actes*, special edition, supplement to no. 17 (Spring 1978).

122   *Phil Cerny*

2 L. Dispot, *La machine à terreur* (Paris: Grasset, 1975).
3 G. Almond and S. Verba, *The Civic Culture: Political Attitudes and Democracy in Five Nations* (Boston: Little, Brown, 1965), pp. 312–13.
4 Consider W. L. Shirer, *The Collapse of the Third Republic* (London: Heinemann, 1969) among others.
5 D. Thomson, *Democracy in France since 1870* (London: Oxford University Press, 5th edn, 1969) and S. Hoffmann, 'Paradoxes of the French Political Community', in Hoffmann, *et al.*, *In Search of France* (Cambridge, Mass.: Harvard University Press, 1963), pp. 1–117.
6 S. Hoffmann, 'Heroic Leadership: The Case of Modern France', in L. J. Edinger, ed., *Political Leadership in Industrialised Societies* (New York: Wiley, 1967), pp. 108–54.
7 R. Rémond, *The Right Wing in France from 1815 to de Gaulle* (Philadelphia: University of Pennsylvania Press, 1966) and J. Touchard, *La gauche en France depuis 1900* (Paris: Seuil, 1977).
8 See P. G. Cerny, 'The New Rules of the Game in France', in P. G. Cerny and M. A. Schain, eds, *French Politics and Public Policy* (London: Frances Pinter; New York: St. Martin's Press, 1980).
9 See M. Crozier, *The Bureaucratic Phenomenon* (London: Tavistock, 1964), Part IV.
10 G. Michelat and M. Simon, *Classe, religion et comportement politique* (Paris: Presses de la Fondation Nationale des Sciences Politiques and Editions Sociales, 1977).
11 J. Marceau, *Class and Status in France: Economic Change and Social Immobility 1945–1975* (Oxford: Oxford University Press, 1977).
12 V. Wright, *The Government and Politics of France* (London: Hutchinson, 1978).
13 See E. R. Curtius, *The Civilisation of France: An Introduction* (New York: Vintage, 1962; originally published 1929).
14 S. Hoffmann, 'The Vichy Circle of French Conservatives', in Hoffmann, *Decline or Renewal? France since the 1930s* (New York: Viking, 1974), pp. 3–25.
15 M. Duverger, *La Ve République* (Paris: Presses Universitaires de France, 1963).
16 For a discussion of de Gaulle's views on leadership, see P. G. Cerny, *The Politics of Grandeur: Ideological Aspects of de Gaulle's Foreign Policy* (Cambridge: Cambridge University Press, 1980), chs 1–3.
17 See chapter 1, *supra*; for a classical Lipsettian view, see H. Waterman, *Political Change in Contemporary France: The Politics of an Industrial Democracy* (Columbus, Ohio: Merrill, 1969).
18 See David S. Bell, ed., *French Political Parties* (London: Croom Helm, 1981).
19 M. A. Schain, *French Communism and Local Power* (London: Frances Pinter, forthcoming, 1982).
20 J.-R. Tournoux, *L'histoire secrète* (Paris: Plon, 1962). Also P. Chairoff, *Dossier B . . . comme barbouzes* (Paris: Alain Moreau, 1975).
21 For an understanding of the army's position, see J. Planchais, *Une histoire politique de l'Armée: de de Gaulle à de Gaulle, 1940–1967* (Paris: Seuil, 1967); cf. O. D. Menard, *The Army and the Fifth Republic* (Lincoln, Neb.: University of Nebraska Press, 1967).
22 For a sympathetic treatment of the FLNA, see F. Fanon, *Sociologie d'une révolution: l'an V de la Révolution algérienne* (Paris: François Maspéro, 1978; originally published 1959).
23 Details of the political context of the Algerian War and independence can be found in P. M. Williams, *French Politicians and Elections 1951–1969* (Cambridge: Cambridge University Press, 1970).
24 Cerny, *The Politics of Grandeur*, pp. 60–1.

25 On the OAS, cf. Tournoux, op. cit., and R. Gaucher, *Les terroristes, de la Russie tsariste à l'O.A.S.* (Paris: Albin Michel, 1965), pp. 279–343.
26 C. Plume and P. Démaret, *Target: De Gaulle* (London: Secker and Warburg, 1974).
27 A. Grosser, *La IVe République et sa politique extérieure* (Paris: Colin, 1961), p. 9.
28 For an example of this paranoia, see R. Moss, *The Collapse of Democracy* (London: Abacus, 1977).
29 For a more detailed comparative treatment, see J. Bowyer Bell, *A Time of Terror: How Democratic Societies Respond to Revolutionary Violence* (New York: Basic Books, 1978).
30 See the three-part series 'La France, terre d'asile', *Le Monde*, 26, 27 and 28/9 November 1976.
31 C. Dobson and R. Payne, *The Carlos Complex: A Study in Terror* (London: Coronet, 1978), pp. 81–2.
32 9 August 1978. The debate on preventive capability and the legal situation will be referred to again in part II of this chapter.
33 *Le Monde*, 2 August 1978.
34 Ibid.; *Le Figaro*, 3 August 1978.
35 *L'Aurore* and *Le Figaro*, 22 May 1978.
36 Dobson and Payne, op. cit., pp. 55–6; *Le Figaro*, 22 May 1978.
37 *Le Monde*, 29 March 1979.
38 *The Observer*, 4 August 1979.
39 *Le Monde*, 2 February 1979.
40 *Le Monde*, 9 February and 3 March 1979.
41 *Le Matin*, 18 October and 24 October 1978.
42 See *Le Point*, 8 May 1978, and Dobson and Payne, op. cit., pp. 84–91. No charges against Curiel were ever proved; indeed the new Socialist Interior Minister found no incriminating evidence on his police file. For a description of how such false rumours became widely accepted even in 'respectable' circles, see Jean-Marie Domenach's 2-part series on 'L'Affaire Curiel', *Le Monde*, 16 and 17/18 May 1981.
43 *Le Point*, 31 October 1977.
44 See *Le Monde*, 6 March 1979.
45 *Libération*, 16 January 1979.
46 *Le Monde*, 27 June 1978 and *Le Figaro*, 1 July 1978.
47 *Le Monde*, 5 July 1978; *Le Figaro*, 27 June 1978.
48 See the 2-part series by Marie-Christine Robert, 'Où va l'autonomisme Breton', *Le Monde*, 6 and 7 May 1981; the 5 demands, presented in a letter to Mitterrand, are detailed in *Le Monde*, 14/15 June 1981.
49 See *Le Monde*, 8 February and 1/2 April 1979. *Le Point*, 2 January 1978, mentions the Corsican who bombed the houses of eight of his wife's lovers. Nonetheless, more bomb attacks were set by Corsicans than by any other group.
50 See the 3-part article, 'La Corse décrispée', *Le Monde*, 19/20, 21 and 22 July 1981.
51 *Le Monde*, 11 January 1979, and 16 September 1978.
52 *Le Matin*, 25 July 1978.
53 *Le Monde*, 5 July 1978.
54 *Le Matin*, 2 May 1979.
55 On these murders, and on the wider activities and structures of SAC, see *Le Monde*, 23 and 26/27 July 1981.
56 *Le Nouvel Observateur*, 14 April 1979; *Le Monde*, 16 January 1979.
57 *Réponses à la violence*. Rapport du comité présidé par Alain Peyrefitte (Paris: Presses-Pocket, 1977), 2 vols. This led to the passage of the 'Security and Liberty Law' in 1980, which the new Socialist Government is pledged to repeal.

58 *Le Monde*, 20 September 1978.
59 *Le Quotidien de Paris*, 28 May 1977; *Le Matin*, 22 October 1977; and *Le Figaro*, 24 October 1977.
60 *Le Monde*, 11, 15 and 24 May 1974; and *Le Figaro*, 11 March 1976.
61 *Le Figaro*, 24 October 1977.
62 *L'Express*, 31 October 1977.
63 *Le Monde*, 28 October 1977.
64 'L'Europe de la répression', op. cit., p. 3.
65 *L'Aurore*, 31 March/1 April 1979.
66 R. Marcellin, *L'ordre public et les groupes révolutionnaires* (Paris: Plon, 1969), pp. 53–64.
67 *Le Monde*, 20 October 1977.
68 M. Laval, 'La Cour de Sûreté de l'Etat'. *Actes*, no. 10 (Spring 1976), pp. 2–6. Also, 'La Cour de Sûreté de l'Etat dans le système judiciaire français', *Actualités-Documents*, Paris, Délégation Générale à l'Information, no. 111 (n.d.). On recent developments, see the articles on the court's history and procedure (all of p. 9) in *Le Monde*, 8 July 1981, and the report of the debate in the National Assembly, *Le Monde*, 19/20 July 1981; on the amnesty and its limitations see *Le Monde*, 13 June 1981.
69 *Le Figaro*, 15 January 1979.
70 *France Nouvelle*, 6 March 1978.
71 *Libération*, 23 February 1978.
72 *Le Monde*, 20 March and 25 June 1971; *Le Figaro*, 4 October 1977.
73 *Le Monde*, 14 December 1978 and 9 January 1979.
74 *Le Nouvel Observateur*, 28 November 1977.
75 'La France, terre d'asile', op. cit.
76 *Le Monde*, 30 October 1976.
77 *Le Figaro*, 21/2 August 1977.
78 *Le Monde*, 20 July 1977.
79 *Le Matin*, 22 September 1977; *Le Monde*, 21 May 1981.
80 F. Julien-Laferrière, 'La Convention européenne pour la répression du terrorisme', *Après-demain*, no. 211 (February 1979), pp. 43–5; 'La Lutte internationale contre le terrorisme', *Problèmes Politiques et Sociaux*, no. 259 (30 May 1975), La Documentation Française, pp. 48–52.
81 On the test case of Tomas Linaza Echevarria, see 'Terrorisme et droits de l'homme', *Le Monde*, 9 June 1981; on the new Government's policy, see the statement by Foreign Minister Claude Cheysson, *Le Monde*, 5/6 July 1981.

I should like to express my gratitude to the British Academy and the Maison des Sciences de l'Homme (Paris) for their financial support during a research visit to France in April 1979 in connection with the preparation of this chapter, and to the Institut d'Etudes Politiques for the use of its research facilities.

6 The Political Construction of Sexuality: The Contraception and Abortion Issues in France, 1965-1975

ANNE BATIOT
Research Student in Government
University of Essex

Introduction

Among various other factors, social movements necessitate a critical mobilising event to turn the individual sense of oppression into a collectively-based political demand resting on some sort of organisational structure. The abortion campaign in France, spreading from the early to middle 1970s, was the critical event around which the French Women's Movement mobilised. Hitherto sparsely organised into small, often isolated, groups of intellectuals and political activists critical of the male chauvinism which they experienced among the many left political groups involved in the events of May 1968, the French feminist movement spread when it challenged politically the ways in which women were sexually discriminated against by French society. Feminists attacked particularly the social and ideological confusion surrounding female sexuality.

Double standards of morality have been criticised by practically every new generation of feminists. However, with the advent of an era of liberation, and indeed of 'sexual liberation', in the 1960s, there emerged a proliferation of discourses on sexuality. These ranged widely from the 'liberating' effects of pornography to the essentialism of female sexuality linked to reproductive functions. These various discourses contributed to a confusion regarding 'sexual liberation' generally felt by all sides of the political spectrum, the feminists included.

The abortion campaign contributed largely to the opening of a public debate on sexuality in French politics. It eventually dragged every single political institution into the folds of its polemics, forcing each in turn to take a position on the issue, but also calling for important political alliances to secure short-term political safety and long-term social changes.

The attempts to liberalise the existing repressive legislation on abortion by liberal-centrists, in the Government and in the Opposition, were intended as a long-overdue reform. The struggles put up by the feminists and their allies in ultra-left groups represented the first major instance of an anti-sexist political construction of sexuality. The previous contraception issue had not involved the public as much as the abortion issue later did. In their struggle for 'Free Abortion on Demand', feminists and their allies made unique political interventions in their attempts to construct non-sexist social categories of sexuality and of women.

It is this general process of the political construction of sexuality which this chapter proposes to analyse — a process which involved several, sometimes opposing social groups and movements.

On Discourse

The process of political construction cannot, however, be reduced to the opposition of two camps, one pushing for liberalisation and the other opposing it; for as we shall see shortly, the liberalisation of contraception and abortion, and opposition to it, was fragmented into numerous nuanced discourses. Nor can the definition of a social movement be limited to the mobilisation of a social group for or against a particular demand, since as well as putting forward definite political requirements, a social movement, by the act of so doing, contributes to society's re-questioning of values hitherto accepted as the *status quo*. It is through this general political process that social movements contribute to the political reconstruction of our social categories.

In the light of these remarks, I propose to demonstrate in the present chapter how the formal acceptance by the French Establishment of a new category of sexuality had to be fought out politically. This new category of sexuality involved the gaining by women of partial control over their reproductive capacities (Contraception Act of 1967 and Abortion Acts of 1975 and 1980).

However, before proceeding with this demonstration, two further points need clarification. The first one concerns the social make-up of a social movement in relation to its ideological motivations, in this case the Women's Movement in relation to the struggle against a sexist categorisation of female sexuality. The second point concerns what is meant by 'discourse'. To begin with the latter, discourse is any activity which produces meaning. It is therefore not restricted to verbal or oral meaning — a partial meaning unfortunately adopted by Foucault in his *History of Sexuality*.[1] Discourse encompasses any meaningful sequence of acts, much in the same way as Roland Barthes describes fashion or love as discursive practices. And so are, for our purposes, public demonstrations, the illegal running of denunciatory abortion centres, the setting up of sexual information centres, or the signing of a public Manifesto admitting to having had an abortion.

Remarks on Abortion and the Women's Movement

With regard to the social make-up of a social movement in relation to its ideological motivations, it needs to be stressed once more that the liberalisation of abortion, although of primary personal relevance to women, was not the sole concern of women alone, since many men took sides either in defence or in opposition to it. Nor did all women support a liberalising reform which could only give them more control over their own lives as well as giving other women more control over theirs.

In other words, women as a readily identifiable social group do not form a unified political group. This point, now recognised by some feminist theorists, nevertheless bears relevance to any theory that still confuses a social group with a political class, a sociological category with a unified political category (for example, Christine Delphy). Of political relevance to women as a social group is the struggle against sexism, a struggle which ought to concern men as well and in which some men partake. The struggle against sexism necessitates the autonomous political organisation of other social groups affected by sexism in our society — gays, children, men, and so on. Whereas all may well be ideally committed to eradicating sexism in our society, this commitment does not make them feminist.

Feminists argue that women's specificity lies in the repression of female sexuality in that it is socially and ideologically organised towards reproduction within the family structure. This equation of repressed female sexuality with reproductive functions is further reinforced by the legal and economic dependence of wives on their husbands, even when in many cases wives are wage-earners. It can be argued here that not all women marry and that this feminist approach therefore aims mostly at married women. But the social and economic pressures put on single parents certainly point out to the importance our society gives to reproduction within marriages.

Foucault

Michel Foucault, however, in his *History of Sexuality*, asserts that the family is not the exclusive guardian of sexuality. Sexuality is also constructed and guarded by legal, medical, pedagogical and scientific discourses. In fact, Foucault insists, repression is not fundamental and over-riding when dealing with sexuality. Whereas the feminists have invested much energy in denouncing the many ways in which female sexuality has been repressed by its equation with reproductive functions and the family, Foucault on the other hand advances the hypothesis of 'a proliferation of discourses, carefully tailored to the requirements of Establishment power'. For although there are repressive laws on sexuality, sex is widely spoken and written about by individuals and by institutions. Whereas in the late sixties and in the seventies, feminists and their allies reacted strongly against the harsh and outdated laws repressing contraception and abortion, as well as other issues related to sexuality, Foucault dismisses what he refers to as a 'juridico–discursive representation of power' — that is, one that attaches analytical importance to legal repression. Power cannot be understood in terms of legal discourse alone, of licit and illicit sexuality, permitted and forbidden acts. If it were, the outcome would be to demonstrate how sex 'suppresses itself for fear of punishment'.[2]

Foucault proposes instead to examine a society which loudly represses sexual pleasure and yet 'speaks verbosely of its own silence'. He sets out to explore the discourses, the will and the strategic intentions which have made and sustained repressive laws on sexuality, and to question whether sexual repression is truly an established historical fact. Therefore of primary interest to Foucault are the ways in which sex is verbalised and 'put into discourse', and how to locate the forms of power that penetrate and control everyday pleasure. These forms of power are not only inherent in the repressive functions of the family for, asserts Foucault, there are multiple forms of policing sexuality in and out of the family. These include the attempts since the nineteenth century to define sexual regularities from sexual irregularities and to identify and categorise patho-logical, sinful sexuality from normal, reproductive sexuality — as well as the multiplication of sexualities, the strengthening of their disparate forms and the multiple implantations of perversions.[3]

Foucault's contribution is twofold. First, he retraces discourse on sexuality in France, from the act of medieval religious confession, which was soon extended to the nineteenth century policing of individual sexual behaviour (such as marriage rules and family organisations), to the emergence of population as a subject of analysis and public control: birth and death rates, fertility and sterility, legitimacy and illegitimacy.[4] In this respect, Foucault provides us with a valuable operational framework to consider for further work: to localise centres of power/knowledge and to uncover the verbal discursive construction of sexuality in French society.

Second, Foucault's contribution is valuable in that he demonstrates amply how sex, popularly regarded as taboo and silenced, became not only a public issue and the subject of scientific enquiry, but that in fact through discourse, sexual norms have been subtly constructed through a strategic *ensemble*. The strategies are the hystericisation of the woman's body, the pedagogising of children's sexuality, the socialisation of reproduction, and the psychiatrisation of perverse pleasure.

The main criticism that can be aimed at Foucault, for our purpose, is that mentioned above — namely that Foucault restricts the concept of discourse to verbal discourse, when in fact he relies himself on much historical evidence of discursive practices regarding sexuality that are non-verbal (e.g. the registration of births to check on legitimacy, degrees of punishment for sexual offences, and so on).

Finally, Foucault's contribution to our understanding of sex as a public issue is limited. This is partly due to the point just made. Foucault has failed to reach one significant conclusion — namely, that since the end of the nineteenth century, sex has become not only a public concern but a political issue. It is worth raising the issue here that this increasing political concern is partly due to the rising feminist political consciousness conjunctural to that period.

Previous discourses on contraception and abortion

Until the eighteenth century, sexuality in France was formally constructed by religious discourse. The mention of previous discursive practices on contraception and abortion is made here to illustrate how discourse on sexuality shifted from the medieval private local centre of power/knowledge (i.e., the relationship between penitent and confessor) to a variety of discursive practices (legal, medical, pedagogical and scientific) contributing to the publicisation of sexuality since the nineteenth century.

Infanticide was commonly practised in medieval France. It was included in the Penitential — a sort of penance scale-book for various sins — and was more severely condemned (twelve years of penance) than was an abortion performed before the embryo's coming of life (one year of penance).[5] Abortion represented then 80 per cent of those sins listed to be especially absolved by someone other than an ordinary priest. And in 1655, the Vicars General of Paris complained to the first President of Law Courts that in one year alone, six hundred women had confessed to have aborted.[6]

But discourse on contraception and abortion was not restricted to the confessional. After all, most women relied on a local network of individuals who practised abortion and knew of various methods of contraception. It was against these popular practices that Pope Sixtus Quint's papal bull *Effraenatal* (1588) was directed. It condemned to death not only any individual who practised or had an abortion, but also any one who made use of contraceptive plants. Although not seriously adopted by theologians and in fact cancelled in 1591 by Sixtus's successor, it nevertheless retained the part concerning the practice of an abortion on an embryo older than forty days.[7]

Until the French Revolution then, sexual and reproductive choices were constructed by two discourses: a religious discourse acting as official discourse and adopted by the Establishment, and a popular discourse. The religious discourse condemned contraceptive and abortive methods as a crime and debated on the theological 'truth' of sex. Popular discourse was based on local knowledge of plants and contraceptive methods, and on networks of individuals who practised abortion. Numerous songs, poems and folk-ballads give ample evidence of this popular tradition.[8] Until 1789, there existed no royal law repressing abortion and the historian Flandrin remarks that there are no known examples of civil tribunals condemning individuals for having practised abortion.

Jurists agreed fully with the Church's legislation. The first law on abortion dates back to 1791. It condemned contraceptive and abortive practices as crimes performed *on* women. Whereas religious discourse held the woman as equally condemnable as her accomplices, the emerging legal discourse posed woman as the victim. Consequently much leniency was shown towards her, in spite of Article 317 of the Penal Code (1810) which punished the woman and her accomplices. It sentenced to hard labour doctors, apothecaries and midwives who assisted in an abortion. But jurists referred mostly to the 1791 text which cleared the woman.[9]

Medical discourse on sexuality appeared in the seventeenth century. It refrained from disclosing whatever practical methods it knew but was more concerned in establishing its own 'scientific truth' about sex and reproduction. Eighteenth century concern with conjugal fertility soon became translated into practical measures. Throughout the nineteenth and twentieth centuries, discourse on abortion became increasingly concerned with questions of legislation, registering of births and deaths, different attitudes towards women and girls who had aborted, and degrees of punishment to be inflicted. Although increasingly anticlerical, French society clung to fundamentally Christian values. Rejecting illegitimacy and suspicious of sexual pleasure, it insisted on the legitimacy of the family.[10]

Following the legislations of 1791 and 1810, legal discourse concerned itself with identifying the victim (the woman) and the guilty ones (her accomplices). Only a few cases were brought to the tribunals' attention. Yet however slight was the number of prosecuted abortions, it is hardly reflective of the frequency with which it was being practised. In 1890, Professor Lacassagne estimated that 600,000 abortions were practised each year in France and by 1914 the number had arisen to 900,000.[11]

The Laws of July 1920 on contraception and of March 1923 on

abortion, swiftly debated and passed with an overwhelming majority, were definitely aimed to combat any propaganda in favour of birth control, on the one hand, and to inflict concrete penalties for the crime of abortion, on the other. Both laws served as a basis of ensuring that juries would no longer be indulgent. Yet they were to remain little applied. There were only 359 prosecutions in 1925, 537 in 1968 and 340 in 1970.[12]

By 1920, the social construction of sexuality in terms of the possibility of sexual and reproductive choices had become a public concern, although it remained politically limited to a small public and it evaded popular political debate. The publicisation of contraceptive methods in France is a recent phenomenon. It has been largely the work of the French branch of the International Movement for Family Planning (MFPF). Created in 1956, operating illegally until 1961, the MFPF was supported at first by the Liberal Party, and later by the emerging Socialist Party. Since then, it has led a campaign to educate and inform the public on methods of contraception and family planning. Its ceaseless work is certainly reflected in the large number of legislative proposals put forward by practically all political groups between 1964 and 1966. Contraception and abortion were gaining a much wider public and political attention. By 1965, François Mitterrand, leader of the left coalition, posed in his election campaign the social problem of backstreet abortions and the need to change the laws of 1920 and 1923.

From Public Concern to Political Discourse

Publicisation

Several factors contributed to the rising public concern in France about contraception and abortion. First of all, medical research made some very significant discoveries. In 1955 Pincus came up with the first contraceptive pill and in 1959 Oppenheimer in Israel and Ota in Japan invented the first modern coils. In 1960 Karman practised the first abortions by aspiration in Los Angeles. Contraceptive methods were becoming increasingly medicalised, yet they were not under the control of the medical profession nor of the law. Second, as we have seen above, the MFPF had been very active in informing and educating the general public, though it was felt then that its work was little compared to what was needed to be done.

Third, during the Second World War, women in France had been drawn into greater employment. Although the rate of female employment decreased after 1946, it increased again significantly after 1962. By 1978, over 75 per cent of women aged twenty-three or over were in employment.[13] In gaining relative economic independence, women began to question seriously the number of children they wished and/or could afford to have. Although relatively accessible in France, childcare nevertheless represents an organisational problem to the working mother. Higher costs of living were also significant in deciding on family size.[14]

Finally, it happens that the two periods of concentrated discourse on contraception and abortion coincide with two periods of elections — the presidential elections of 1965 and the legislative elections of 1967; and the presidential elections of March 1974 and the legislative elections of 1973 and 1978. It is worth noting here that it is following the legislative elections of March 1967 that the contraception law was passed (28 December 1967). The abortion law was voted through in December 1974.

In this process of publicisation of sexuality, the media played an important role, for it highlighted contraception and abortion as *political* issues. From the middle sixties onwards, there emerged in the press a public debate on sexuality that reached national dimensions. Public and political discourses on sexuality widened. An increasing number of spokespersons of different status publicly intervened on these issues. Politics was used by the press as a sort of clutch to bridge the gap between sexuality as a private sphere and as a public concern.

A study of the debate on abortion in the press had demonstrated how discourse on sexuality was represented between 1965 and 1974 by various arguments.[15] Chronologically, scientific and technical controversies, as well as demographical arguments, were raised mainly between 1965 and 1967, showing that there has existed a definite link between scientific progress on contraception and the general social movement leading to the liberalisation of abortion. New contraceptive techniques gave the start to such a movement but the liberalisation of the legislation itself was in the hands of political institutions and social forces. Furthermore, greater pressure from the press was required to push the theme of abortion (38 per cent of the material analysed) in 1967 than had been formerly necessary to push that of contraception (30.7 per cent) in 1965.[16] Contraception and abortion did not become political concerns until 1967 whereas they remained a regular moral concern from 1962 (25 per cent) to 1974 (23 per cent). Although posed primarily as a source of technical enquiry, contraception and especially abortion became important social matters between 1972 and 1974.[17] The most significant progression however is that of the theme of contraception and abortion as political concerns.

Of all daily papers analysed, *L'Humanité* came last in the frequency of entries on abortion, reaching only a total of 1,046, compared to *La Croix*'s total of 7,286. The authors conclude that *L'Humanité* was little interested during that period in the problem of abortion, and when it was, it was so mainly on its own terrain of political and social problems. *Le Monde* refused categorically to politicise abortion but tended rather to moralise the problem while showing moderate attention to abortion as a social problem. *France-Soir* fluctuated between the theme of quality of legislation and that of scientific information. *L'Aurore* concentrated mostly on the scientific controversies regarding the pill, while ignoring most of the other themes.[18]

Political discourse

The political discourse on sexuality emerging after 1964 was characterised by its pragmatism. Initiated by the centrists from the liberal right and the centre-left, and backed by the progressive faction of the medical profession, this emerging political discourse relied on a widely varied factual argumentation and led to political propositions usually oriented towards institutional pragmatism. Insisting on the role of the legislator and of public institutions, it was nevertheless preoccupied with the condition of women in French society and with the social problem of backstreet abortions. It expected contraception to become the main means of family planning, thus reducing the practice of abortions.[19] Its main political aim was to publicise information on sexuality, legalise contraception and control the practice of abortion by making it legal, and medically safe and restricted.

This liberal discourse on sexuality met opposition from two moral discourses. One came from the right-wing traditional Catholics who not only opposed any reform in the existing repressive legislation on contraception and abortion but insisted to some extent that the existing laws should be more strictly enforced. This religious ethical discourse held morality as universal and as being religious, a morality that respects the right to life and considers the embryo to be a living being. It therefore condemned abortion. Although not the most frequent of all discourses, it was statistically the most coherent, constituting a real ideological blockage in which biological, moral and religious arguments appeared to be strongly integrated, and establishing around abortion a sort of doctrinal fortress.[20]

However, Isambert and Ladrière point out that, although the Catholic daily newspaper *La Croix* contributed largely to the moral discourse against any form of liberalisation, nevertheless abortion emerged in the national debate primarily as a political issue rather than a moral concern. Furthermore, even excluding *La Croix*'s contribution in posing abortion as a moral concern, other newspapers' contributions on the subject remained substantial. The point to be drawn here is that the militant Catholic paper *itself* was not the main determinant in posing abortion as a moral problem.[21]

This brings us to a second moral discourse on sexuality. Although not religious, this discourse insisted on the legitimacy of the traditional family and moral values. Worried by the discourse of 'sexual liberation' emerging in the 1960s, this moral discourse denounced abortion as an easy solution for young unmarried women who did not respect traditional values. It ignored the fact that abortion was practised by a significant number of married women of varying ages who did not want any more children (see note 14). This non-religious moral discourse was practised by various political formations − from the Communist Party, who at first posed abortion as an anti-working-class issue, to the Gaullist RPR, who simply opposed any attack on the legitimacy of the traditional family.

A third major discourse on sexuality was that termed by Isambert and Ladrière as libertarian. It opposed the liberal reformist and both moral discourses in demanding moral and sexual freedom and in rejecting the Church's authority, the universality of religious morals and traditional values. It called for the total repeal of the laws of 1920 and 1923, and demanded free contraception and abortion for women. This libertarian discourse was statistically less coherent, showing rates of error between 4.79 per cent and 11.85 per cent.[22] It was practised by the Women's Movement, some groups of the ultra-left such as the former *Ligue Communiste Revolutionnaire* (Trotskyite) and the Unified Socialist Party (PSU) as well as individual members of the Socialist Party (PS). Specialised bodies created to lead the struggle for the liberalisation of abortion also adhered to this discourse, including an association of left-wing doctors and medical students called *Groupe Information Santé* (GIS), who later participated in the setting up of the *Mouvement pour la Libération de l'Avortement et de la Contraception* (MLAC); CHOISIR, created by the feminist lawyer Gisèle Halimi to mobilise support during the abortion trials of Bobigny; and the left wing of the MFPF.

It is important to note here that although political parties and organisations took definite political positions on the issue of contraception and abortion after 1972–3, political mobilisation on these issues is best understood in terms of individual choices rather than party adherence. Nevertheless, the position adopted by parties and organisations certainly played a significant role in challenging individual attitudes towards sexuality as a political issue. Professional and voluntary associations also contributed to this process.[23]

Two further points need to be made. First of all, contrary to Foucault's advocacy to avoid what he calls a juridico-discursive analytics of sexuality, we find that, at least as far as the press is concerned, the questions of legislation on abortion (9.6 per cent), the role of the legislator (6.7 per cent), the quality of the legislation (4.5 per cent) and information on the law (3.7 per cent) came up as the four first priorities within the analytical category of political discourse discerned by the study mentioned above. Political discourse itself came up as the main theme granted attention by the press in the national debate on abortion.[24] However, it must be remembered that these priorities do not necessarily reflect the opinions and discourses of the general public as a whole but rather *the attention granted by the press* to this national debate. Such priorities cannot be discarded as of little interest since the press can rightly be seen as an important instrument in shaping the main dimensions of this national debate.

Second, in spite of the positions which parties, trade unions and voluntary associations took on the question of abortion, they remained seriously split on the issue right up to the time when the first temporary legislation was passed in 1975. By the time the law was to be finally passed five years later, these organisations (except for the traditional Catholic ones) had accepted the need for the reform. By 1979, the debate had died down compared to its earlier fury, although the Catholic opposition had retained all of its former strength. But it did not have the political weight to reverse the 1975 legislation.

The Political Construction of Sexuality:
The Fight for the Liberalisation of Contraception and Abortion

Contraception

Contraception and abortion were publicly posed as a political concern by Mitterrand during the president elections of 1965 when he demanded the modification of the existing laws. In 1966 a special committee was constituted to discuss a text on contraception presented by M. Neuwirth, UDR (Gaullist) deputy for the Loire. His law proposal was finally adopted as law on 28 December 1967. It cancelled the former law of 1920, permitted the controlled use of contraception, and forbade any propaganda on contraception. Although contraception was legalised in 1967, its distribution was left totally unorganised until 1972, at which date

M. Neuwirth proposed to create a Superior Council of Sexual Information, Birth Control and Family Education. It took one year, from 30 June 1972 to 11 July 1973, for this law to be passed. This delay was due mainly to M. Foyer's opposition, to be found again three years later during the abortion debate.[25]

On 4 April 1974, the Chirac Government, conscious of the short-comings of the 1967 law, proposed a new law that included minors as beneficiaries of the contraception law, allowed for publicity and introduced reimbursement by the *Sécurité Sociale* (the French National Health). This revised text was adopted by the National Assembly without any opposition. The Senate showed reticence but finally accepted it. The law was definitely passed on 28 June 1974. It had taken seven years for the Government to make possible the implementation of the law on contraception passed in 1967. Until then, contraception had remained a formal right, but no practical measures had been taken to ensure the availability of information on it or its distribution.

The fact that it was a UDR[26] Deputy from the Loire who proposed the contraception law is surprising, for the national political majority formed by the UDR and the centrists until 1981 had first sided with the Catholic Church and part of the Reformed Church in opposition to any liberalisation concerning contraception. After all, Gaullist leader Michel Debré wanted French population numbers to reach 100 millions; Louis Terrenoire wanted many children to contribute to the funds of the *Sécurité Sociale*, chronically in deficit; and many others invoked alarmingly the fact that French population was getting old.[27] But part of the UDR and centre later came to accept contraception as a lesser evil than abortion. After having done everything politically in their power to fight against the liberalisation of contraception, they were suprised a few years later that it was not more widely used and that women had to resort to abortion.[28]

The same argument was used by the French Medical Council (*Conseil de l'Ordre*) in its resistance against legalising abortion. Created under the Vichy Régime, and counting 77,000 doctors in France alone (i.e., excluding Overseas Territories) in 1974, its political resistance had an impact incommensurate with its numerical size. But then, doctors are well represented in the French Parliament and they keep close ties with the monopoly of the pharmaceutical industry.[29] Eventually split on the issue, the medical profession had to reach some sort of compromise. The right wing of the Council managed to obtain that sexual matters be dealt with exclusively within the terms of their competence, while the minority left and libertarian wings of the Council lent their practical and political support to their respective organisations, mostly within the PS and the MFPF with regard to the former, and within the specialist groups such as MLAC, GIS, CHOISIR, and the Mouvement de Libération des Femmes (MLF), with regard to the latter.

The pressing for the need to change the contraception law was owed to the liberal wing of the majority — people like Peyret, Neuwirth, Poniatowski and Taittinger. The passing of the law was made possible through the support lent by the Socialist Party to the majority on that specific issue, while the Communist Party voted against it. Protestants, liberals and Freemasons were also typically representative of this modernist current which, however, was left behind when specialised associations and movements became politicised on the issue of sexuality. They had contributed to the establishment of the MFPF — which they left after 1973, following its further radicalisation, to move closer to government positions and to moderate associations like the National Association of Abortion Research (ANEA).

Quite distinctively from its counterparts in other countries, the MFPF had become radically politicised since 1967 and especially so since 1973. It was the first institutionalised organisation to pose the problem of contraception in a perspective of personal liberation, not of population control, and to link it to the themes of sexual information, abortion, the liberation of women and the modification of the status of the family.[30] First forced into clandestine action (late fifties) and then systematically opposed by public institutions (early sixties), the MFPF has been confronted since 1970 with the problem of being integrated into official structures. In 1967 it counted 10,000 members, 33,000 in 1971 and 45,000 in 1974.[31] Implanted in every *département* and comprising three hundred and fifty centres in 1974, the MFPF has *cadres* who intervene in schools, hospitals, Centres for the Protection of Mothers and Children (PMI), dispensaries, constituencies (*quartiers*), factories and firms. By 1973 it was the only independent association to have built its experience altogether on contraception, sexual information, matrimonial advice and abortion.

As to the feminist movement, there was in 1967 none to speak of in France. There existed only small pockets of women militants in left groups, mostly Trotskyist groups, who had been either involved in the anti-imperialist struggles in France with regard to Algeria and Vietnam, or who had been following the beginnings of the Women's Liberation Movement in the USA.

Abortion

By 1969 the ANEA, composed mainly of GPs, presented a first series of legislative proposals on abortion which came to be known as the Peyret text. This text was presented to the National Assembly in June 1970. In November of the same year, the association *Laissez-les-vivre* (Let Them Live) was created to mobilise against the liberalisation of abortion. Its initiator, M. Foyer, had fiercely debated against the contraception law in 1967.

After the Peyret proposal, there followed a series of events which directly stirred public opinion. In 1970 the first large public demonstration of the MLF took place: women's 'problems' were taken out on the street. In 1971 the Homosexual Front of Revolutionary Action (FHAR) was created, and in October of the same year unmarried mothers rebelled in the Plessis-Robinson centre. The publication in April 1971 by *Le Nouvel Observateur* of a manifesto signed by 343 women was the first and most significant event. Celebrities and non-celebrities, among whom was Simone de Beauvoir, declared having had an abortion and asked for free abortion on demand. By taking public responsibility for an abortion which they had — or had not — experienced, these three hundred and forty-three women publicised the importance of abortion as a social issue. But also the fact that the event was widely reviewed in *Le Monde* gave a new public meaning to abortion: it was possible to admit to its existence publicly and openly, in defiance of law, morality, medical knowledge, or closed-door debates. One immediate reaction to this act of defiance was reference to the 'three hundred and forty-three sluts'.

Several other incidents followed, such as the distribution of tracts in schools and the taking of disciplinary action against teachers who raised the subject of sexual information in class. The second most significant event was the Bobigny trial (October–November 1972) in which a girl of seventeen, her mother and two friends were prosecuted for having performed an abortion. The trial became the focus of public attention: well-known actresses, celebrities and politicians came to bear witness at the trial and defended the cause of the accused — who were cleared. The public debate was now in full sway, and all political organisations had to take a position. From then on, events concerning abortion rolled on. I shall mention only the most important ones to illustrate how politically intense this debate on abortion was to become in 1973–74.

During a press conference in 1973, President Pompidou admitted that the law of 1923 was out of date and had to be revised after the coming parliamentary elections. In the summer of 1973, the film *The Story of A.* (on backstreet abortions) was denied public showing. It was, however, widely circulated in underground shows. On 4 February 1973, three hundred and thirty-one GPs (there were to be seven hundred and thirty in April) admitted to having practised abortions and signed a manifesto asking for the legalisation of abortion up to the eighth week of pregnancy. These doctors mostly belonged to, and were backed by, the GIS. Created in 1969, the GIS regrouped doctors who were critical of capitalist medicine for being concerned only to 'repair' people, as opposed to showing a real interest in the welfare of their clients. The GIS also denounced the huge profits made by GPs, private clinics and especially the pharmaceutical industry, and publicly criticised the close relationship existing between these.[32]

On 7 February 1973, the ANEA published a chart signed by two hundred diverse personalities, and which defined six particular cases in which abortion should be legalised. On 18 February, the newspaper *Le Monde* published an article criticising the 'silence of the political world' in the face of the on-going debate and in view of the coming legislative election to be held on 4 and 11 March. On 27 March, the French television programme *Les dossiers de l'écran* (equivalent to Robin Day's *Question Time*) organised a live debate on abortion which ended up in utter confusion.

It was in April 1973 that the MLAC was created by militants from the MLF, the GIS, CHOISIR, and members of the MFPF. Its aim was overtly political — to create a common front for all groups intervening on questions of sexuality and particularly on contraception and abortion. Soon it involved militants from trade unions, from the PSU, the ex-LCR and other groups. Apart from the CFDT, which is politically related to the Socialist Party, and the PSU, most of these political groups had originated from the events of May 1968 and were under violent attack from the traditional left, particularly the PCF (French Communist Party). Yet most of the mobilising issues since 1971 (immigrant workers, housing, sexuality, education, and so on) were initiated by these groups. Unsatisfied with the function of simply providing electoral platforms to the traditional left, these groups, while accepting to struggle at the legal level, also contributed to producing another conception of the political and of the hierarchy of social contradictions. While the traditional left insisted on the class struggle as the main political contradiction, these specialised groups introduced other political contradictions and insisted that these did not always stand in secondary position to the class struggle.

Most of the political resistance to established norms on sexuality came from the MLAC which acted as coordinator of all the groups and individuals who made it up. Immediately the MLAC set up a Centre of Sexual Information in central Paris where it also initiated a spontaneous network of GPs, medical students, nurses and individuals willing to perform Karman-method abortions for free or very little money. These 'flying' abortions, performed by sympathetic GPs in hospitals and disguised as miscarriages, were used as denunciatory practices against the Government's cowardice in the face of the debate. The MLAC also set up self-help groups of women to learn how to perform the Karman abortion outside of hospital structures.

If the MLAC was the organisational structure on which rested feminist discursive practices on abortion, the MLF was its think-tank. There was in the French feminist movement of the early 1970s a resistance to centring the politicisation of women exclusively on the issue of abortion. After 1973–4, the MLF penetrated new areas of struggle — battered women, rape, homosexuality, and economic independence. Yet abortion remained an important cornerstone of early feminist politics, not so much because it is an experience which can affect all women in relation to their body, their sexuality and motherhood, but because free abortion was part of the general feminist discourse on sexuality — control over one's body and women not being 'condemned' to childbearing but free to choose. The abortion issue, initiated by the liberal centrists, was now on the cards; it became a good first mobilising event for a feminist movement yet to be born.

Feminist discourse on abortion did not limit itself to the legal question of the number of weeks after which an abortion may not be practised, or the role of the GP in counselling the individual woman in her decision to have an abortion, or the role of the legislator in passing a new law liberalising abortion. It called for a woman's right to have an abortion during the safest possible period, limited the role of the GP as one of the possible counsellors only in the woman's interest — and not in that of morality — and denounced the hypocrisy of the narrow straight-jacket within which abortion was discussed by the government, legislators, institutions and political parties alike.

The traditional left was slow in responding to the public issues of sexuality. We have seen how the debate on contraception was started by Mitterrand in 1965, and how the Socialist Party was all in favour of liberalising contraception. But when, in 1973, it came to questions of liberalising abortion, the PS at first showed reluctance to pronounce itself. It finally helped the majority to vote in the abortion law of 1974. Without its support, the law could not have been passed by the liberal majority alone.

The PCF, ambiguous on demographical questions and equating the sexual liberation discourse of the 1960s with a new form of bourgeois degeneration, actually opposed the legislative proposals on contraception.

It was finally pushed into the abortion debate in 1973–74, when the conflict became increasingly polarised, the Government was blocking the legalisation process and women outside and inside the Party were recognising abortion as *their* struggle.

In May 1973, a test case was brought up in Grenoble against a 'flying' abortion; a GP was prosecuted for having performed an abortion and having made it public knowledge. All the specialised organisations – GIS, MLAC, CHOISIR, MFPF – and the MLF organised a common front and mobilised some ten thousand people (more according to the militants).[33] Following the Grenoble trial, the Government announced that a bill would be debated in the National Assembly in the near future, while it also proposed to take a series of measures to permit the distribution of contraception. It was between 1973 and 1974 that the Government established state-controlled Centres of Matrimonial Information and Consultation and Centres for Family Planning and Education to counteract the radicalised MFPF centres.

Just days before the debate on abortion was to take place in the National Assembly, the moral antagonists of liberalization attempted to make their own political impact on the forthcoming debate. Mobilised by *Laissez-les-vivre* and under the initiative of the *Association des Médecins pour le Respect de la Vie* (*Doctors' Association for the Respect of Life*), over ten thousand GPs signed a manifesto asserting that abortion could not be morally considered a medical act. And on 22 June, the Bishops' Council published a 'white book' recalling the position of the Catholic Church in its opposition to any taking away of life. Recognising the incompatibility between the present legislation and emerging social values, they nevertheless denounced the Government's project as risking a 'total liberalisation'.

In its legislation on abortion, the Government attempted to reach a balanced compromise inspired by the basic ideals that abortion is a medical act to be practised in hospitals or clinics only; that it is a problem of responsibility for the woman who is the only person to decide; that it is a problem of conscience for the GP who acts as counsellor to the woman and informs her if her situation comes under one of the possibilities prescribed by the law; and that abortion is an extreme solution, 'dictated by the failure of contraception, and not a substitute to birth control'.[34] When it is known that less than 40 per cent of women of reproductive age in France practised some sort of contraception in 1974, and that contraception was under strong and restricting medical control anyway, one questions the extent to which abortion was not still to be used as a form of birth control. As it stood then, and still stands now, the liberalisation of abortion was little more than a political compromise between various institutions and political parties. But definite gains were achieved by and for women. Unwillingly forced into such legislation by the political uproar created by the MLF, MLAC, GIS, CHOISIR, MFPF and some of the ultra-left since 1970, the Pompidou government passed decrees in 1973–74 which were to represent the first breach in the traditional status of the family. Although still strongly related to reproduction, sexuality was defined and legislated to include illegitimacy. Sexuality outside marriage and the family was being acknowledged by the Establishment, although little was done in the way of extending other forms of support to single-parent families.

Conclusion

In retracing briefly the shift from religious to public and later political discourse on contraception and abortion, this chapter has demonstrated that, although this discourse is not as recent a phenomenon as is popularly believed, it is only recently that the social production of these sexual categories has involved an open political struggle in which the public, and more importantly women themselves, have actively participated.

Taking Foucault's operational framework of local centres of power/knowledge as a starting point, I have shown that an analysis of discourse on sexuality cannot limit itself to verbal discourse. Furthermore, when taking into account the variety of discursive practices involved in the political construction of sexuality, one must acknowledge that the Establishment's over-all strategy centres on the legislation concerning, and the control of, abortion.

The legislation of 1975 measures the compromise made between social and political forces on the issue of abortion. Although it cannot be relied on as the *sole* indicator of that process, it is indicative of the political process involved in the construction of sexuality. Other indicators include changes in family patterns, childbearing patterns, medical, legal and social definitions of various sexualities, changes in the representation of female/male sexualities, the commercialisation of the female/male body (advertising, and so on), and the institutionalisation of sexuality by state-controlled sexocrats. Unfortunately, the conjunctural analysis of these factors could not be covered within the scope of this chapter.

Notes

1 Michel Foucault, *History of Sexuality*, vol. I (London: Allen Lane, 1979).

2 Ibid., p. 6.

3 Ibid., pp. 37-8.

4 Ibid., p. 24.

5 Jean-Louis Flandrin, 'Un entretien avec Jean-Louis Flandrin', *Le Nouvel Observateur*, 22 October 1979.

6 Flandrin, 'Introduction' in 'L'histoire de l'avortement', special issue of *L'Histoire*, no. 16 (October, 1979), p. 33.

7 Ibid., p. 34.

8 See Flandrin, *Les amours paysannes (XVIe-XIXe siècle)* (Paris: Gallimard/Julliard, 1975); and Flandrin, *Le sexe et l'Occident: évolution des attitudes et des comportements* (Paris: Seuil, 1981).

9 Jeanne Gaillard, 'Le médecin et l'avortement au XIXe siècle', *L'Histoire*, no. 16 (October, 1979), p. 36.

10 Ibid., pp. 35-7.

11 Roger-Henri Guerrand, '900 000 avortements en 1914?', *L'Histoire*, no. 16 (October, 1979), p. 38.

12 Henry Berger, *L'avortement, histoire d'un débat* (Paris: Flammarion, 1975), p. 36.

13 Janine Mossuz-Laveau and Mariette Sineau, 'Women's Political Participation', in Joni Lovenduski and Jill Hills, eds., *The Politics of the Second Electorate: Women and Public Participation* (London: Routledge and Kegan Paul, 1981), p. 114.

14 Berger, op. cit., p. 115, quotes the following figures. The MFPF had a study made by an English private clinic of the French women who came to them for an abortion. Out of 1,509 women,
   − 54 per cent were single, 38 per cent were married,
   − 48 per cent were Catholic,
   − 48 per cent already had children,
   − 360 were aged 20 years and under,
   − 532 were aged 21-25 years,
   − 240 were aged 26-30 years, and
   − about 350 were aged 30 years and over.

15 François Isambert and Paul Ladrière, *Contraception et avortement: dix ans de débat dans la presse, 1965-1974* (Paris: Editions du CNRS, 1979), *passim*.

16 Ibid., pp. 22 and 34-5.

17 Ibid., pp. 34-6.

18 Ibid., pp. 32-3.

19 Ibid., p. 90.

20 Ibid., p. 73.

21 Ibid., p. 29.

22 Ibid., p. 77.

23 In July 1973, the Cultural Affairs Committee started a series of hearings in which it interviewed the representatives and spokespersons of some one hundred and forty professional organisations and voluntary associations.

   Of those in favour of the legalisation of abortion and its total control by the medical profession and the Government were the Research Centre in New Birth Biology, the National Academy of Medicine, the Confederation of French Medical Unions, the Federation of French General Practitioners, the Magistrature Union, the Director of the National Institute of Demographic Studies, the National Union of Family Associations (UNAF), the National Confederation of Working-Class Family Associations (CNAPF), Menie Gregoire (journalist, *Marie-Claire*), Suzanne Gauthier (journalist, *France-Inter* radio), Claude Ullin (journalist, *Femmes d'Aujourd'hui*), Marie-France Leclerc (journalist, *Elle*), Christiane Gilles (CGT), Jeannette Laot (CFDT), Union of French Women (UFF), Father Roquelpo (Catholic priest, CHOISIR), Rabbi Guggenheim, Rvd. Longeiret (Independent Evangelical Reformed Churches), Father Pohier (ANEA).

The nuances in propositions to change the law varied in the number of weeks permissible to practise an abortion (between eight and fourteen generally speaking) and in the conditions under which an abortion may be legally permitted and medically performed. Most of the individuals or organisations in favour of some liberalisation mostly expressed their discontentment with the existing repressive legislation and with the fact that it did not prevent backstreet abortions in any way.

Opposed to the reform were the National Council of the Order; Dr. Sourdille of the National Academy of Medicine; M. Braunschweig speaking for the Federal Union of Magistrates; M. Fedou of the French Association of Magistrates for Youth and Family Affairs; Cardinal Renard (Archbishop of Lyons); M. Alfred Sauvy, Professor at the Collège de France; the National Confederation of Christian Families; the National Confederation of Catholic Family Associations; M. Vie; Florence d'Harcourt on behalf of the Feminine Centre of Study and Information 'Future Woman'; SOS Future Mothers; the Association of Jurists for the Respect of Life; the Association of Arts and Humanities Professors for the Respect of Life; Women's Union for the Respect of Life; National Women's Association 'Life and Freedom'; the Nurses' Association for the Respect of Life.

Opposition to the reform ranged from comparing the open practice of abortion with the open practice of concentration camps, referring to both as 'acts of death' — to raising legal questions concerning the conceived child's lawful eligibility to the father's inheritance and therefore abortion being a breach of inheritance law. Abortion was given, along with euthanisia, infanticide, pornography, murder, the selfishness of women, and decline in the birth rate, as one of the reasons for social and moral decline in society. Finally, relying on demographical arguments, others argued that it was not the right time to take such measures.

The *Fédération Couple et Famille* and the Association for the Study of Birth Problems (presided by Dr. Lagrous Weill-Halle, formerly of the MFPF) were still undecided at the time these hearings were taking place. (Berger, op. cit., pp. 56–137.)

24 Ibid., p. 21.
25 Ibid., p. 36.
26 The Gaullist party was named the UNR (Union for the New Republic) from 1958–67, the UDR (first the Union for the Defence of the Republic and then the Union of Democrats for the Republic) from 1967–76, and RPR (Rally for the Republic) since 1976; see P. G. Cerny, 'Gaullism, Advanced Capitalism and the Fifth Republic', in David S. Bell, ed., *French Political Parties* (London: Croom Helm, 1981).
27 PARTISANS, *Libération des femmes* (Paris: François Maspéro, 1974), p. 36.
28 Dominique Wolton, *Le nouvel ordre sexuel* (Paris: Seuil, 1974), p. 24.
29 Ibid., pp. 24–5.
30 Ibid., pp. 53–4.
31 Ibid., p. 53.
32 Ibid., p. 19.
33 Berger, op. cit., p. 39.
34 Ibid., pp. 40–1; and pp. 284–91. Article 317 of the Penal Code was suspended for a period of five years. Abortion became legally permitted if performed before the end of the tenth week by a doctor in a hospital or a clinic. The GP must inform the woman of the medical risks she takes for herself and any future pregnancies. He must hand out to the woman a list of the rights and social advantages given to married and single mothers and their children, as well as information on the possibility of adoption.

The woman must then consult a centre of Family Advice, Social Services or Family Planning which will give her a doctor's certificate. A GP cannot accept to perform an abortion unless s/he receives a written confirmation of the woman's desire to do so; this must be received no sooner than one week following the initial visit.

A single under-age woman must have the written authorisation from her parent(s) or guardian. A GP is never bound to accept a woman's request to have an abortion, but s/he must inform the woman of her/his decision (however no time limit is imposed on this last procedure). Immigrant women with valid residence permits only may benefit from the above law.

PAUL HAINSWORTH
Lecturer in Politics
Ulster Polytechnic

Introduction

The French obsession with digging up the past and imposing it on contemporary political perspectives is legendary. For almost two centuries,
arguments have reverberated which, at the end of the day, can be reduced
to disputes about *les deux Frances*. Embers of former conflicts are revived
periodically and ideas, thought by some to be *dépassé*, have a tendency
to be resurrected. The traditional appetite for social and political discussion ensures a lively debate.

The post-Gaullist era, for reasons we shall discuss, provided a fertile
breeding ground for doctrines temporarily in hibernation. Ghosts from the
heady days of *Algérie française* and proscribed right-wing extremist
groups resurfaced, sometimes to join ideological hands with the emergent,
so-called 'New Right' or even to haunt the corridors of power. This
chapter proposes to explore the revival of right-wing extremism in contemporary France as typified primarily by neo-fascist, anti-semitic and
New Right manifestations. What forms has this revival taken? What has
been the response to this revival from *les pouvoirs*, i.e. those in positions
of authority? How might we explain what has been termed *un véritable
risorgimento*?[1]

From electoralism to provocation

The extreme right in France has vacillated between overt violence, protest
politics and participation in elections. This strategic dilemma has resulted
from its extremist ideology, small size and internecine conflict. Accuracy
about the numbers involved in French contemporary right-wing extremism,
neo-fascism and anti-semitism is however virtually impossible. A fairly
recent report[2] put the figure at twenty-five thousand individuals. For the
late fifties to early sixties, Malcolm Anderson[3] estimated that over one

thousand groups existed belonging to this political family. This period straddled the traumatic years of the Algerian War and typical examples of such groups were the Secret Army Organisation (OAS), *Jeune Nation* and the *Phalange Française*.

Between 1958 and 1962, several of these groups were proscribed,[4] their successors meeting the same fate — *Occident* (in 1968) and *Ordre Nouveau* (in 1973). In practical terms, proscription is not always effective. First, it entails 'useful' publicity and notoriety, and second, it may be circumvented by reconstitution under alternative names and guises. For these reasons, in 1980, Mark Frederiksen virtually welcomed the ban on his organisation FANE (the National Federation of European Action). He hoped the ban might serve as a springboard for wider unity incorporating the two principal extreme right-wing organisations, i.e. the National Front and the *Parti des Forces Nouvelles* (PFN); but both these parties (led respectively by Jean-Marie Le Pen and Pascal Gauchon) marked their distances from the FANE.

Electoral contests (local, legislative, presidential and European) were seen as more suitable propaganda channels than the neo-fascist parades of the FANE. Nevertheless, along with other organisations, all these bodies represented the extreme right-wing political family. Anderson's criteria of definition could be applied to all:

. . . they were unlike the groups involved in direct political action. The main function of the programme of these . . . groups was to exacerbate political conflict, raise the temperature of debate by aggressive slogans and encourage the polarisation of opinion to the benefit of those who proposed extreme solutions to the country's problems.[5]

In their more extreme forms, these groups ranged from *groupuscules* and commando groups of OAS inspiration such as the 'Delta Organisation', which claimed the assassination of Henri Curiel in 1978, and an attack on *Le Monde* editor Jacques Fauvet in 1981, to groups named after SS leaders, such as the 'Vengeance Peiper Group'. They included neo-fascist groups (e.g. the FANE), police support groups (e.g. *Honneur de la Police*), anti-American organisations (e.g. the *Mouvement Nationaliste Révolutionnaire*) and anti-semitic bodies (e.g. *L'Oeuvre Française*). Many had connections with other sympathetic groups abroad. The term 'black international' became commonplace in the left-wing press, particularly in 1980 after the wave of European violence which included incidents in France and fatal bombings in Munich and Bologna. However, although European links could be traced back quite easily to at least 1951, it was probably an exaggeration to talk of a 'black international' despite ongoing European and international contacts.

Anderson depicted the postwar history of the extreme right as 'a confused record of feuds, violence and inefficiency'.[6] This divided, squabbling image is a traditional characteristic of the extreme right in France. As various spokesmen made political compromises they were subsequently rejected and other groups and spokesmen emerged to claim their places. In 1979, the alliance between the PFN and the well-known right-wing lawyer and former presidential candidate Jean-Louis Tixier-Vignancour for the European Assembly elections tended to marginalise some extremist groups and irritate the National Front. In desperation, the latter attempted to 'raise the temperature of the debate'. The National Front objected to Simone Veil's leadership of the assorted Giscardian forces (as Giscard's Minister of Health, she had 'foisted' the abortion law on France), and to draw attention to themselves, they interrupted her campaign: eggs were thrown, behaviour was rowdy and cries of 'dirty Jew' — against at least one of her supporters — were heard. Veil ridiculed the meagre support for the National Front and spoke of '*SS aux petits pieds*'. Her subsequent electoral success and elevation to the presidency of the European Parliament added insult to injury. A spokesman for the National Front interpreted it as 'a crime against the women of France'.[7]

The general rowdiness of the extreme right and the drift towards violence by some extremists should not, however, distract from another inherent trait prevalent in the post-Algerian War phase — electoralism. After de Gaulle's Algerian settlement, the extreme right wing became gradually, perhaps superficially, integrated into the Fifth Republic. The story of Tixier-Vignancour provides a colourful example of this trend. A former Vichyite and OAS apologist, Tixier defended General Salan in the famous barricades trial. In the 1965 presidential election, Tixier mustered 5.3 per cent of the vote (1.3 million votes). This figure represented the high-water mark of extreme right-wing electoralism in the Fifth Republic. On this occasion, Tixier was eager to punish de Gaulle for abandoning Algeria; although he was the spokesman of the *pieds noirs* and *Algérie française*, he recommended that his voters transfer their votes on the second ballot to François Mitterrand. By 1968–69, however, he had rallied to the Gaullist–Pompidolian camp, and his *ralliement* meant loss of credibility as the spokesman of the extreme right. Militant groups such as *Occident* and its successor, *Ordre Nouveau*, claimed his mantle, but their proscription meant the search for ideological homes in such bodies as the National Front (born 1972) and the PFN (1974).

Electoralism yielded little joy for the extreme right wing. The success of 1965 was not to be repeated. In the parliamentary elections of 1967, almost 200,000 votes (0.87 per cent) were polled on the extreme right but a year later this poll slumped to 29,000. The threat posed by the events of May 1968, Pompidou's vote-catching amnesty for OAS prisoners, the Gaullist call for unity and the increased repatriation of the *pieds noirs* accelerated extreme right-wing integration into French politics. In the presidential elections of 1969, Pompidou took 82 per cent of their vote on the second ballot with only 14 per cent going to centrist rival Alain Poher. (This *désistement* in favour of the candidate of the *majorité* was a pointer towards future extreme right trends in the seventies.) In the parliamentary elections of 1973, the extreme right polled only 2 per cent of the vote, followed by a derisory 0.75 per cent in 1974 for Le Pen's presidential bid. In the 1978 legislative elections, the extreme right could not manage 1 per cent of the vote.

In 1981, none of the potential extreme right candidates could draw on the required five hundred 'notable' signatures to enable them to contest the presidential election. Cantonal (county council) elections were equally discouraging. These statistics indicate the decline in votes and seats at the level of the General Councils in the *départements*.

Table 7.1

	1961	1964	1967	1970	1973	1976
seats	21	15	7	6	–	7
%	2.8	1.5	0.5	0.4	–	0.6

(Taken from John Frears, *Political Parties and Elections in the French Fifth Republic* (London: C. Hurst, 1977), p. 231. Note that only half of the total number of general council seats comes up for election at each three-year interval.)

The 1976 returns at least gently reversed the trend for the extreme right but the European Assembly elections gave the extreme right wing more cause for satisfaction. The 'Euro-Right' alliance of Tixier-Vignancour and the PFN also included the *Movimento Sociale Italiano* (MSI) and the Spanish *Fuerzas Nuevas* (Spain being a non-member of the European Community, this *Franquiste* group did not, of course, contest the elections). With the National Front left politically stranded, a rival extreme right coalition was headed by Philippe Malaud, Pierre Poujade and Jacques Médecin. Their *Union de Défense Interprofessionnelle* campaigned for fewer taxes, less statism, and less technocracy. This mini-Poujadist revival secured 1.4 per cent of the poll — 283,000 votes. Tixier-Vignancour and the PFN, campaigning to swing Europe further towards the right, won

1.31 per cent of the poll — 265,000 votes. Thus the extreme right could claim a fair improvement on the scores of 1973, 1974 and 1978. Pascal Gauchon interpreted the result as a big success considering the limited finances available to the extreme right. Other spokesmen rejoiced in the best electoral result for a decade. In some of the Paris districts returns for the Euro-Right were promising — 3.45 per cent (in the 8th *arrondissement*), 3.17 per cent (in the 6th), 2.95 per cent (in the 7th), 2.50 per cent (in the 17th) and 2.24 per cent (in the 1st). Outside Paris, the best results were in the Var (2.11 per cent), Alpes-Maritimes (2.09 per cent), Bas-Rhin and the Vaucluse (both 1.68 per cent).[8]

The Euro-Right list included — beside Tixier-Vignancour and Gauchon — Alain Robert (ex-Secretary General of *Ordre Nouveau*), Joseph Ortiz (*rapatrié* and co-founder of the Algiers Committee of Public Safety) and a declared member of extremist right-wing *Groupe Union Défense* (GUD). The latter organisation is renowned for its commando style raids such as the one on Nanterre students in December 1980. In 1979, Tixier-Vignancour went to great lengths to distinguish the Euro-Right from rowdy and National Front tactics, even sending a telegram of sympathy to Simone Veil! The Euro-Right fended off accusations from various quarters that the MSI and Spanish allies were neo-fascist bodies and, to boot, boasted the nominal exclusion from their ranks of all neo-fascists.

The National Front urged voters to abstain. Once again, Tixier-Vignancour's claim to represent the extreme right was questioned. As to the PFN, the FANE accused them of being the 'hard wing' of the governmental *majorité*: 'They are *notables*. They are always ready to please the Government. For example, they do not hesitate to stick up Chirac's posters'.[9] Indeed, the PFN backed Jacques Chirac in 1977 in his successful campaign to become Mayor of Paris and again in the presidential campaign of 1981, but it would be wrong to see him as a spokesman for this party. However, deprived of a single MEP, the PFN could legitimately claim the MSI as their mouthpiece inside the European Parliament. Inside France, the PFN endeavoured to cash in on their own modest European Assembly vote. The PFN interpretation was that: 'the right exists. We have proved it. The right is a force in the country'.[10] The electoral returns represented *'une base de départ* . . . which would enable our political family to be present in all the struggles to come'.[11] This claim was interesting since it boasted a familial rather than a personal victory. It underlined the message that, despite perennial divisions and differences, the whole extreme right could draw inspiration from the European Assembly elections. Heartened by the break-up of the left and supported by patient extreme right re-organisation and strengthening in the seventies, the whole of the extreme right appeared to demonstrate a new-found confidence and aggression. By 1980, the National Front felt able to move on to the offensive. Their press spokesman, Michel Collinot, announced that 'the era of provocations has arrived'.[12]

The Era of Provocations

The 'era of provocations' had a distinctly anti-semitic tone in France. Whether one could point to a widespread revival of anti-semitism among the French population is questionable and, without doubt, racialism *vis-à-vis* Arabs and blacks was of a more serious order. However, that there was a revival of anti-semitic outrages was undeniable. Thus, in September 1980, President Giscard intervened in an eleventh hour bid to reassure *all* minorities, following several months of attacks upon Jewish individuals and establishments. The President denied that there existed a 'diffusion in the French body politic of perverse, racialist or fascist ideas'.[13] School teachers were instructed to give extra lessons on 'the pluralist, fraternal and tolerant character of French society'. Recent attacks and disturbances were blamed on a few small groups. This was a reasonable estimation of these specific incidents, but French socio-political history is sufficiently endowed with analogous events to suggest that anti-semitism, at least, constitutes a familiar skeleton in the French cupboard. The Dreyfus Affair, the activities of the Leagues in the thirties, the abrogation of the 'loi Marchandeau' (passed in 1939, this law forbade all anti-semitic propaganda in the press; by 1940, it had become an empty letter), the Vichy period, 'the rumour of Orleans', the 1980 incidents, etc., provide a conspicuous anti-semitic minefield. The unfortunate response of no less a figure than Jean Jaurès to the Dreyfus Affair reminds us that anti-semitism is not simply a preserve of the extreme right.[14]

Despite the many obvious examples which spring to mind (e.g. Bucard, Maurras, Doriot, the Leagues, and so on), Nazism or fascism is less easily placed than anti-semitism within French political culture. For the French Jewish community, vigilance prevails against *both* doctrines especially since both have often combined; indeed, in the later phase of Giscard's presidency (1974–1981), vigilance was deemed necessary by Jewish spokesmen who expressed fears of vulnerability and railed against lack of protection.

The 550,000 Jews in France are not a united community. Ashkenazy Jews of East European and Polish descent are primarily refugees from pogroms of the twenties and thirties; in the fifties and sixties, Sephardic Jews from North Africa arrived to alter the complexion of French Jewry.

The former were reasonably well assimilated. Many had made widely acknowledged contributions to French society. The latter — about 150,000 — are distinguished more by their poorer economic status, greater sense of separate identity and militant postures. Organisations such as the 'Representative Council of Jewish Institutions in France' (CRIF) — under Alain de Rothschild's leadership — represent the former, whilst the latter are more likely to be critical of traditional leadership and, therefore, more sympathetic to bodies such as Henry Hadjenberg's *Mouvement de Renouveau* (started in 1979) or the *Collectif d'Initiative des Juifs de Gauche* (born 1980). But despite differing tendencies and political choices, *all* French Jews were unsettled by the direction of the Fifth Republic's Arab policy after 1967. In 1981, the *Ligue Internationale contre le Racisme et l'Anti-sémitisme* (LICRA) lobbied presidential candidates to declare their positions on Arab–Israeli matters, anti-semitism and racialism. And *all* Jews (and other minorities) were similarly disturbed about the revival of neo-fascism and anti-semitism in France.

In 1980, Jewish feelings reached their zenith after the bomb attack on the synagogue in Paris's rue Copernic. Four people were killed on this occasion and the attack prompted Giscard's aforementioned intervention. The synagogue represents an obvious target for graffiti artists and aggressors. Synagogues elsewhere (e.g. Nice and Antibes) suffered anti-semitic attacks. Anti-semitism was not, however, confined to the synagogue: Jewish schools, war memorials, boutiques, crèches, offices, restaurants, tombs, travel agencies and shops were further targets. In 1981, on the eve of the Presidential election and the thirty-sixth anniversary of the liberation of the concentration camps a number of Jewish tombs were profaned at Bagneux (Hauts-de-Seine). In recognised Jewish areas, e.g. the Paris *Marais*, Jews were subject to vicious attacks. Sometimes these attacks were fatal. In 1979, for example, the group *Honneur de la Police* claimed the assassination of the left-wing Jewish intellectual, Pierre Goldmann; indeed, the same group was linked with the death of the manager of the well-known clown Coluche, one-time 1981 presidential hopeful. In Nice, the South of France and the South-West, prominent Jews received threatening telephone calls and warning letters, bearing the inscription *Notre dieu Hitler*.

Organisations which defended the rights of Jews and other minorities — the LICRA, the *Mouvement Contre le Racisme et pour l'Amitié entre les Peuples* (MRAP), the Henri Curiel Association, the French Communist Party (PCF), *The Ligue Française des Droits de l'Homme* and the *Amicale des Algériens en France* — were also subject to various attacks. Between 1977 and 1980, the Paris office of MRAP was bombed ten times. After the attack on Jacques Fauvet in March 1981, the Henri Curiel Association declared that since June 1977, two hundred and seventy-three fascist and racist attacks had been treated with 'total indifference' by the Government.[15]

Preventive and punitive legislation — passed in 1936, reinforced in 1972 — graced the statute books but anti-semitic groups proliferated in the seventies. In Grenoble and Strasbourg, the street ciculation of anti-semitic tracts resulted in prosecutions filed by LICRA, but in Nice, the local *Nice-Enchaîné* propagated anti-semitism freely. In Paris, the FANE sported Nazi-style uniforms and held parades until banned for incitement to racial discrimination, violent demonstrations and the propagation of Nazi goals. Other forms of anti-semitism were less strident and, accused of laxity and complacency, the Minister of the Interior was compelled to refer to press freedom and to recall the exacting terms of the 1936 and 1972 legislation.

For French Jews, the revival of anti-semitic and neo-fascist threats evoked unpleasant memories. Non-Jews seemed unable to appreciate the mood and tensions within the Jewish community. The French Jew was suspicious of relatively innocuous contact. A Jewish correspondent to *Le Monde* expressed his astonishment on being contacted by the *Institut National d'Études Démographiques* as part of a general survey.[16] Did this mean that dossiers were kept on Jews, as in the Vichy period? The Minister of the Interior, Christian Bonnet, denied this but many Jews retained their apprehensions. Other Jews were surprised to receive free postal copies of the PCF's bulletin *Oui, la liberté: Bulletin d'échanges du PCF avec la Population juive*. Did this mean that political parties kept private dossiers and addresses of Jews? Denials and protestations of innocence generally failed to satisfy in a period of tension and vigilance. The Chief Rabbi, Jacob Kaplan, summed up the mood in the French Jewish community in 1980: 'Since the last World War the doctrines of hatred — whether they be neo-Nazism, racism or anti-semitism — have never been propagated with so much evil intent and audacity than in our time'.[17]

Civil rights groups and spokesmen for minorities echoed these sentiments. The main political parties counselled against confusing the extremist behaviour of a few small groups with any *general* wave of anti-semitism and neo-fascism. Nevertheless, the unquestionable revival of *incidents* merited some explanation. What prompted this so-called 'era of provocations'?

First, the poor electoral returns of the extreme right political family made a resort to other channels always likely for some groups. Electoralism was not the favoured instrument of all right-wing extremists and the 1979 European Assembly election had ambiguous implications. For some interpreters it coincided with extreme right-wing ascendancy, while for others it heralded this trend. Second, the shock of May 1968 *and* the awful reality of left-wing unity around the Common Programme of Government was seen as necessitating an extreme right-wing riposte. By the time the Common Programme alliance snapped, the extreme right had a decade's stocktaking behind them.

Third, the passage of time distanced an increasing proportion of the French population from the Vichy period with its anti-semitic and neo-fascist trappings. The historic manifestations of these doctrines became less and less tangible. Potential members of neo-fascist and anti-semitic groups were often raw recruits. Attempts by the media to recall the fascist era were liable to backfire. For example, the screening of the epic 'Holocaust' series was resented by many French Jews as a media intrusion into sacrosanct memories. In addition, neo-fascist and anti-semitic beds were ruffled thereby encouraging these forces to take up the gauntlet. They endeavoured to counter the 'falsified' televised presentation of Jewish wartime history. Mark Frederiksen and his colleagues queued up to deny the existence of the gas chambers. Equally significant, French authors and Jewish spokesmen have felt compelled to go to great lengths to prove that the chambers did exist, as in the intense discussions provoked by Georges Wellers's *Les chambres à gaz, ils ont existé* (Paris: Gallimard, 1981). A moribund issue suddenly became a debate.

A fourth element of explanation is the persistent and deepening economic crisis. Rising levels of unemployment, inflation, youth disaffection and the like helped to create a favourable climate for extremist solutions. Broad parallels with the thirties became *à la mode*. In the words of Eric Hobsbawm,

> We live in times of insecurity and nerves. We also live in times when civility is on the retreat before barbarism. It is a serious matter for all of us when civilisation, after a generation of partial recovery, looks as though it may again go into reverse in the matter of anti-semitism. It is not surprising that a people with the Jews' historical experience looks at the future with foreboding.[18]

Parallels with the 1930s should take into account at least two crucial differences when assessing anti-semitic revivals: the reality of the holocaust, and the creation of the state of Israel. Both factors have introduced new dimensions into postwar anti-semitism. The experience of the holocaust worked generally against anti-semitic resurgence — except where it was not accepted or was, for various reasons, resented.[19] This rider would apply obviously to neo-Nazi groups, but some left-wing forces have referred unkindly to the Jewish 'monopoly of martyrdom'. Jewish opinion has often complained about left-wing groups using anti-Zionism as a cover for anti-semitism and although these accusations merit closer examination, the left needs to guard against posing anti-racialism against anti-semitism instead of combating all forms of racism.[20] From another angle, conservative forces resent Jewish support for left-wing causes. If the French Jewish vote is seen as predominantly *Mitterrandiste* or left-wing this is likely to affect the reflexes of conservatives in power — a point we shall return to later.

Two final themes need exploring in order to reach a better understanding of neo-fascist, anti-semitic and racist tendencies in contemporary France. The first involves an examination of the so-called 'New Right'; and the second deals with the semi-official, political rehabilitation of the extreme right political family under Giscard d'Estaing's manangement of the state.

The New Right

Malcolm Anderson sees the literacy of the extreme right as 'perhaps its most outstanding feature and its greatest contribution to political life in France'.[21] Intellectually, the elevation of the New Right in France has revived traditions which had lapsed with the demise of Charles Maurras. Raymond Aron does not hesitate to associate the writings of the New Right with the revival of anti-semitic outrages.[22] Indeed, in a letter to *Le Monde*, Mark Frederiksen showed positive interest in the analyses of the New Right.[23] However, Alain de Benoist, the New Right's guru, rejects any assimilation between his own and FANE's ideas. Interviewed by *Le Matin*, de Benoist insisted that 'the positions of this group are the opposite of my own'.[24] What, then, are the positions of the New Right?

The New Right defies accurate description. Various components are even divided over acceptance or rejection of the label 'New Right' — but, like 'Eurocommunism', it has stuck. The link with Eurocommunism does not stop here, for, like all good Eurocommunists, the New Right draws upon the ideas of Antonio Gramsci. In a Gramscian sense, de Benoist and his colleagues contest the ideological supremacy of the French left and pose a hegemonical alternative to left-wing ideas. They hope to buttress the 'Weberian' *political* power of the right with the intellectual force of ideas. As one observer puts it, de Benoist and his colleagues set themselves the task of reversing the unwritten French law by which 'the right rules and the left thinks'.[25] The New Right proposes to contest the left on its own ground. According to veteran Maurice Bardèche, the goal is 'an open breach in the front line of intellectual terrorism' practised by the left.[26] Pierre Vial, a spokesman for the Research and Study Group for European Civilisation (GRECE), looks back to pre-French Revolution sources and forward to the twenty-first century for inspiration:

> As the freemasons as a school of thought prepared minds for the 1789 Revolution so the GRECE as a school of thought intends to prepare the minds for the 21st century revolution which will link the oldest spiritual heritage with the most progressive technology.[27]

For Louis Pauwels (the editor of *Figaro-Magazine*), it is time to forsake *les idéologies sèches* (Marxism, human sciences) and *les idéologies moitiés* (Rousseauism, neo-Christianity).[28] Utopian, messianic recipes must give way to the rediscovery of Ancient Greek polytheist doctrine or Indo-European civilisation. Charles Maurras's interest in Catholicism was in its scope as an ordered social system rather than as a redemptionist creed. The New Right of Pauwels and de Benoist goes a step further: biological justifications for hierarchy and elitism should replace Roman Catholic dogma. In any case, the latter shares with Marxism and Christianity the cardinal sin — i.e., 'false ideas about equality'. Jensen, Lorenz, Eysenck, Burt, Nietzsche, and Spengler figure high on the roll call for New Right 'scientific' theories of elitism, race, hierarchy and order, but de Benoist, at least, draws on Gramsci and Althusser to supplement an eclectic struggle against egalitarian ideology.

The same themes — elitism, bio-politics, race theory, inequality, Indo-European heritage — straddle the whole of the extreme and New Right forces. The methods of application, however, differ considerably. Neo-fascist parades, anti-semitic attacks, electoral platforms, street pamphleteering, journalistic presentations, academic contributions, the publishing house, the *groupuscule* and the dinner-debate provide an inexhaustible variety of propaganda instruments. De Benoist's favourite channels include the columns of *Figaro-Magazine* and the printing press of *Editions Copernic*. The former constituted a significant coup for the New Right. It popularised the ideas propagated, and thereby fulfilled a longstanding goal of the extreme right. De Benoist's route to *Figaro-Magazine* led from *Nouvelle École* and, formerly, the neo-fascist journal of the 1960s — *Europe-Action* — which he edited. Other refugees from *Europe-Action* joined GRECE, set up in the late sixties to counter the *gauchisme* of that period and develop a New Right counter-culture. Other New Right forces favoured the *Club de l'Horloge*, founded after the Common Programme alliance threatened to realise a left-wing electoral victory. The *raison d'être* of this *Club Jean Moulin de droite*[29] was 'to keep up the battle of words and ideas by injecting the fundamentals of a new social logic and by forging the concepts of a new political language'.[30]

The club united intellectuals, technocrats, civil servants, politicians from the *majorité* and other elites. Traditional pillars of French society formed the backbone of *les horlogistes*: the *École Nationale d'Administration* (ENA), the *École Polytechnique*, other *grandes écoles*, liberal professions, big business, *notables*, etc. The main instruments of influence were to be neither the barricade nor the ballot box, but rather the dinner-debate, the publishing house, the political cabinet and the corridors of power. The list of invited speakers included Michel Poniatowski, Jacques Médecin, Philippe Malaud and Manuel Fraga Iribarne — but also Michel Debré, Ionesco and Barrault. The club aimed to shift the *majorité* to the right and spearhead 'a conservative revolution'. The teething ground for some *horlogistes* spanned *Occident*, GUD and other extreme right-wing groups; but, by the late seventies, according to Kathleen Evin, 'the iron bar, the Celtic cross and the motorbike helmet have been replaced for the better by the biro, the notice in 'Who's Who' and *le carnet des rélations.*'[31]

Close contacts developed between the *Club de l'Horloge*, GRECE, *Figaro-Magazine* and members of the *majorité*. Giscard himself underlined these by giving an extended interview to Louis Pauwels virtually on the eve of announcing his candidature for the 1981 election.[32] Yves Blot explained that the *Club de l'Horloge* was an 'ideas bank': 'We are a political club which proposes to be a laboratory of ideas for the current *majorité*'.[33] Bernard Stasi, a leading Christian Democrat within the Giscardian *majorité*, rejects this theory: 'Between us and the supporters of the New Right ... there is an incompatibility of nature'.[34] However, for de Benoist, the *entriste*, Trojan Horse tactic was a longstanding proposition. As early as 1969, he formulated the strategy: 'What we need is men of influence, placed in today's spheres of decision making and even better in tomorrow's [spheres]'.[35] For Maurice Bardèche, too, de Benoist's *realpolitik* was the only way out of the 'ghetto'.[36]

Given the positions and intellectual offensive of the New Right, and notwithstanding the marking of distance from the behaviour and ideas of certain neo-Fascist and anti-semitic groups, the question must at least be posed: Is it possible to marginalise the behaviour of the extremist right wing and propose a total divorce from the ideas of the New Right?

Does the elevation of the New Right entail the renaissance of ideological and philosophical alibis for the extreme right family? Can the intellectualising of pseudo-scientific theories be separated from the consequences of vulgarisation or popularisation of these themes? Thus in 1974, Pascal Gauchon appealed to his New Right contemporaries to recognise that they were all from the same family. The collective make-up of the New Right bears some consideration: activists create a 'strategy of tension'[37] at the base; the legalised PFN and National Front propose programmes and contest elections; the New Right, for its part, formulates hegemonic themes, which form the cultural backbone of the 'conservative revolution'. The relationship of these groups and strategies to the state is less tangible, however, and we can agree with Vincent Wright that 'the relationship between the state and . . . groups during the Fifth Republic is like the rest of government — infinitely complex and intrinsically untidy'.[38] This is an area which merits attention, and it will therefore be examined in the next section.

Rehabilitation, Repression, Racism

The regained confidence of the New Right was essentially a child of the Giscardian rather than the Gaullist Fifth Republic. It complemented the increasing confidence of the whole extreme right political family. Paradoxically, the 'advanced liberal' society of Giscard gave the extreme right greater scope for rehabilitation and influence than had been possible throughout most of the Gaullist decade. The closeness of the 1974 Presidential election contest emphasised Giscard's need for allies. As already suggested above, some previous extreme right opponents of de Gaulle rallied to Gaullism in crisis. May 1968 enabled an amnesty for OAS extremists and pushed the extreme right towards reorganisation. By the time of the 1973 and 1974 elections, new right-wing parties were formed. Pascal Gauchon threw his hat in with Giscard in 1974 — and Chirac later!

Giscard's declared aim was to establish an advanced, liberal, democratic, pluralist society. Nowhere is this theme better illustrated than in his own *Démocratie française* (Paris: Fayard, 1976). His ascendancy facilitated the continuing integration of the centre with the *majorité*; leaders like Jean Lecanuet had found it difficult to compromise with de Gaulle or even Pompidou but were favourably predisposed to Giscard's ideas. They shared liberal, pluralist goals. However, Giscard's liberal society also signalled the integration into the pluralist system of the extreme right wing.

The Vichy period and the Algerian War had led to the ostracism of the extreme right from the mainstream of French political activity. With Giscard's success, the extreme right found itself on the winning side for the first time since Vichy. In his book *Ici et maintenant*, François Mitterrand complains that members of extreme right-wing organisations were either open collaborators with the President, or adopted as *députés*, or recruited as policemen. 'At the time of a debate with Giscard d'Estaing on Europe 1 in 1974, . . . [Mitterrand] was astonished to recognise amongst the guests some armed commandos of the extreme right or former members of the OAS' acting as Giscard's bodyguard.[39] From the PCF came similar, if predictable accusations:

> In fact, between the classical right and what we modestly call the extreme right there is more than a parental link. The President of the Republic himself was the candidate of all the right including fascists at the second round of the last presidential elections.[40]

The columns of the left-wing press and journals carried the same charges. For instance *Les Temps Modernes* attempted to place this theme in its historical context:

> It does not matter whether paternity is actual or symbolic. We know that the combat of the OAS forms part of a larger history of which Algeria was only an episode — that it had precursors and successors. When the extreme right finds accomplices at the heart of power, or fascism is reborn from the ashes, or the defence of democracy — having been reduced to a minimum — becomes the first priority, there will undoubtedly be better things to do than to look for justifications in a dubious parallel with the OAS.[41]

Finally, *Le Nouvel Observateur* drew attention to the rehabilitation of the extreme right since 1968: 'Reintegrated into the national mainstream in 1968, and doing well in 1974, the old right has simply masked its cheap and tarnished façade in the impeccable three-piece suit of Giscardian respectability'.[42]

Attempts to tar Giscard's 'liberal society' with the brush of rehabilitating the extreme right wing became a standard weapon in the left-wing armoury of criticisms. It was also a useful distraction from the left's own divisions and problems. Certain deputies were 'named' on account of their extremist past or connections, e.g. Gerard Longuet (Meuse), Alain Madelin (Île-et-Vilaine), Thierry Guyot-Sestier (Alpes-Maritimes) and Giscard's campaign manager, Hubert Bassot (Orme). The road from the OAS and *Occident* apparently led to the benches of the *majorité*.

Michel Poniatowski, ex-Minister of the Interior, OAS sympathiser and Giscardian 'baron', was a favourite *bête noire* of the left. His own writings echoed New Right themes. During his control of the Interior, it was alleged, the rehabilitation of the extreme right was accelerated. Jewish and immigrant groups asked why Poniatowski and his successor, Christian Bonnet, were slow to reprimand anti-semitic or racialist elements.

Les pouvoirs publics stood accused of laxity, complacency, complicity and forbearing *vis-à-vis* neo-fascism and anti-semitism. How did the Government respond to these accusations? How extensive were these charges? Firstly, it is worth recalling that the revival of anti-semitism and neo-fascism coincided with a virus of scandals which dogged the Giscardian administration. Poniatowski (*via* the 'De Broglie Affair')[43] and Giscard (notably *via* 'the Bokassa affair[s]')[44] were at the centre of these. None of the scandals falls directly within the scope of the present enquiry but, collectively, they soured the image of Giscard's 'liberal society'. The scandals, the revival of anti-semitic outrages and extreme right-wing provocateurs contributed to a general decline in respect for the President. Thus, in the 1981 presidential campaign, various opponents of Giscard campaigned for the restoration of prestige and respect for French (or Gaullist) institutions. The candidate of the MRG (left-wing Radicals), Michel Crépeau, used his allotted television time to attack Giscard's links with ex-Emperor Bokassa and the South American dictators Pinochet and Videla.

The charge of complacency was rejected by Christian Bonnet, who pointed to occasions when he had intervened to ban neo-fascist conferences, rallies, and so on.[45] Like Giscard, he counselled against over-dramatisation and panic responses; if measures were to be taken they needed to be effective. As we have indicated (see above), publicity can be counter-productive and banned groups may reconstitute themselves. For example, in 1973, the ban on *Ligue Communiste* led to the direct formation of another Trotskyist formation, the *Ligue Communiste Révolutionnaire*. The FANE, prior to its banning, threatened to have two substitute bodies waiting in the wings. Indeed, a number of extremist organisations were reputed to be operating from FANE's headquarters. This not only illustrates the problem facing Ministers of the Interior, it also shows how statistics on extremist groups may be unreliable in view of parallel organisations, pseudonyms, dual membership, etc.

Leaders of the French Jewish community, such as Alain de Rothschild, followed suit and frowned upon panic responses. Rumours of Jewish commando and self-defence groups earned condemnations. Nevertheless, many Jews and minority groups saw the ban on FANE and the subsequent leniency of the courts as symptomatic of official policy — too little, too late and too half-hearted. Minority feeling was that the state was insufficiently protective towards minorities; a distinct lack of sensitivity was discernible *en haut*. Did the Government's Middle East policy create a temperament conducive to anti-semitism? Why did the President tease Jews over their divided loyalties? Why were attacks on minorities not condemned immediately? These kind of questions were asked time and again.

Moreover, when *le pouvoir* did respond, Freudian slips of the tongue left the real attitudes of those in power open to question. For instance, after the incident in rue Copernic, Premier Raymond Barre regretted 'the attack which also killed three innocent Frenchmen'.[46] Giscard, too, spoke of four dead including 'three passers-by'.[47] Were Jews, by implication, 'guilty' citizens? Were the deaths of passers-by more lamentable than that of a Jew at prayer? These were the natural reflexes of a community under pressure. Unfortunately-worded epitaphs only further reinforced the ghetto mentality; insensitivity worked against the continuing integration of the Jew into French society. A classic example of this insensitivity allegedly occurred with the choice of dates for the 1981 election. This slip was exploited by the (then) opposition when Charles Hernu (Socialist Party) called it an 'unthinkable negligence' and an insult to the Jewish religion that the first ballot of the elections coincided with a Jewish holy day.[48] Devotional duties could keep practising Jews away from the polling booths, Hernu explained. Again, the charge was insensitivity, although some critics suggested that it represented an intentional ploy to deprive François Mitterrand of the expected Jewish vote.[49]

The list of accusations was not confined to attacks on the Government. Raymond Aron, a Giscardian supporter, brandished the stick further: 'The assassins of rue Copernic are inspired by the police and by the writings of Alain de Benoist and Louis Pauwels'.[50] The New Right we have looked at. As regards the police, an oft-asked question was: 'Is there a fifth column in the police force?' The police trade unions were patently disturbed by such queries and anxious to purge their ranks of known neo-fascists in order to bolster their flagging public image. They complained repeatedly that the Minister of the Interior failed to act on information and names proffered. When FANE was banned it transpired that about twenty per cent of the one hundred and fifty or so members were police officers. All had been reported *previously* to the Minister of the Interior by police trade unions. One policeman and FANE ideologist (a recruit to the Minister of Interior's special *Renseignements*

Généraux) was eventually suspended. In 1980, he was picked up in connection with the Bologna railway station bombing. Formerly, however, he had been entrusted with guarding prominent Jewish individuals — despite his professed neo-fascist ideas! In the wake of the ban on FANE, the rue Copernic incident and the great deal of subsequent publicity, mud began to fly. The police were not only accused of sheltering or ignoring right-wing extremist suspects, but immigrant and civil rights groups recalled the number of aggressions committed by policemen against North Africans, blacks and other minorities.

The MRAP designated 1980 as 'the year of neo-Nazi violence'.[51] Their secretary-general, Albert Lévy, raised the familiar theme of police bias: 'It should be emphasized that police inquiries against the extreme right always come to nothing'.[52] The MRAP demanded more effective police action against neo-Nazi and anti-semitic groups: 'It is necessary to demand from the authorities measures effective enough to dismantle the fascist groups'.[53] For 'political reasons', anti-fascism and anti-racism lay dormant. What were these political reasons? One may well be the 'red herring' strategy; for example, it has been claimed that: 'Fascist groups are useful to the authorities because they turn attention away from genuine struggles by accusing foreigners or Jews of being responsible for all our troubles as in the 1930s'.[54] As Cerny suggests,[55] such groups may not be serious threats in themselves, and in this respect, the Giscard–Bonnet de-dramatisation policy may be seen as a practical response. However, the existence of such groups may force the state to subvert itself by eroding liberal and democratic values. The West German practice of *berufsverbot* testifies to this.

The collective baggage of security and anti-immigrant legislation introduced by Ministers Peyrefitte (Justice), Stoléru (Immigrants) and Bonnet can be seen in this context. The various proposals[56] were roundly condemned by civil rights groups, trade unions, immigrant bodies and political opponents and (in some instances) questioned by the Constitutional Council. Taken together they indicated the movement of 'early' Giscardian liberalism towards a more illiberal *étatisme*. Some opponents — not only on the left — accused the Giscardian *majorité* of cultivating a 'strategy of tension' capable of sponsoring a political back-lash favourable to the established order. In 1981, Brice Lalonde, the ecologist presidential candidate, fully condemned the airport bomb attack which coincided with Giscard's campaign visit to Corsica. However, he rejected the incident as a pretext 'for maintaining a climate of fear and calling for a reinforcement of repression in France'.[57]

In such a climate, controversial legislation can be rushed through and the search for scapegoats escalated. The response of the Mayor of Ajaccio (Corsica) was understandable in view of Corsican nationalist violence — 'they are acts of *gauchistes* which carry the mark of international terrorism'[58] — but this, too, needs to be related to the search for scapegoats. Once the ground has been prepared, the hunt can be narrowed down to foreigners, immigrants, Jews, *gauchistes*, etc. After the rue Copernic incident, the search for suspects turned inevitably towards 'strangers in our midst' — a Cypriot? a Libyan? or some other alien? In a society which values the right of political asylum, the 'myth' of a foreign terrorist is often real enough but such a concept can easily distract from serious analysis.

The concept may also provide a convenient smokescreen for the prevalence and rehabilitation of right-wing extremism *inside* France. Critics maintained that the authorities had no problem inventing scapegoats or threats. The opinion polls obliged by indicating the disturbing levels of intolerance (especially towards North Africans) in French society.[59] When it comes to apprehending real culprits complacency or complicity ruled and magistrates complained of police opposition to investigations of right-wing and neo-Fascist extremism inside the police forces.[60]

From the late 1970s, in particular, fears resounded from several quarters that *specific* attacks on immigrants and Jews would be used to support repressive legislation *in general*. The measures — which threatened repatriation of second generation immigrants, harsh penalisation of demonstrators protesting against steel industry redundancies, progressive institutionalisation of widespread security checks, widening of the state's geographical jurisdiction through Giscard's proposal for a 'European Judicial Area', expulsion of 'troublesome' immigrant trade unionists or editors (e.g. Simon Malley of *France-Asie*), an attitude of harassment towards newspapers such as *Canard Enchaîné* and *Le Monde*, and so on — all served to reinforce suspicions.

For some years, now, immigrants in France have been under pressure. Attacks on Arabs have increased, occasionally reaching high levels — at the time of the 'oil crisis', or, from time to time, in the Marseilles area. Civil rights groups complain that attacks of a racist nature are too easily banalised by the authorities. 'High spirits' or 'irrational impulses' are given as *causes* for such attacks. After a vicious gang attack on a young Jewish boy in the rue des Rosiers (Paris), the police explained that it was merely 'a drunken quarrel which turned out badly'.[61] In an incident at Saint Chamas (Bouches-du-Rhône), after a series of attacks on young North Africans, the deputy Mayor and a local karate teacher were arrested. In their defence, the Mayor of nearby Cuques pleaded that: 'One should not speak of racism. They had a little too much to drink'.[62]

Such incidents were bizarre but not untypical in their occurrence or explanation. For threatened minorities, such interpretations ignored the wider framework of analysis required and were tantamount to whitewash. For Jews, immigrants and other targets the situation demands a more serious assessment. According to M. Belper, of the *Association d'Aide aux Travailleurs d'Outre-mer* (ATOM):

> We are faced with a change in mentalities, a disturbing evolution . . . The change today is that racism's xenephobic character is disguised; justification and support for racism are often found in ambiguous political statements — including one by the Government — and in a climate of dangerous attitudes and ideas.[63]

All the political parties have condemned the doctrines discussed in this chapter. When the MRAP organised a large demonstration after the rue Copernic incident all parties were represented amongst the hundred thousand demonstrators. (The MRAP, who organised the demonstration, put the figure at three hundred thousand: *Droit et Liberté* [MRAP monthly], no. 395, October 1980.) The regional and central press organs of the parties published articles sympathetic to victims of anti-semitic and racist attacks. Condemnations abounded — not least in the National Assembly. It was unfortunate, therefore, that too many of the parties opposing anti-semitic, racist or neo-fascist behaviour diluted their efforts from time to time for political gain. Two brief examples illustrate this point.

In 1976, the following demagogic statement made by Jacques Chirac was hardly conducive to good community relations: 'A country with 900,000 unemployed and 2 million immigrant workers should logically have no trouble about employment'.[64] This represents a Gaullist response. However, by 1980–1, the French Communist Party was saying virtually the same thing and campaigning for the presidential election using themes distasteful to many immigrants. Here is not the place to exploit this particular theme,[65] but it is worth noting that Jean-Marie Le Pen, for instance, 'protested' against other candidates stealing National Front clothes.[66] One African journal spoke of Ku Klux Klan-like behaviour[67] and other critics rubbed salt in by coining the phrase *fascisme aux couleurs de la France*.[68] According to Jean-François Revel, 'there is one fascist party, and only one amongst the main parties in France today: the French Communist Party'.[69]

Without doubt, these were exaggerated anti-PCF reflexes, largely wallowing in the luxury of 'kicking the dog while he's down'. It was tragic for the PCF that such allegations *could* be made since the Party claimed to have been in the vanguard contesting ideas and measures which threatened individual liberties. Between the 1978 election and the campaign for the 1981 election, Communist Party *députés* intervened thirty times in matters of racialism or neo-Nazi acts, through questions to the Government, press releases, letters to Ministers, Parliamentary speeches and three private members bills. Every outrage prompted some form of response — public statements, press conferences, rallies, petitions, demonstrations, press releases, etc. To quote one PCF activist: 'Documents testifying to our activity in this field would fill volumes'.[70]

Conclusion

The opposition to neo-Nazism, anti-semitism, racism and New Right ideology testified to the diversely held fears, often exaggerated but none-theless real, evoked by potential or actual revival of these ideas in French society. The extreme right wing and the New Right welcomed the publicity incurred, although de Benoist and his colleagues protested that it was impossible to be openly right-wing without being labelled fascist. The mood of the New Right is captured by the confident assertiveness of Henri de Lesquen (*Horlogiste*, GRECE, ENA, *École Polytechnique*, Ministry of the Interior):

> We are the first generation who, because we were born after the war, can accept the heritage of the right . . . The Nazis? That does not at all concern us. They are excessive and stupid. Yes, we are from the right and we are going to prove that this is neither disgraceful nor *dépassé*. Marxism and the ideologies of the left are generally on the decline. The way is open for us.[71]

Nevertheless, de Benoist admitted that it would be tantamount to '*angélisme*'[72] not to recognise that ideas propagated by the New Right would achieve political dimensions. De Lesquen's verbal aggression concurred with the claims of those extreme right groups, such as the PFN, which purported to be fighting a neo-Gramscian 'war of positions'. Contemporary '*camelots du roi*' continued to seek their intellectual and political alibis. By 1981, the PFN had deserted Giscard for Chirac and many of Pascal Gauchon's supporters adhered to Philippe Malaud's *Centre National des Indépendants et Paysans*, which, formerly, was close to Giscard. Pascal Gauchon considered a *rassemblement* around Chirac to be the best guarantee of PFN ideas. Philippe Malaud looked one step further ahead: in the event of a Mitterrand victory, the conditions would be tailor-made for a new 'prince' — the *rassemblement* of the *whole* of the French right around Chirac.[73] The likelihood of this strategy being adopted was enhanced by Mitterrand's success and by Chirac's respectable 18 per cent of the vote on the first ballot.

The electoral context and the assertiveness of the extreme right/New Right introduced a further important consideration. To what extent has the left contributed to the development of the trends discussed in this chapter? According to Jean-François Kahn, 'since 1968, a certain intellectual left has, by incoherence, facility or demagogy built up so many errors that it is not astonishing that today a thinking right . . . comes to occupy part of the ground lost by his left'.[74] However, the poverty of philosophy argument should not be pushed too far. May 1968 and the post-68 society promoted a number of creative socio-political movements, e.g. ecologists, *autogestionnaires*, feminists, etc. More crucial, the failings of the *political* left were a more serious factor as this force struggled to fill the vacuum left by the break-up of the Communist-Socialist alliance. No doubt, the PCF's retreat from Eurocommunism and the divisions within the Socialist Party had spin-off effects in the extreme right political family. In this light, it is perhaps unsurprising that initiatives and assertiveness developed outside the political left. By 1980, Alain Touraine (on the left) was formulating his *L'après-socialisme* and retrospectively applying a familiar slogan to the left in 1978: *'Dix ans, ça suffit'*.[75] However, Mitterrand's presidential victory — after twenty-three years of uninterrupted right-wing rule — indicates that a more detailed look at the complex question of left-wing 'failure' is required.

Whilst Touraine propagated his remedies for the left in post-industrial society, the extreme right returned to largely *dépassé* ideas. De Benoist was skilled in throwing new angles on old ideas and the neo-Gramscian tendencies were innovatory, but the term 'New Right' was nevertheless something of a misnomer. The themes developed were principally *déjàvu*. We began by noting the French propensity to exhume the past; indeed, the ideas of the resuscitated extreme/New Right would qualify as old wine in new bottles. Yet there was novelty in the openness, assertiveness and audacity of this political family compared with the understandable defensiveness of the previous three decades. By the late seventies, shyness had deserted the extreme right and the man who had been the Vichy Minister of Jewish Affairs, Darquier de Pellepoix, could scandalise opinion through an unrepentant interview.[76] As we have seen, provocation and offensiveness were the order of the day, and the lessons of the past seemed to have lost some of their impact — raising once again the spectre of the manipulation of racism for political gain. Bernard-Henri Lévy's sober words spring to mind: 'History . . . teaches us that an amnesiac people . . . is a people in chains'.[77]

Certainly, the world since the 1930s and 1940s has changed so much that parallels with that period need to be made with the greatest of caution. On the optimistic side, the French political culture continues to demonstrate what Cerny calls a 'credibility gap' *vis-à-vis* fascist authoritarianism;[78] premature alarm bells can be counterproductive. Nevertheless, an obvious but apparently indigestible lesson is that the inability to solve social problems should not lead to their banalisation or utilisation for political gain; nor should the criticism of defective responses to real problems by the authorities be used as a pretext for introducing more repressive apparatus. Where qualitative reforms are called for, quantitative retreat behind the shield of law and order carries no recipe of hope for the future. In conclusion, anything short of vigilance offers little consolation to French citizens conscious of their existing liberties and rights, and apprehensive about any movement towards a more authoritarian state.

Notes

1 *Le Nouvel Observateur*, 2–8 July 1980.
2 *The Sunday Times*, 17 August 1980.
3 Malcolm Anderson, *Conservative Politics in France* (London: Allen and Unwin, 1974), pp. 280–3.
4 For a full list of proscribed parties, see *Le Monde*, 6 September 1980.
5 Anderson, op. cit., p. 297.
6 Ibid.
7 For the election campaign cf. *Le Monde*, 28 May–13 June 1979.
8 *Le Monde*, 14 August 1980.
9 See *Le Monde*, 13 June 1979.
10 *Le Monde*, 12 June 1979.
11 *Le Monde*, 13 June 1979.
12 *Le Monde*, 4 July 1980.
13 *The Guardian*, 9 September 1980.
14 Jaurès's initial estimation projected Dreyfus as a rich Jew guilty of traitorous activity.
15 *Le Monde*, 7 March 1981.
16 Roger Klein, *Le Monde*, 3 September 1980.
17 *Le Matin*, 6 September 1980.
18 E. J. Hobsbawm, 'Are we entering a new era of anti-semitism?', *New Society*, 11 December 1980, pp. 503–5.
19 For an interesting example of this see the interview with Darquier de Pellepoix, *L'Express*, 27 October 1978.
20 See the chapter on left-wing anti-semitism in France in André Harris and Alain de Sédouy, *Juifs et Français* (Paris: Grasset, 1979).
21 Anderson, op. cit., p. 299.
22 See Raymond Aron, 'Antisémitisme et terrorisme', *L'Express*, 18 October 1980.
23 *Le Monde*, 11 July 1980.

24 *Le Matin*, 2 July 1980.
25 Mona Ozouf and Jean-Paul Enthoven, 'Quand la droite pense', *Le Nouvel Observateur*, 22–29 April 1979, pp. 36–8.
26 Maurice Bardèche in *Défense de l'Occident*, no. 170 (December 1979), p. 29.
27 *Le Monde*, 24 August 1979.
28 Louis Pauwels, *et al.*, *Maiastra Renaissance de l'Occident* (Paris: Plon, 1979), pp. 22–3.
29 K. Evin, 'Les jeunes loups de la Nouvelle Droite', *Le Nouvel Observateur*, 23–29 April 1979.
30 Ibid.
31 Ibid., *Jeune Nation* used the Celtic cross as an emblem.
32 *Le Figaro-Magazine*, 28 February 1981.
33 *Le Matin*, 25 July 1979.
34 *Le Monde*, 12 July 1979.
35 Alain de Benoist, 'Itinéraire', *Nouvelle École*, no. 9 (Summer 1969).
36 Bardèche, op. cit.
37 This key concept was favoured by François Duprat, founder of the Groupes Nationaux Révolutionnaires (GNR) – and National Front member: cf. P. Chairoff, *Dossier néo-nazisme* (Paris: Éditions Ramsay, 1977); F. Laurent, *L'orchestre noir* (Paris: Stock, 1978); F. Duprat, *Les mouvements d'extrême droite en France depuis 1944* (Paris: Éditions Albatross, 1972).
38 Vincent Wright, *The Government and Politics of France* (London: Hutchinson, 1978), p. 198.
39 François Mitterrand, *Ici et maintenant* (Paris: Fayard, 1980), p. 119.
40 *L'Humanité*, 13 August 1980.
41 François George, 'Un exemple d'analogie malheureuse', *Les Temps Modernes* (September 1980), pp. 555–9.
42 Ozouf and Enthoven, loc. cit.
43 See Jacques Bachelin, *L'affaire Broglie* (Paris: Jean Picollec, 1981).
44 See Roger Delpey, *La manipulation* (Paris: Jacquer Grancher, 1981).
45 *L'Express*, 18 October 1980.
46 Ibid.
47 Ibid.
48 *Le Monde*, 3 February 1981.
49 Some Jewish organisations had advised against voting for Giscard whilst Mitterand was expected to be the main beneficiary of the Jewish vote.
50 Aron, op. cit.
51 *Le Matin*, 2 July 1980.
52 See *Le Monde*, 6 September 1980.
53 *Le Matin*, 2 July 1980.
54 *The Guardian*, 6 October 1980.
55 See chapter 5, pp. 99.
56 Cf., *inter alia*: Syndicat de la Magisture, *Justice sous influence* (Paris: François Maspéro, 1981); Brian Fitzpatrick, 'Immigrants' in John Flower, ed., *France Today* (London: Methuen, 1980); Hommes et Libertés, *Les droits de l'homme en France 1974–1981: livre noir d'un septennat* (Paris, 1981).
57 *Le Matin*, 18 April 1981.
58 Ibid.
59 The following poll from *L'Express* indicates French public opinion *vis-à-vis* minorities, anti-semitism, the role of the police, etc. It should of course be realised that the poll was taken at an 'exceptional' time, i.e. shortly after the incident in rue Copernic. For a later poll on racism, attitude to immigrants, etc. cf. *Le Matin*, 4 March 1981.

Table 7.2

Tolerance and Intolerance
'For each of these categories of people, say if you think that there are too many of them in France.'

	Yes 1980	Yes 1977
North Africans	49 per cent	63 per cent
Spaniards	16	27
African blacks	28	25
Jews	12	17
Corsicans	6	6
Protestants	4	5
Foreigners in general	43	61

French Jews
'In your opinion, is a Jew just as French as any other French person?'

	1980	1977
Yes	87 per cent	65 per cent
No	10	22
No opinion	3	13

Antisemitism
'In your opinion, is antisemitism — the feeling of hostility towards Jews — in France . . .'

	1980		
Very widespread	13	=	55 per cent
Fairly widespread	42		
Not very widespread	34	=	38
Not widespread at all	4		
No opinion	7		

Reasons for the recent attacks
'For each of the following reasons, indicate whether you think it might explain the recent antisemitic attacks in France?'

	Yes	No	No opinion
The economic crisis and unemployment	35	60	5 per cent
French policy towards Israel and the Arab countries	30	53	17
Police inefficiency	40	50	10
Publicity given to the ideas of the extreme right	42	36	22
A longstanding French tradition of antisemitism	33	55	12
The presence of terrorist networks directed from abroad	69	16	15

The President of the Republic
'The day following the attack, a ceremony took place in front of the synagogue in rue Copernic in Paris. In your opinion, should Valéry Giscard d'Estaing have been present or not?'

Should have been present	44 per cent
Should not have been present	37
No opinion	19

The political parties
'Which of the following political parties seem to you to be the most responsive to the worries of the Jewish community?'

UDF	15 per cent	
RPR	17	(Total higher than
PS	30	because of
PC	20	multiple replies.)
None of these	16	
No opinion	37	

The police
'In the struggle against French neo-Nazi movements, would you say that the police . . .'

Have done everything that they ought to have done	19
Have not done all that they ought to have done	57
No opinion	24

The Minister of the Interior
'After the events of the past few days, certain people think that Christian Bonnet, the Minister of the Interior, ought to resign. Do you personally . . .'

Agree	24 per cent
Disagree	52
No opinion	24

Escalation
'Do you think it legitimate for French Jewish organisations to reply to violence by violence?'

Yes	7 per cent
No	90
No opinion	3

(Source: *L'Express*, 18 October 1980. This survey was carried out on 7 and 8 October 1980 by l'Institut Louis-Harris France at the request of *L'Express*, using a sample of one thousand people representative of the French population aged eighteen and over.)

60 Such as M. Guy Jolly (magistrate) in *Le Canard Echaîné*, 15 October 1980.
61 *Le Matin*, 2 August 1980.
62 *L'Humanité*, 17 September 1980.
63 *Le Monde*, 14 March 1981.
64 *The Guardian*, 15 March 1981.
65 For a study of the 1981 election which assesses the left, see the article by Paul Hainsworth in *Parliamentary Affairs* (forthcoming Autumn, 1981).
66 See *Le Droit de Vivre* (MRAP monthly) (April 1981).
67 Hainsworth, op. cit.
68 Ibid.
69 *L'Express*, 26 February 1981.
70 Statement from P. le Corré, whom I would like to thank for helping me to clarify PCF thinking on these matters.
71 Quoted by Evin, op. cit.; cf. Pierre Vial, *Le GRECE prend la parole: pour une renaissance culturelle* (Paris: Copernic, 1979).
72 Alain de Benoist, *Les idées à l'endroit* (Paris: Hallier, 1979), p. 21.
73 cf. Pascal Krop, 'L'extrême-droite avec Chirac', *Le Matin*, 24 April 1981.

74 Jean-François Kahn, 'Nouvelle réflexion sur une droite dite'nouvelle', *Le Matin* (supplément), 7–8 July 1979.
75 Alain Touraine, *L'après-socialisme* (Paris; Grasset, 1980), p. 268.
76 Darquier de Pellepoix, op. cit. One particularly upsetting comment for French Jews read: 'À Auschwitz, on n'a gazé que des poux'. (At Auschwitz, they only gassed lice.)
77 Bernard-Henri Lévy, *L'idéologie française* (Paris: Grasset, 1981), p. 12.
78 See chapter 5, loc. cit.

8 Protest in Brittany from the Fourth to the Fifth Republics: From a Regionalist to a Regional Social Movement?

JILL LOVECY
Lecturer in European Studies
University of Manchester Institute
of Science and Technology

Over the last thirty years regionalism has been a potent political force in Brittany, and one that has, moreover, assumed a wide variety of manifestations. This chapter will be concerned with investigating and accounting for the differences, and also the linkages, between what have constituted three distinct phases of regionalist activity within this period: first, the emergence of CELIB (the *Comité d'Études et de Liaison des Intérêts Bretons*, founded in 1950), and with it the establishment of a new, and specifically regional, political elite in the early to mid-1950s; second, the series of dramatic social mobilisations around regionalist themes which marked the early years of the following decade; and third, the pair of prolonged and bitter strike movements which took place, one in the agricultural sector and the other in industry, in the early 1970s. By clarifying what has been the nature and causality of regionalist protest in Brittany in its various guises in the period since the war, and by examining the sources and carriers of regionalist ideology and the extent, and nature, of its appeal to different elements of the population concerned at these three points in time, it should be possible to elucidate the circumstances in which specifically regionalist social movements have occurred in Brittany.

These several issues, in turn, feed into a wider debate concerning the competing claims of different theoretical frameworks employed in the social sciences and of their associated methodologies. A further concern of this chapter will therefore be to explore a number of problems relating to theory and method raised by the attempt to account for the occurrence of regionalist movements. While the term 'region' certainly designates 'a geographical unit', it is also the central organising concept of regionalist ideology and as such is an artefact of men's minds. The question, 'Where is Brittany?' is thus of less importance here than to ask, 'Who has sought to construct this idea of a Breton regional identity?; in what circumstances?; and for what purpose?'[1] At the heart of regionalism as a political phenomenon lies a double claim: on the one hand, that in a specified geographical area a shared regional identity — however this be defined — does exist, endowing the inhabitants of this area with some unity of interest and purpose which sets them apart from their fellow citizens; and, on the other, that this shared identity requires the modification of existing institutions of the state, so as to incorporate processes of representation which will both ensure the input of interests specific to that region into the policy-making process, and also legitimise the ensuing policy-outcomes in a new way.[2]

These features of regionalism have particular implications for elaborating an appropriate research strategy for the empirical investigation of such movements. Quite specifically, in so far as the populations of certain areas are characterised as forming separate and distinct entities within the wider social formation which corresponds to the existing 'nation-state' institutions, regionalist movements in France (and elsewhere) draw on a mode of conceptualising the internal differentiation within their national societies which is not dissimilar to that informing the established institutions of the state. Regionalist discourse prioritises the 'vertical' divisions between geographically-defined units over the 'horizontal' divisions constituted by social class — and it is precisely through the principle of territorial representation that the exercise of state power is legitimised in liberal democratic regimes.[3] Therefore, even though regionalism is normally associated with opposition to the policies and procedures of the established state, research into regionalism should not ignore the ways in which the perceptions of crucial relationships and problems by different elements within the population may be influenced by their experiences within a political system in which consensus-building has traditionally been founded on the representation of a variety of territorial units. Nor should it preclude the hypothesis that in certain circumstances regionalist themes, and indeed the concept of a regionalist unit requiring appropriate representation, may be available for the state to employ for its *own* purposes.[4]

Considerations such as these raise questions as to the validity of an underlying conceptual approach present in a broad range of literature not only on regionalism, but also, more generally, on local political processes. This is an approach that can be characterised as basing itself on a geographical mode of conceptualisation, since what is offered is a problematic focusing on the relationship between two major analytic categories, normally designated as *centre* and *periphery*, that are defined in terms of their geographical location and separation. What is questionable here is the way in which the *method* of conceputalisation adopted, by taking as its starting point the establishment of the concepts 'centre' and 'periphery' (or variants on the latter such as local or regional society) as separate and distinct units, itself serves to write into the analysis what ought to be the proper object of investigation — i.e. what *kind* of shared interest may indeed exist at the regional level in any specified historical context, and whether, therefore, 'regional society' can be taken to constitute an appropriate unit of analysis.

The implications consequent upon adopting this type of conceptual approach will be explored here with particular reference to the major work of Renaud Dulong on Brittany, *La question bretonne*, as well as to his *La région, l'état et la société locale.*[5] For while these works are notable not only for their concern to deal explicitly with the broader problems of theory and methodology that are involved, but also for the innovative interpretative frameworks which they develop within a sophisticated Marxian discourse, it will be argued here that in crucial respects the methodology which Dulong adopts is indeed informed by what is, fundamentally, a geographical mode of conceptualisation. His analysis thus becomes entangled in issues of social geography at the expense of providing an adequate elucidation of the dynamics of social class. We shall argue here that the development of social movements in Brittany can be better explained by a class analysis — set within a specific *regional* context — rather than by positing the existence of a regional identity or common interest which transcends or supersedes class distinctions (i.e. a supposed 'regional*ism*').

Dulong's Analysis of Regionalism

In *La question bretonne*, Dulong starts by discussing the social scientist's problems in developing an appropriate research strategy for investigating regionalist movements. He argues that the essential task is that of demystifying the key terms of regionalist discourse — 'Brittany' and 'the Bretons' — through an analysis of divisions of interest within the region (here he identifies territorial, linguistic and political as well as economic divisions) and of the different components of Breton regionalism. This he breaks down into three distinct components: 1. CELIB with its particular concern to establish an economic and political consensus; 2. the Breton movement of cultural and linguistic defence; and 3. the region's worker-peasant social movements.[6] In addition, it is characteristic of his approach that he seeks from the outset to elucidate an underlying 'content' shared by these three different forms of regionalism; and this, he suggests, is to be found 'at the level of the evolution of Brittany's economic structure'.[7] This approach subsequently enables him to establish, as his major hypothesis, that regionalist movements have arisen in the 1950s and 1960s primarily in response to a transformation of the mode of production in Brittany: 'Regionalism really expresses the Bretons' resistance to the dismantling of a whole social structure'.[8]

What needs to be noted here is the method Dulong adopts in establishing the central hypothesis of his research. Even though he declares his intention of breaking with the 'Breton character' thesis, his methodology is nevertheless one which is primarily concerned with understanding the various manifestations of Breton regionalism by placing them 'within the social life of the region taken as a whole', and thus endowing the region's inhabitants with a unifying identity which, for a certain historical period at least, does effectively set them apart from other Frenchmen by virtue of their geographical location.[9] First and foremost, people living in Brittany are portrayed as members of 'a specific society', of 'a precapitalist island within the period of liberal capitalism', which has hitherto enjoyed a marked degree of autonomous structuring, but which from 1945 onwards was to be progressively dismantled as economic activities within the region were integrated by sectors of monopoly capital now emerging to dominance at the national level.[10] Quite apart from his failure to substantiate adequately — in terms of empirical data — this analysis of the region as 'a predominantly pre-capitalist society', what should concern us here is the issue of Dulong's method.[11]

For it is his method which arbitrarily limits the type of hypothesis that he can investigate through this case-study. In Dulong's work, Breton regionalism is ultimately to be accounted for by factors which are quite specific to this geographical area — by an internal economic structuring and social and political process which are clearly demarcated from, and find themselves in confrontation with, those obtaining in the rest of France.[12] One consequence of his method is that it logically entails an overall characterisation of Breton regionalism as a movement of resistance and defence, even though on numerous occasions Dulong's analyses of particular developments in the regionalist movement point to other insights into its nature. Until political actors who are themselves members of the 'techno-Bourgeoisie' emerge at the forefront of the regional stage in the late 1960s (when CELIB is thereby transformed into an instrument of domination), regionalism in Brittany cannot be said to constitute a real social movement in the sense that Touraine uses this term — one with its own 'historicity' — for, as Dulong argues, it has centred on 'a secondary contradiction'.[13]

At issue here is the way in which Dulong presents, in respect to Brittany, what is essentially a geographical conceptualisation of the Marxian categories of modes of production — in which he bypasses the question of whether the experiences of social groups and classes in Brittany before the mid-1960s linked them with any similar groups and classes elsewhere in France, ones for which the pre-capitalist characterisation would be manifestly inappropriate. His approach has equally significant implications for his political analysis. It leads him to treat the economic regionalism of CELIB in isolation from similar developments elsewhere in France under the Fourth Republic, and obviates the need to explore in any systematic fashion the interaction between regionalism in Brittany and political and ideological developments at the level of the French national state. The crucial relationship in his account is the confrontation between two sets of geographically-located economic forces, those of Brittany's precapitalist social forces and the emergent hegemonic fraction of monopoly capitalism in France as a whole. As a consequence, the state's role cannot, for Dulong, be of central importance, for 'the Breton movement poses its problem outside of the arena where the primary contradiction (that opposing capital to labour), which the state by its existence seeks to regulate, takes place'.[14]

In a number of respects Dulong's work thus exhibits features which are characteristic of a broader body of literature that focuses on 'centre-periphery' relations, even though these features are present in his work in somewhat distinctive forms.[15] In the first place, local societies, situated in the periphery, are taken to constitute a distinct analytic category. In Dulong's work, where it is married into a Marxian framework, this proposition is argued through in terms of the specificity of the economic and social structures present in the region, whereas in a number of works concerned with France's local politico-administrative systems, as J. Médard has recently observed, this proposition is introduced without any formal attempt to substantiate it empirically. The particular patterns of socio-economic forces present in a given locality are in effect assumed to constitute distinct units within the national society for purposes of analysis.[16] Second, the 'centre', located elsewhere, is adopted as a separate analytic category. In other works, where this is taken to comprise, or include, the centralised institutions of the French state, the state is thus 'exteriorised' from the social order of the periphery and, as a consequence, this conceptual approach serves to preclude an understanding of the state, not as a set of formal institutions, but as the institutionalisation of relations of authority in society, as the focus for those processes through which a negotiated order, comprised of collective goals backed by sanctions, and of the values which inform them, is established out of the conflicts of interest in that society. In the case of Dulong, it is the hegemonic forces of monopoly capitalism that constitute the 'centre', and the state is viewed as operating in close relationship to these; and while in his work the state is therefore not exteriorised from French society as a whole, it is marginalised from the account he offers of developments in Brittany, since here the primary contradiction between capital and labour is displaced by the secondary contradiction posed by regionalism.[17] Finally, it is the relationship between these two distinct units of analysis, 'centre' and 'periphery', which is posed as the appropriate problematic for understanding contemporary political processes at the local or regional level.

The empirical evidence available, however, does not justify the separating out of what Dulong claims to be 'the regional society' of Brittany as a unit of analysis — despite the fact that the configuration of social and economic forces present in much of the area concerned in the post-war period was in important respects distinctive.[18] As a result, Dulong's interpretation of this period does not succeed in unravelling and 'explain [ing] the confusion of image and reality so that the living contradictions with which people had to contend emerge'.[19] Nor does a reading of the publications associated with CELIB for this period support Dulong's interpretation of its role as being primarily one of *resistance* to the economic changes underway.[20] Moreover, since CELIB's economic regionalist ideology was not peculiar to this organisation in the 1950s but was shared by a range of similar bodies in other areas of France, it does not seem valid to adopt a method, and a working hypothesis, which concentrate on accounting for Breton regionalism in terms of factors that are portrayed as unique to Brittany, to the exclusion of a more general explanatory framework.[21]

CELIB and the Development of Early Regional Demands on the State

That the successful launching in 1950 of CELIB marked a decisive turning-point for subsequent developments in Brittany is therefore not in dispute, even though CELIB itself was not associated with any large-scale social mobilisation in the 1950s.[22] What is at issue is the character and historical function of CELIB's economic regionalism, and how it may be most appropriately accounted for. What CELIB mobilised was an elite stratum within the four departments, drawn from politics, the different economic sectors, personnel of the major ministries' field services, the prefectoral staffs and the regional university. Political notables, already established at the local level in the four departments, now sought to restructure the basis of their 'representativity' and establish a correspondingly new form of legitimacy around a distinctive conception of Brittany's regional identity, portrayed in terms of the region's unity of economic interest.[23]

CELIB's success was thus bound up with the emergence of new *regional* political 'notables' in Brittany. In the following period these notables pursued piecemeal lobbying on many issues of a purely protective character on behalf of a variety of economic activities in the region. However, as intermediaries between the French state and organised interests and public opinion in the region, their primary historical function was not, as Dulong suggests, to act as the focus of a defensive struggle, of a backward-looking resistance to economic change. Instead, and increasingly, this regional political elite, organised within CELIB, acted as disseminators, within a traditionalist and primarily rural area, of the national planners' modernising ideological climate of economic growth and rationality. In this way they directly contributed to promoting the two processes of industrial decentralisation and agricultural integration by which economic activities located in this region were restructured in the post-war period under the aegis of national, and indeed international, industrial and finance capital.[24]

It was CELIB's decision in 1952 to embark on its most ambitious project, the elaboration of a regional plan for Brittany, the first of its kind in France, that was decisive in this process, enabling CELIB to contribute to shaping the attitudes and expectations of wider layers of social actors. Its contribution in this respect can be summarised in terms of three crucial perspectives developed in the First Breton Plan.[25] First, CELIB developed the argument that the region's problems were, at least in part, of the region's own making; certainly the French state was at fault and should now adopt different policies and different procedures for policy-making – but it was also incumbent on the Bretons themselves to abandon their old ways and to make the necessary sacrifices.[26] Second, the region's crisis was now redefined as hinging crucially on the problem of depopulation: the solution therefore lay in new employment opportunities, and this meant that overriding priority needed to be given to industrial decentralisation – the way forward lay in an alliance with large-scale private sector employers from outside the region, and the Bretons could help to stimulate this alliance, in conjunction with the state, by offering appropriate fiscal and other incentives, together with a disciplined, hard-working labour force.[27]

Finally, in elaborating perspectives for agriculture, the Plan gave rise to a critical confrontation between the traditionalist farmers' leaders in the region, allied to local officials of the Ministry of Agriculture — who were committed to the national policy of price support and social investments in the countryside of the FNSEA (*Fédération Nationale des Syndicats d'Exploitants Agricoles*) — and representatives of the Planning Commissariat who argued that priority for investment be given to rationalising agricultural production and improving its quality. This confrontation, resulting in defeat for the traditionalists, may have fed into the new policies of structural reform being developed within the JAC (*Jeunesse Agricole Chrétienne*) and CNJA (*Centre National des Jeunes Agriculteurs*) by a younger generation of farmers in some parts of Brittany. Certainly CELIB's economic regionalism could readily be absorbed into their concern to achieve commercial viability through a strategy combining emphasis on technological innovation and structural reforms with cooperative organisation.[28]

In seeking to account for the appeal which these ideas had, a number of factors need to be considered — not least the influence of the region's distinctive cultural heritage and the memory within certain groups and political tendencies of previous historical mobilisations in the name of a specifically Breton regional or national identity.[29] However, the crucial causality at work would seem to have been one operating not at the regional but at the national level. In the first place, the immediate political conjuncture of the early 1950s needs to be borne in mind, following the shift to a Third Force alliance at governmental level after the end of Tripartism. Politicians drawn from the spectrum of centre-left to centre-right parties that were predominant in these four departments were especially sensitive to the need at this stage to reproduce this governmental alliance at the electoral level, but also aware of the strength of the policy issues which traditionally divided them. The locally-based political notables who now succeeded in establishing their credentials as a regional political elite were not at all cut off from national political and ideological trends; quite on the contrary, a number, including René Pleven, who was to retain the presidency of CELIB for twenty years, were heavily involved in national governmental responsibilities.[30] CELIB, with its apolitical vocabulary of economic regionalism and conciliatory aspirations, 'took off' precisely at the time of the 1950 National Assembly elections and served to offset the sharp clerical/anti-clerical divide which made it difficult to produce departmental party-list alliances corresponding to these current national strategic priorities.[31]

More fundamentally, the emergence of the ideological construct of economic regionalism in Brittany and elsewhere is to be explained in terms of broad developments both of an economic and of a political-ideological order, for which the French state provided the organisational framework. Special attention therefore needs to be paid, on the one hand, to the restructuring of French capitalism underway from the early post-war period, a process centring on sustaining economic growth and achieving international competitiveness through concentration, specialisation and increased labour productivity; and on the other, to the emergence of the ideal of 'a concerted economy' with its consensus-building ethos and tendency towards claims, however pragmatically expressed, of rational resource utilisation — with the Plan and the planners acting both as the major agents of restructuring and as the disseminators, mainly at elite level in French society (covering representatives of the main sectors of the French economy and leading civil servants), of new attitudes and expectations.[32]

The most significant implications of this process of restructuring French capitalism, in relation to the emergent regionalist movements in Brittany and elsewhere, were twofold, resulting in problems of adaptation and demise for whole sectors of small-scale, family-owned industrial and agricultural units of production and commercial establishments; and concomitant with this, a significant expansion of France's working class, with the introduction of altered conditions of labour for that class. These were, moreover, geographically uneven processes, unsettling and reorganising relations between rural and urban areas, and between eastern and western France. In particular, in that area to which the term Brittany came to be increasingly commonly applied in this period (that is the four departments of Ille-et-Vilaine, Côtes-du-Nord, Finistère and Morbihan), the features of family ownership, limited scale and a low level of investment were to be found widely in agriculture, industry and commerce.[33] This meant that quite large numbers of those active in each of these sectors would at some stage face acute problems of commercial viability and lose their status as self-employed; that small and medium-sized farms, factories and shops would be integrated by various means into the ownership or control of large-scale capital; that relations of economic interdependence hitherto obtaining in this area would be broken.

For the most part, it should be noted, such developments were to get underway only from the mid-to-late 1950s, well after the successful establishment of CELIB.[34] By the early 1960s, however, these developments meant that a dual, and quite specific, process of proletarianisation was underway in this area with, on the one hand, the rapid expansion of unskilled, manual industrial work provided by manufacturing industries decentralised to the region and to a lesser degree by the introduction of new types of food processing industry; and, on the other, the emergence of a whole stratum of proletarianised farmers, who were in effect merely outworkers for large-scale food firms, both private and cooperative, neither owning nor controlling the key means of production with which they now worked.[35] At the same time the population of this area continued in its long-standing role as an exporter of manual workers to the major growth centres of the French economy.

These economic changes might, indeed, have been expected to generate resistance, but only if they were experienced in isolation from wider political and ideological currents in France; that they were not is testified to by the genesis of the Breton Plan. This initiative originated with certain industries in the region seeking state aid for their own modernisation plans, and with Michel Phlipponneau, an applied geographer at the University of Rennes.[36] It was the new ethos of 'the concerted economy', with its stress on the urgency and desirability of initiating a process of economic modernisation in France, which would constitute a common and longer-term interest for all French people that is of critical importance for understanding the subsequent development of regionalist movements in Brittany. The new modes of state intervention in the economy raised the expectation that available resources could, and would, be rationally utilised, and it was this optimistic note that was translated by the economic regionalist movement in France into the theme of winning 'modernisation on our terms' – into a voluntarist faith in the possibility of promoting a harmonious interregional pattern of development.[37]

It must, however, be emphasised that in Brittany, as elsewhere, the economic regionalist construct was a complex one, and not without ambiguities. In this it reflected the contradictory influences of a number of factors. If much of CELIB's activities in the mid-to-late 1950s were eminently concordant with the actual patterns of economic restructuring being promoted by France's planners at the national level (for example: the major perspectives adopted in the First Breton Plan; CELIB's activity as an agency of industrial decentralisation from the mid-1950s; and its close early involvement in launching the SDRB, the regional investment agency), this was combined with regionalist protest centring on the state's failure to direct appropriate resources to the region – a failure which CELIB portrayed as stemming above all from the absence of procedures in France for the consultation of the political and economic representatives of regional interests. But this position, in turn, could easily merge into a rather different argument drawing on the traditional principle of *la justice distributive* – that the region should receive a share of state expenditure equivalent to its proportion of the population of France.[38]

Moreover, the planners' own ideal of *une économie concertée* was not without contradictory features. For while they were careful to adopt cautious and pragmatic formulations, tensions arose between a practice which came to prioritise the task of rendering French capital internationally competitive, and a certain logic in their role as planners that led them, at the same time, to seek to impart greater comprehensiveness and greater internal coherence to the national plan and to legitimise their activities in terms of rational utilisation of resources as well as consensus-building procedures.[39] CELIB and its sister organisations in other areas of France posed a dilemma for the planners: there is evidence that they were themselves only too aware of the growing and 'hidden' economic costs entailed by the concentration of growth in limited areas (most notably around Paris) and were also sensitive to the possible value of organisations of the CELIB type as agents of social control — reproducing the consensus-building procedures of the national plan at the regional level as the unsettling effects of restructuring penetrated ever wider circles of economic activities in France. However, the rhetoric of economic regionalism also raised potentially dangerous expectations as to the ability of the planners to control the process of economic modernisation and to achieve a more equitable regional distribution of employment and wealth.[40]

The Mobilisation of Regional Protest

In certain respects this account of economic regionalism in Brittany lies closer to Touraine's observations on the ambiguous character of populism as combining a modernising outlook and acceptance of change with the attempt to reassert a threatened collective social identity. For Touraine, populist movements do have the potential to develop into social movements, by directing their collective action against, not the state, but 'what is, properly speaking, a social adversary' and in the historical period into which France had entered by the 1960s, this meant developing into specifically anti-technocratic struggles. Populism is presented as one of the components of regional movements, and the potential for these latter to develop into social movements is by no means discounted by Touraine, as it is by Dulong, for whom regionalism, by definition, involves the displacement of the primary contradiction in contemporary society by a secondary one.[41] (Touraine does not, however, make the distinction that is developed here between *regionalist* and *regional* social movements.)

Brittany, however, was to be the scene of a complex series of very militant, large-scale social mobilisations of the early 1960s around key regionalist themes. A number of distinct strands can be identified in this period, of which three are of particular interest here. In a first phase, activity centred on farmers in the region and their activism was to be intermittently revived into the mid-1960s on specific issues of agricultural policy, in addition to their participation in other struggles in the region. The second strand of regionalist mobilisation in the early 1960s developed from August 1961 with the decision of CELIB's *Commission Régionale d'Expansion Economique* (CREE) to prepare a Second Plan for Brittany. The third strand in this period which needs to be considered, centring on trade union struggles in industry, emerged with the Government's announcement of the imminent closure of the Forges d'Hennebont in the autumn of 1961.

Agricultural Mobilisation

In order to account for the mobilisation of militant farmers in Brittany in these years, Dulong offers a tightly argued analysis of successive phases by which capitalism penetrated Breton agriculture from the 1950s to the late 1960s, and here many of his detailed points of analysis are persuasive. However his central thesis concerning Brittany's pre-capitalist economic formation leads him to stress the continuing relative homogeneity of the region's agriculture well into the 1960s, and he does not develop the linkage suggested here between the modernising farmers and CELIB's economic regionalism.[42] In dealing with the events of 1960–62, his account centres on the state as the major focus of the farmer's discontent, for state intervention was vital to achieving new forms of marketing organisation that would enable medium-scale farmers to consolidate their commercial viability and sustain the hopes of a stratum of smaller farmers of following them. Dulong argues that while a new pattern of internal differentiation among Brittany's farmers was now underway, their actions at this stage were indeed informed by an objective regional unity of interest embracing the region's farmers and setting them apart from the large-scale capitalist farmers of the Paris Basin and the North.[43]

His account thus mirrors the regionalist claims of leading activists, who portrayed their adversary as an external one (the centralised, technocratic Gaullist state; and large-scale farmers in other regions), developing a variant on the CNJA's challenge to the 'myth' of peasant unity, in which this unity was retained as a regional phenomenon but denied any reality at national level. Dulong fails to acknowledge that marketing reform, and the related objective of 'disciplining' production, was a deeply divisive issue in rural Brittany.[44] While the burning of ballot boxes at Pont l'Abbé in May 1961, and the demonstration of four thousand farmers in Morlaix in June which culminated in the seizure of the subprefecture, caught the headlines in this period, other types of direct action were also recorded which set Bretons, not against the state, but against other Bretons. Militant farmers destroyed the produce of other farmers, burnt down a private-sector slaughterhouse, attacked the premises of private wholesalers, occupied farm lands acquired by non-farmer *'cumulards'*.[45] If some farmers in this region protested bitterly at the Government's failure to implement the 1960 Agricultural Orientation Law, it was because they needed the state to help them and their cooperative organisations — at the expense of other farmers and of a section of private commerce in the region with which these were linked — who were competing with the farmer cooperatives.

Here, surely, is a regionalist movement that requires 'demystification' through an analysis of the antagonisms of social interests present within the region. The activists may themselves have believed passionately in the cause of 'Brittany'; and their sense of their own contribution to that cause can only have been enhanced by the similarity between their strategy and the general perspectives that CELIB's brand of economic regionalism had developed for the region. But what was crystallised out in the large-scale mobilisation of small and medium farmers in the region in 1960–62 was a new, historically specific, social grouping acting collectively to defend its own interests against those of other strata of the regional population.

The essential ambiguity of economic regionalism as an ideological construct can be seen here: not only did it provide the mobilising themes for a social group the unity of which was subsequently to prove illusory, but it mobilised that group under the banner of regional unity at the very moment when the divisions between that group and other elements of the regional population were emerging in acute form for the first time. Touraine's approach, in contrast, serves to pinpoint precisely this ambiguity — that the movement was able only to designate the state as the target of its action, and could not at this stage articulate social divisions of interest among farmers in the region. But whereas Touraine's problematic notion of the 'programmed society' would point to the later emergence of region-alist social mobilisations in which an historically new social category will appear with its own 'project' seeking to gain 'the social direction of historicity' through its anti-technocratic struggles, what Brittany was to witness ten years later in the agricultural sector — with the milk strikes of 1972 — was what might more appropriately be described as a *regional* social movement, a variant on what Touraine characterises as the 'old' working-class social movement of 'industrial society'.[46]

Planning and Rising Expectations

As regards the second strand of regionalist ferment in this period which accompanied the drawing up of the Second Breton Plan, this was stimulated by a number of issues centring on transport within the region and its road and rail communications with Paris. The Paris–Le Mans motorway envisaged in the First Plan had still not been budgeted for in 1961 when the SNCF made public its decision to raise freight and passenger tariffs for peripheral and deficitary networks, including Brittany's. The height of this activism was reached in September 1962 with the 'Battle for the Railway'; CREE's warning to the Government that the tariff increases were unacceptable for the region was followed by a fortnight of meetings, demonstrations and unofficial action when major road and rail links were blocked and telephone lines cut, and a number of the region's mayors threatened to resign in protest.[47]

Dulong covers the developments of 1961–63 primarily for the purpose of providing a background to the crisis of 1964 when CELIB reaffirmed its 'apolitical' stance against the challenge of those on the left seeking political confrontation with the Gaullist regime.[48] For Dulong the decisive new feature of the opening years of the Fifth Republic was the state's closer dependence on the monopolistic sector and the increased stability of the executive. Brittany's declining rural bourgeoisie, in Dulong's account, could only now sustain their political dominance in the region by aligning themselves with the political and economic strategy of the state. It is therefore only at this point that Dulong is able to analyse the role of this rural bourgeoisie in terms similar to those developed here in relation to the emergence of a regional political elite in Brittany by 1953–54:

> . . . a game of complicity was now established, in which CELIB agreed to confine itself to a servicing role for the central state at the regional level . . . it was the Government that was, in the final analysis, in control of the game.[49]

Because this relationship is, for Dulong, a new one, the Second Breton Plan and the regionalist activism that accompanied it are of marginal interest in comparison to the subsequent internal crisis in CELIB. However, from the perspective developed here, it is precisely *because* there is a fundamental point of comparison between CELIB's role in the mid-1950s and in the early 1960s that the points of *contrast* with the earlier period would seem to require closer investigation. The elaboration of the Second Breton Plan at no stage involved any member of the staff of the national Planning Commissariat, on however informal a basis. Neither, however, was it confined to a restricted circle of experts and well-established members of the region's economic and political notability. The CREE (now under the chairmanship of Professor Phlipponneau) provided a forum for a much wider process of participation, the initiative here coming from the new generation of militant young farmers and from trade unionists, with affiliation finally won from the CGT. Indeed CELIB now achieved an improbable degree of regional unity, temporarily embracing all shades of political opinion from the Communists to the Gaullists, with the backing of the four departmental councils, some nine hundred municipal councils (including twenty-six municipal authorities in Loire-Atlantique), and all the main professional and cultural interest groups in the region.[50] Moreover, at this stage, when the pursuit of modernisation with which CELIB had so closely associated itself was producing a ferment of social tension in Brittany as the expectations it had raised of greater, not less, security failed to be met and as a new pattern of social and economic differentiation began to emerge in the region, the regional political notables could only reaffirm their claims about regional unity and sustain their political leadership by taking up demands from below and aggregating those onto the state in the form of the draft Second Breton Plan. Nevertheless, the central theme of the Second Plan remained that of creating new jobs through an accelerated programme of industrial decentralisation.[51] It should be stressed therefore that CELIB's brand of economic regionalism sustained an essentially positive attitude to the region's relationship to major externally-based firms which could be expected to bring new employment to the area. As with our analysis of the farmers' direct actions of 1960–62, the powerful and essentially ambiguous appeal of regional unity in this period – when the emergent patterns of differentiation and division had not yet crystallised into new forms of class consciousness – would seem to need underlining.

As regards the region's political elite, regionalism – in the context of the Fourth Republic when they were 'insiders' at the national level of politics – proved itself well suited to consolidating their role as agents of social control, filtering demands onto the state, defending what limited gains the state could allow, and channelling expectations towards aims that were compatible with national priorities. In the early years of the Fifth Republic, however, when they were less well placed to influence the substantive content of governmental policies, accelerating economic and social changes threatened to 'derail' regionalism, catching the political elite up in a spiral of rising expectations. From early 1963, they seem to have become increasingly taken up with focusing on piecemeal gains and attempting to develop perspectives for the region that might realistically be won from the Government in Paris. In this sense, and in spite of continuing friction between the regime and surviving members of the previous regime's political notability of the Radical and Christian-Democrat centre, Brittany's regional political elite did renew their traditional alignment with national priorities and thus their role as agents of social control. The presence within CELIB of increasing numbers of deputies loyal to the presidential majority was of importance here, as was the subsequent establishment of the consultative CODER, in which CELIB's leading figures, participated, with the exception of Michel Phlipponneau; so too, was the way in which their economic regionalist construct had already made them advocates of a process of economic modernisation in the region that was informed by similar priorities to those which were shaping the restructuring of French capitalism at the national level.[52]

Worker Protest

The third, distinctive strand of regionalist activism in these and subsequent years was precipitated by the decision to close the foundry at Hennebont in Morbihan. That this should have given rise to widespread declarations of opposition and, somewhat later, to militant regionalist demonstrations is not in itself surprising. At the minimum, the loss of 1,500 jobs would affect the economic security of a large number of those living and working in the immediate vicinity (shopkeepers, industrial sub-contractors, various public sector workers), and would deprive food-canning factories in a wider area of a cheap source of tin plate. Beyond this, however, job losses on this scale presented a major challenge to the credibility of CELIB's strategy of modernisation and expanded industrial employment in the region — a strategy dear to the more militant farmers' leaders because it promised to facilitate that reduction in the number of independent farmers in Brittany which was crucial to their strategy for achieving commercial viability! On the availability of other social groups for mobilisation on this issue, Dulong's analysis is clear. What does require further investigation, however, is the way in which this wider regionalist response linked itself into the local *Comité de Défense des Forges*, based on the CGT-organised workforce and the two PCF-run municipalities of Hennebont and Lochrist in Morbihan. Dulong does note the PCF's rapid change of stance (which he dates from late 1963), explaining it in terms of the party's concern to provide a new anti-capitalist orientation to the regionalist movement — in part under pressure from the CGT. The latter, he suggests, had already found it increasingly necessary to develop perspectives of its own for the region in the period of large-scale social mobilisations from 1961, but he takes this analysis no further.[53]

In the early 1960s, the relevant question would seem to have been what strategy the CGT could credibly have offered to save the foundry from closure. Any attempt to answer this immediately takes us away from the peculiarities of Brittany and its class structure and confronts us with the wider issue of the weakness of the French working class and its organised labour movement. As early as 1954 and 1957 the Forges had been under threat of closure, but on neither occasion had the CGT been able to organise an effective campaign linking workers in the Hennebont foundry with those in other steelmaking areas in the north and east. In part this was because the foundry was originally an independent firm, only coming into the orbit of the large Wendel group through quite major loans from the latter (as well as from the state) in 1957, but still not formally integrated into the group; but in any case no effective joint trade union organisation existed in this or any other steel group capable of resisting their state-backed programme of rationalisation and restructuring in what was traditionally a highly cartelised industrial sector.

In contrast, a number of parliamentarians in Brittany had in 1957 taken up the defence of the Forges, proposing, unsuccessfully, that the Government should seek aid for the firm from the European Coal and Steel Community. Now, in 1961, direct militant actions organised around regionalist themes were forcing the Government to make at least piecemeal concessions on a number of fronts.[54] It was in this context that the departmental leaderships of the CGT shifted their position, followed by the PCF which for the first time participated in CELIB's activities by attending the Auray meeting in November 1962, at which all the prospective candidates were solemnly asked to pledge themselves to ensuring the implementation of a promised *loi-programme* incorporating the Second Breton Plan.[55] In June 1963, the *Comité des Forges d'Hennebont* produced its document on 'The Truth about the Hennebont Ironworks', in which emphasis was placed on the need for organised resistance not only by the Hennebont workforce itself 'with their legendary Breton stubbornness', but more generally by 'Breton workers' as a whole — and indeed by a broad alliance of the region's population — to save this 'important element of the economy of Brittany'.[56]

This shift from the language of class to one focusing on a specifically Breton identity was subsequently modified. In its brochure 'For a Happy Brittany within a Democratic France', published in the autumn of 1963, the PCF maintained the idea of a broad-based alliance 'of all Bretons' on limited issues of immediate concern, but argued that a fuller development of Brittany's resources would only be gained by breaking the power of large-scale capital which in turn would first require political change in France as a whole. In pursuit of this perspective the PCF then became involved in the short-lived CAB (*Comité d'Action pour le Bretagne*), an attempted left-wing alliance in the five departments. Meanwhile demonstrations on the Forges issue increasingly focused not on saving the works but on securing adequate sources of alternative employment, and when even these did not materialise, active opposition finally fizzled out before the closure in 1967.[57]

The Development of New Political Strategies and the 1972 Strikes

The early 1960s thus witnessed a series of militant collective actions in the region that can justifiably be characterised as regionalist social movements. These were actions informed by the ideal of a shared regional identity and interest, and the credibility of this ideal was founded, at least in part, on the availability of a common external adversary against whom various groupings in the region could be mobilised, *viz.* the centralised French state machine. Even though the dual process of proletarianisation underway was already at this stage giving rise to new patterns of social differentiation and social conflict, as has been seen, it was CELIB's brand of economic regionalism that supplied the major perspectives and themes for these collective actions.

However, following this period, the tensions engendered by economic modernisation were to be reflected in a number of challenges to the economic regionalist construct from different components within the left and the organised labour movement in Brittany, and these developments were to contribute in important ways to the renewal of doctrine and strategy within the French left from the mid-1960s.[58] From within CELIB Professor Phlipponneau argued that the organisation's failure to win the implementation of either its first or second Breton Plans dictated that priority now be given to fighting for radical reform of the policy-making processes of the French state. This would entail their refusal to participate in the new CODER and their alignment with the French left, so as to combat the Gaullist regime more effectively and, at the same time, win the left to a serious commitment to regional reform. His departure from CELIB and adherence to the SFIO however involved a challenge to CELIB's leadership rather than to the strategy of winning 'modernisation on our terms' that underpinned CELIB's economic regionalism.[59]

A further development on the political left, dating from 1964, was the founding of the UDB (*Union Démocratique de la Bretagne*), formed following a split within the nationalist umbrella organisation, the MOB. This initially small and primarily student-based grouping was to exercise an impact disproportionate to its size in terms of the key themes which it popularised in Brittany, most notably the concept of the region as constituting 'an internal colony' of French capitalism. The UDB's concern to develop a strategy of regional organisation and action informed by class analysis marked a rupture with economic regionalism in that the shared identity on which it focused was that uniting workers in all economic sectors in Brittany against capital, rather than against the French state, and this involved acknowledging the antagonisms of interest between different social classes present in the region. At the same time, however, the UDB emphasised that wider alliances were available within the region to aid the struggle of Breton workers both to overcome their cultural oppression as Bretons and to combat the exceptionally poor conditions to which labour in the region was subjected. In this sense the UDB did then sustain a regionalist ideology, albeit in a form that excluded *de facto* some groups present within the region from participating in this redefined identity of the Breton people as 'an oppressed proletarian nation'.[60]

In addition to these developments, from the mid-1960s the old Catholic trade union, now secularised into the CFDT (*Confédération Démocratique Française du Travail*), built up a growing presence in the region — particularly, it would appear, among recent recruits to the industrial labour force from the region's rural population. As it did so, and within the framework of doctrinal and strategic perspectives adopted nationally — which by the end of the decade, focused on the goal of building a 'socialism based on workers' participation' — the CFDT's regional and local leaderships in Brittany increasingly addressed themselves to the specific problems encountered by those undertaking unskilled or semi-skilled work in firms which had been attracted to the region or were expanding within it not only because of the material inducements available under regional development policies, but also, and especially, because of the reputation of the region — assiduously cultivated by CELIB among others — as offering a docile (i.e., poorly organised and cheap) and industrious work-force.[61] The CFDT thus also took up the issue of the distinctive character of much of Brittany's working-class population and tended to be sensitive to, and to emphasise, the availability of other social actors in the region as allies of industrial workers attempting to organise and improve their conditions of work.[62]

Finally, it should be added that the PSU (*Parti Socialiste Unifié*) enjoyed some strongholds in Brittany, not only in the Côtes-du-Nord but also in the fifth department, Loire-Atlantique.[63] It was here, in the hinterland of the Nantes-Saint Nazaire conurbation, that in conjunction with the political perspectives offered by the PSU in the early 1960s, the leading figure of the 'Paysans-Travailleurs' movement, Bernard Lambert, emerged to prominence arguing that the bulk of small and medium-sized farmers, even those who owned rather than rented their land, were now effectively being reduced to proletarian status as outworkers of 'agribusiness'. Farmers of this type should therefore adopt, with suitable modifications, the organisational forms and tactics of organised labour in industry and the tertiary sector, and give priority to the development of strategic alliances with these groups.[64] Here too analysis focused on class and was applicable to developments in France generally, although clearly of particular pertinence to regions where, for historical reasons, large numbers of small-scale farming units had survived. This then was an analysis which (like that of the CFDT) underlined the extent to which the terms of labour were subject to geographical variations and could therefore be expected to give rise to regionally distinctive organisations, forms of actions and alliances that might blur into *regionalist* social movements.

The 1960s thus witnessed the popularisation of new themes and analyses on the left in Brittany which provided, for certain sectors of its population, alternative explanations of the nature of the region's predicament and alternative perspectives for action to those afforded by the economic regionalist construct of CELIB and those variants on its theme of 'modernisation on our terms' to which the region's political notability continued to subscribe, from within a political spectrum ranging from the rump of the Radical and Christian-Democrat centre, surviving uneasily in the institutional and ideological framework of the Fifth Republic, through Independent Republicans to Gaullists. These political and ideological developments, and the underlying economic trends which they sought to account for, provided the changed context for a third phase of large-scale social mobilisations in the early 1970s, in particular the two strikes of 1972.

The Joint Français Strike

The first of these strikes involved the workforce of the Joint Français rubber factory at St. Brieuc, one of the major industrial decentralisation operations from which the region had benefitted in the early 1960s.[65] The strike started on 13 March and was to last two months, with the strikers, a majority of whom were women, pursuing parity with the main Joint

Français factory at Bezons. The involvement of sections of the region's farmers in an alliance with CFDT-led workers, around platforms that highlighted the distinctive problems which both these groups faced in the specific context of this region, had created growing difficulties for the development of an effective alliance between the two main trade union organisations in Brittany, and these were to develop in acute form during the Joint Français strike.[66] In order to account for these divisions, Dulong provides an interesting interpretation of the differences in the nature of their respective memberships, which is persuasive to a degree (although lacking in supporting data). The CGT is portrayed as being based, in Brittany, in longer-established, relatively well-organised sections of the workforce, for the most part employed by the state, and thus disposed to combine a trade union strategy of economic advance with a specifically political strategy directed at *the state*. The CFDT, in contrast, is said to have recruited primarily in the 'new' working class employed in decentralised industries, drawn for the most part from a rural background and bringing with them a deep-seated opposition to capitalism as the expropriator of the peasantry, and therefore readily available for mobilisation around themes portraying the region and its population as the victims of *capitalism*.[67]

However, what is offered here again is an approach which privileges exclusively regional factors at the expense of exploring the impact on working-class struggles in this region of national divisions of policy and strategy between the two main unions. As regards the conduct of the strike, the majority union in the factory was the CFDT, and its national trade union strategy was undoubtedly important — as was the intransigence of the national management — in radicalising and extending the dispute.[68] As with the struggle to save the Forges d'Hennebont a decade earlier, the interplay between the Joint Français strikers and the nature of the alliances available to them requires careful examination. For those employed a decade later in this and similar decentralised factories, the raised expectations of the early 1960s had been deceived: only limited, poorly paid and, it seemed, vulnerable sources of industrial employment had been won. What leverage could these workers use to win their case? They were aware that their low pay was directly related to the terms on which firms like theirs had been encouraged to decentralise.[69] In the absence of a trade union combine in the parent company strong enough to impose the strikers' case on management, they pursued other types of action which were undoubtedly less effective in terms of their impact on the head office of CGE, but which did enable the strikers to hold out until the management was finally prepared to cede a good part of their claim on 6 May.[70]

The strike eventually attracted very broad support within the region, covering the whole political spectrum. Much of this was expressed in the cross-class language of regionalism and focused on the fact that the employers concerned were based outside of the region.[71] But this regionalism blurred into a more specifically anti-capitalist theme concerning the region's 'colonial' status as a pool of cheap, unskilled labour for large French and multi-national firms. The very active support of local farmers organised in the CDJA (*Centre Départmental de Jeunes Agriculteurs*), moreover, led that organisation later that year officially to adopt, for the first time, the analysis of the *Paysans-Travailleurs* tendency:

> The essential lesson to be learned from our intervention in the Joint Français strike is that we share the same struggle, that of remunerating our labour, and that we shall only suceed if we create a new balance of forces against those who own capital (that is, those who exploit us).[72]

However, although the region itself, and in particular the department of Côtes-du-Nord, was the most important source of financial support for the strikers, if the total collected, amounting to some 1.6 million francs, is broken down not on a geographical but on an occupational basis, the largest single component — 42 per cent — is seen to have been provided by the trade union movement, and this trade union financial support extended well beyond the region primarily to areas with large chemical industries, or where the CFDT was strongly organised.[73] The Joint Français strike thus developed several overlapping dimensions in terms of the nature of the support it mobilised. The points discussed here suggest that, in terms of the class basis of the core of the support which it mobilised, and also of the generally limited geographical scope of that class mobilisation, the Joint Français strike warrants being interpreted as a *regional* social movement. While it acquired — though only in a fragmented and limited fashion — some of the resonance of a *national* social movement, it nonetheless served to sustain specifically regionalist themes and perspectives among certain political groupings and social strata within the region. Thus it could be argued that, at the same time, it provided the focus for what was, in part, a *regionalist* social movement.

The Milk Strike

As the St. Brieuc strike ended, a second, quite unprecedented strike movement got underway in the region's agricultural sector. The 'Milk Strike' involved some fifty thousand small and medium-sized dairy farmers who refused to deliver milk to the cooperative and private sector dairies to which they were under contract. They were mobilised in support of new payment policies which would guarantee them an income at least equivalent to the nationally negotiated minimum for industrial workers, and against what they designated as an adversary coalition comprised not only of the management of both cooperative and private sector dairies, but also of the larger dairy farmers, who enjoyed particularly advantageous terms under the contracts in force in both sectors. This coalition, it was claimed, had accepted the logic of profitability dictated by the monopoly sectors of French industrial and financial capital and had incorporated it in local and regional policies which protected the interests of each component of the coalition at the expense of the majority of the dairy farmers whose status was thereby reduced to that of proletarianised 'outworkers' for private and cooperative firms, working on a piecework basis.[74]

Dulong, in analysing the milk strike, is curiously unwilling to accept that there was an objective clash of class interests between what he insists on terming, even in this later period, the region's 'medium peasantry' and 'those peasants in a transitional situation'.[75] Although his initial account of the transition in agriculture in the region (and of the periodisation of this transition) from a 'precapitalist' to a 'capitalist' mode of production does allow for the possibility of some part of his 'upper stratum' of medium-sized farmers turning themselves into capitalist entrepeneurs, his brief remarks on this strike movement are largely taken up with denying that this was the case, but without reference to any empirical data at all. In spite of the penetration of the forces of modern capitalism into rural Brittany, therefore, what we still have here is a 'peasantry', one that is differentiated into 'a prosperous fraction and a lower fraction for which no transition is possible', and indeed between these and a third stratum of purely artisanal production. The crucial factor in his analysis is that Brittany's better-off farmers remain working farmers (*chefs d'exploitation*) unlike the agrarian capitalists of the Paris Basin and the north; he does not here develop any analysis of the different forms of contracts adopted by both cooperative and private sector farms, nor does he raise the issue of whether these contracts provide for a qualitatively different relationship to the means of food production as between larger and smaller farmers.[76]

This is somewhat paradoxical: regionalism was initially identified by him as tending to 'displace the real opposition (of class) by a geographical opposition . . . to replace the principal contradiction by a secondary one'.[77] However, faced with *Paysans-Travailleurs* tendency's pursuit of an alliance between themselves, as a specific component of the working class, and other sectors of the working class in the region, Dulong argues that the primary cause of the failure of Brittany's peasantry to maintain a strategy reflecting their underlying unity of interest 'as farmers' is the penetration into sections of the region's farmers of a quite particular 'trade union ideology', developed by that section of the working class in the region which was organised by the CFDT. It is this which explains why the upper stratum of farmers developed, instead, an alliance with fractions of the region's industrial and commercial bourgeoisie.[78] What is discounted without serious examination by Dulong is the possibility that the process by which food production in this region has been integrated under the control of large-scale French and multinational capital, has resulted in the creation of a new component of the French working class, one subject to quite distinctive terms of labour.

In the 'Milk Strike' of 1972, the lines of demarcation that emerged were ones not easily susceptible to regionalist interpretation, even though the farmers involved, like the Joint Français strikers, were themselves convinced that their peculiarly unfavourable circumstances were in some way linked to their regional location. If the 'Milk Strike' — like that at Joint Français, only to a greater degree — warrants being characterised as a regional, rather than a regionalist social movement, this is not to accept Dulong's problematic of principal versus secondary contradictions, for we have been concerned here precisely with social movements which, while also having a geographical appearance, have in fact had a class basis.

Conclusion

In respect of regionalism in Brittany this chapter has therefore pointed to its contradictory and ambiguous character and has offered a quite different pattern of relationships from those, suggested by Dulong, between regionalism and the contending class forces in this area of France in the post-war period.

The optimistic, modernising content of economic regionalism in the 1950s, it has been suggested, served to consolidate the new regional political elite's role of social control and to bind the region's population into an economic strategy consonant with the national priorities being developed by the state for French capitalism. In the early 1960s, the possibilities open to CELIB's political notables for sustaining their role were threatened, as rising social tensions forced them to take up larger demands from the region. Nevertheless, a strategy of regional unity centring on the need for modernisation and, above all, industrial decentralisation retained its appeal for important sectors of farmers, and could also appeal to isolated and relatively weak groups of workers threatened by the process of capital restructuring. By the early 1970s, however, it has been argued, while the region's political notables still sought to use the unifying appeal of regionalism, albeit in much modified form, there was now the basis for more classical forms of class struggle to develop — if in a distinctive regional form — among workers in industry and agriculture for whom broader alliances, with corresponding groups elsewhere in France, were not easy to develop.

Notes

1 The argument here is similar to that concerning the *nationalist* ideological construct of 'Wales' developed in Gwyn A. Williams, *When Was Wales?* (Cardiff: BBC Publications, 1980). The issue of *where* Brittany is, and whether or not it incorporates the fifth, southern department of Loire-Atlantique, has been controversial, but differing positions in this issue largely reflect deeper differences as to the purpose for which the regional identity of Brittany is being constructed; see below, pp. 174–177.

2 It is therefore on this second count that regionalist movements should be distinguished from nationalist ones, which seek to break from existing nation-state institutions and create a separate, independent state. In the postwar period, Brittany has seen nationalist as well as regionalist organisations, in particular the MOB (*Mouvement pour l'Organisation de la Bretagne*, founded in 1957) and the FLB (*Front de la Libération de la Bretagne*, dating from 1956) and its successor groupings. On these, see in particular J. E. Reece, *The Bretons Against France: Ethnic Minority Nationalism in the Twentieth Century* (Chapel Hill: University of North Carolina Press, 1977), chs. 8 and 9.

3 The development of political ideologies and parties, informed by a geographical mode of conceptualisation insofar as the nation-state is concerned but combining this with other, non-geographical, forms of identity, modified the operation of -this principle from the outset. More recently, it has also been supplemented by the increasing recognition of organised interests as providing 'a second pillar of representation' and by procedures which serve to institutionalise corporatist forms of representation.

4 This point is effectively recognised, although its implications are not pursued, in many works on the emergence of regional development policies in France. One case of a member of the prefectoral corps taking up the task of promoting the development of a regional identity is that of P. Blanc-Gonnet and CEBANOR (*Le Comité Régional d'Expansion de Basse-Normandie*); see Blanc-Gonnet, *L'administration régionale en Basse-Normandie* (Paris: Cujas, 1969). A later example of the Gaullist state's use of regionalist themes for its own purpose is documented by Sidney Tarrow in his 'Regional Policy, Ideology and Peripheral Defence: The Case of Fos-sur-Mer', in S. Tarrow, *et al., Territorial Politics in Industrial Nations* (New York: Praeger, 1978).

5 *La question bretonne* (Paris: Presses de la Fondation Nationale des Sciences Politiques, 1975); this is a revised edition of his earlier work, *Le régionalisme en Bretagne* (Paris: CORDES Report for the Commissariat Général du Plan, 1973). Also *Les régions, l'Etat et la société locale* Paris: Presses Universitaires de France, 1978).

6 *La question bretonne*, op. cit., pp. 14–30.

7 Ibid., p. 31: '. . . it is indeed the economic question to which they each refer even though they deal with it through different ideological modes.'

8 Ibid., pp. 35–8.

9 Ibid., p. 9.

10 Ibid., pp. 34 and 70.

11 His analysis centres on the relative homogeneity and backwardness of farming in the region. The region's long-standing industrial sector, based on what are clearly capitalist social relations, is incorporated into this 'precapitalist' formation by virtue of its location; the relationship of much of it, up or down-stream, to agricultural production; and above all the social ties linking it into the rural population; see especially ibid., pp. 40–2. Although in this version he introduces the concept of uneven development and notes in places that the regional society and its mode of production are at the same time, to a degree, integrated into 'France taken as a whole', this has little bearing on the main lines of his analysis or on his central hypothesis which stresses the region's degree of autonomy and internal coherence.

12 Dulong, in his preface, seems to suggest that it is the case-study method in itself which constrains him in terms of the problematic which he can appropriately investigate. Here it is being argued that it is his conceptualisation of the problem of Breton regionalism which is limiting. Ibid.

13 Ibid., p. 35; see also pp. 9 and 203. On Touraine's analysis of social movements see in particular A. Touraine, *La voix et le regard* (Paris: Seuil, 1978), ch. 4.

14 R. Dulong, *La question bretonne*, p. 203. This formulation raises wider problems since it involves a particularly constrictive interpretation of the relationship between state and society.

15 This type of conceptualisation is most clearly adopted in the literature on internal colonialism; see for example, R. Lafont, *La révolution régionaliste* (Paris: Gallimard, 1967), and M. Hechter, *Internal Colonialism: the Celtic Fringe in British National Development 1536-1966* (London: Routledge and Kegan Paul, 1975). It is also present, I would argue, in the works of P. Grémion, J.-P. Worms and J.-C. Thoenig, in which it is married to Michel Crozier's approach to organisation theory. For a fuller discussion of the following points see my 'Problems in the Study of France's Regional Political Elites: The Case of Post-War Brittany', in Jolyon Howorth and P. G. Cerny, eds, *Elites in France: Origins, Reproduction and Power* (London: Frances Pinter Ltd., 1981).

16 See J. Médard, 'Political Clientelism in a Non-Clientelist Political System: The Case of France', paper presented to the workshop on *Clientelism*, European Consortium for Political Research, Joint Sessions of Workshops, Florence, March, 1980; also J. Becquart-Leclerc, *Paradoxes du Pouvoir Local* (Paris: Presses de la Fondation Nationale des Sciences Politiques, 1976).

17 See above, p. 176 and n.14; and pp. 194–6, below.

18 Cf. n. 10. At issue here is the degree to which economic activities in the region were already by the Second World War, and increasingly from the early 1950s, integrated into the national economy in terms of capital ownership, location of market(s), and the source and characteristics of factors of production (including labour). This in turn raises further questions concerning the relationship that had previously obtained between regional and national developments and its causality, for the patterns of activities present in the region are to be accounted for in some measure historically as the product of the French nation-state's pursuit of protectionist policies over the preceding century.

19 D. Smith, 'Wales Through the Looking Glass' in D. Smith, ed., *A People and a Proletariat* (London: Pluto Press, 1980).

20 Primarily, *La vie bretonne*, independent journal under the control of J. Martray, founder and General Secretary of CELIB. Also *Rapport d'ensemble sur un plan*

d'aménagement, de modernisation et d'équipement de la Bretagne 1954–1958 (*Le Rapport Vert*) (La Baule: CELIB, 1953) and later, R. Pleven, *L'avenir de la Bretagne* (Paris: Calmann-Lévy, 1961).

21 See below, pp. 177–80. On the similar bodies which participated in the 'Conférence Nationale des Economies Régionales', founded in October 1952, see J. Tessier, 'Les comités régionaux d'expansion économique et leur conférence nationale', in *Revue Administrative*, vol. 8, no. 48 (November–December, 1955), pp. 593–8.

22 The major mobilisations that did occur in this period centred on the participation of the region's farmers in the national FNSEA (Fédération Nationale des Syndicats d'Exploitants Agricoles) campaigns in favour of price support and the index-linking of agricultural prices.

23 See my unpublished doctoral thesis, *Regionalism, Regional Development Policies and the 'Economie Concertée': A Case Study of Brittany* (University of Sussex, 1978), ch. 2.

24 CELIB's contribution to these processes was developed through its involvement in the establishment of both the *Société de Développement Régional de la Bretagne* (SDRB) and the *Société d'Economie Mixte d'Aménagement et d'Equipement de la Bretagne* (SEMAEB), and through its own specialised agency, the *Bureau d'Etudes Industrielles et Artisanales* (BEIA), which acted as a broker between local authorities and prospective decentralising industries. In addition, see p. 179 for its role *vis-à-vis* agriculture in the region.

25 400 delegates were present at the St. Brieuc 'Etats-Généraux' when the final draft plan was adopted in March 1953. The Planning Commissariat was closely involved especially in the discussion and drafting of the section on agricultural perspectives, but insisted that the Breton Plan remained a strictly unofficial undertaking. *L'Ouest-France*, the region's leading daily paper, campaigned in its columns for the plan, giving it much publicity.

26 Joseph Martray was clear in his Foreword to the Plan: 'our task is to convince public opinion in Brittany', and he reminded the Bretons of 'their own responsibility for the economic backwardness of their region'. *Le Rapport Vert*, op. cit., p. 8.

27 Cf. n. 24. Subsequently CELIB also edited a brochure directed at industrial firms in the Paris region entitled *Bretagne, pays de main-d'oeuvre: région-pilote de la décentralisation* (1956).

28 On these developments in Breton agriculture, see in particular, G. Wright, *Rural Revolution in France: The Peasantry in the Twentieth Century* (Stanford, Cal.: Stanford University Press, 1964), esp. pp. 149–54.

29 See J. E. Reece, op. cit. The Vichy period itself is of particular importance. See also Y. Gicquel, *Le Comité Consultatif de Bretagne (1940–43)* (Rennes: Simon, 1961), of which Martray was a member. Some active elements in the Breton cultural movement where later to be closely associated with the nationalists and later with the left-wing *Union Démocratique de la Bretagne* (UDB). On these see Reece, op. cit., ch. 8.

30 Earlier ministerial participants from the region, Tanguy-Prigent, SFIO (Socialist) Deputy for Finistère, and P. Ihuel, MRP (Christian Democrat) from Morbihan actively supported CELIB from 1950. The then ex-Prime Minister, R. Pleven (from the small radical grouping, *Union Démocratique et Socialiste de la Résistance*), based in Côtes-du-Nord, became interested in CELIB in 1951 when he was Minister of Defence; shortly afterwards he was re-invested as Prime Minister.

31 All candidates in the 4 departments, except those of the Communist Party, signed CELIB's 'pledge' on regional action before the 1951 elections. Only Pleven, in the Côtes-du-Nord, was able to put together a Third Force alliance list (UDSR, SFIO, MRP).

32 For a succinct account of the concept of a 'concerted economy' by one of its foremost exponents, see F. Bloch-Laîné, *A la recherche d'une 'économie concertée'* (Paris: Editions de l'Epargne, 1964, 3rd edn.); for a critical review of its operation, see S. Cohen, *Modern Capitalist Planning: The French Model* (London: Weidenfeld and Nicolson, 1969).

33 The historical capital of Brittany was Nantes (now part of the department of Loire-Atlantique, and seat of the regional prefecture of the Pays de Loire); however, the Nantes-St. Nazaire industrial conurbation itself does not fit easily with this problematic of backwardness on which CELIB came to focus.

34 For a detailed account of the economy and demography of the four departments in the fifties, see M. Phlipponneau, *Debout Bretagne!* (St. Brieuc: Presses Universitaires de la Bretagne, 1970).

35 On these developments in agriculture, see in particular C. Canevet, *L'agriculture de groupe en Bretagne* (Rennes: Université de la Haute Bretagne, 1970). Dulong's discussion of the new industrial working class as the basis for the 'regionalist trade union ideology' of the CFDT is discussed below, p. 190; his account of developments in agriculture, however, focuses on the survival of 'a peasantry' internally divided, but not in terms of class, see below, pp. 194-5.

36 On the origins of the First Breton Plan, see my 'Problems in the Study of France's Regional Political Elites', op. cit.

37 See above, n. 20.

38 This argument frequently appears in *La Vie Bretonne* and is also employed in M. Phlipponneau, op. cit.

39 See S. Cohen, op. cit., part IV.

40 Indicative of these concerns are the two series of articles which appeared in special issues of the *Revue Economique* and the *Revue Française de Science Politique* in 1956.

41 A. Touraine, op. cit., pp. 33-6 and 105-8.

42 R. Dulong, *La question bretonne*, op. cit., esp. pp. 54-67.

43 'The period in which transition (to capitalism) was still possible', ibid., pp. 63-5. Only subsistence farmers are by this stage excluded from this regional unity.

44 On 'the "natural" regionalism of peasant movements', see ibid., pp. 157-8.

45 See *Le Monde*, 26 May-23 June 1961, 16-17 October 1960, and June 1960. Also J.-P. Le Dantec, *Bretagne: renaissance d'un peuple* (Paris: Gallimard, 1974), ch. 2, and G. Wright, op. cit., p. 167; see also S. Quiers-Valette, 'Les causes économiques du mécontentement des agriculteurs français en 1961', and H. Mendras, 'Les manifestations de juin 1961', both in *Revue Française de Science Politique*, vol. XII, no. 3 (September, 1962), pp. 555-99 and 647-71.

46 See A. Touraine, op. cit.

47 For further details, see *L'année politique, économique et sociale, 1962* (Paris: Presses Universitaires de France, 1963), pp. 239-44; *La Vie Bretonne*, no. 63 (December, 1962); and *Le Monde*, September 1962. The issues involved here were ones which directly affected not only the regional workforce of the SNCF, farmers, related cooperative and private wholesalers and processing firms (and many other industries), but also the travelling public more generally.

48 The immediate issue sparking this confrontation was that of deciding how CELIB should respond to the new consultative body introduced under the regional reform decrees of March 1964 — the CODER (*Commission de Développement Economique Régional*); see J. E. S. Hayward, 'From Functional Regionalism to Functional Representation: The Battle of Brittany', *Political Studies*, vol. XVII, no. 1 (March, 1969), pp. 48-75.

49 R. Dulong, *La question bretonne*, op. cit., p. 112.

50 On the PCF's involvement, see below, pp. 187-9. At the Auray meeting organised by CELIB, eighty-four candidates from the five departments pledged their

support for the framework-law on special development policies for Western France which Pleven and Ihuel had tabled in the budget in June 1962. The Loire-Atlantique departmental council passed a resolution in February 1962 requesting that it be included in any special programme adopted for Brittany. The twenty-six local councils in this department did not seek affiliation to CELIB until early 1963. By this time, it should be noted, six out of a total of eight deputies representing seats in Loire-Atlantique had joined CELIB's Parliamentary Commission (five of the six being Gaullists).

51 The Second Breton Plan was adopted at CELIB's annual general meeting held at Lorient in June 1962.

52 On the presence of Gaullist deputies from the fifth department, see above, n. 49; the Gaullists and their allies now held fourteen of the four departments' twenty-five seats. On the CODER, see above, n. 47. The Government increasingly attempted to substitute the more amorphous unit of 'Western France' for that of Brittany in formulating its development policies for the region. Electoral considerations were also relevant. While the vote for components of the centre and right outside of the presidential majority remained higher in Brittany than nationally in November 1962, as it had in 1958 (and conversely the Gaullist vote was somewhat lower), politicians of these tendencies needed to take into account the exceptionally high vote for the October constitutional reform referendum in these four departments (over 57 per cent of the registered electorate, as compared to 46 per cent in France as a whole, approving de Gaulle's proposals).

53 R. Dulong, *La question bretonne*, op. cit., p. 136.

54 In June 1961 the Government promised action on the motorway, and the Minister of Interior received a delegation of CELIB's Parliamentary Commission. In early October the Minister of Public Works met representatives of CELIB's executive committee and offered road and rail concession. Late in October P. Ihuel was received by President de Gaulle.

55 The November 1962 legislative elections provided the occasion for the PCF to develop an informal electoral alliance at the national level with the SFIO for the first time, thus breaking the party's 'ghettoisation'.

56 Reprinted in *La Vie Bretonne* (1963).

57 R. Dulong, *La question bretonne*, op. cit., pp. 161–4 and 166–8.

58 Regional decentralisation, through directly elected assemblies with extended powers, was to be an important part of the new programmatic commitments developed by the Communist and Socialist parties in the 1970s, and is the object of a major reform package, including reducing the powers of the prefectoral corps, being prepared by the Mauroy Government in 1981. Equally, growth in both membership of and electoral support for the Socialist Party after 1969 in Brittany was to be a notable feature of that party's renewal in the 1970s.

59 For details on the 1964 annual general meeting of CELIB held at Brest, at which Professor Phlipponneau was persuaded to withdraw his motion of opposition in the name of regional unity, see *La Vie Bretonne*, nos. 79–80 (June–July 1964), and J. E. S. Hayward, loc. cit.

60 On the UDB, see in particular J. E. Reece, op. cit., ch. 8, and the organisation's journal, *Le Peuple Breton*.

61 See above, note 26.

62 On the positions of the CFDT in the region and nationally, see J. Capdevielle, E. Dupoirier and G. Lorant, *La grève du Joint Français* (Paris: Presses de la Fondation Nationale des Sciences Politiques, 1975), pp. 7–15 and 105–18. The CFDT was organised at the regional level, whereas the CGT only had departmental organisations above its local branches.

63 From 1962 Y. Le Foll held the St. Brieuc seat in the Côtes-du-Nord for the PSU.

64 For a full exposition of the argument of the *Paysans-Travailleurs* tendency, see

B. Lambert, *Les paysans dans la lutte des classes* (Paris: Seuil, 1970). S. Mallet, *Les Paysans contre le passé* (Paris: Seuil, 1963) is an earlier contribution by a leading PSU activist to the debate on changes taking place in French agriculture.

65 The Joint Français itself came under the ownership of CGE (the *Compagnie Générale d'Electricité*) in the year in which the St. Brieuc factory opened. The original terms for Joint Français's decentralisation were negotiated through SEMEAB by the then centre-right municipal council, and were subsequently ratified, not without some dissension, by the new PSU-led majority.

The following section draws on J. Capdevielle *et al.*, op. cit.; M. Phlipponneau, *Au Joint Français, les ouvriers bretons . . .* (St. Brieuc: Presses Universitaires de Bretagne, 1972); and J.-P. Le Dantec, op. cit.

66 On the disunity and recriminations between the two unions during the strike, see J. Capdevielle, *et al.*, op. cit., pp. 110–12. A year later 3 CFDT members of the works committee voted in support of the management's decision to sack a CGT shop-steward; ibid., p. 136.

67 R. Dulong, *La question bretonne*, op. cit., pp. 90–2.

68 See above, n. 60.

69 CGE paid a nominal 1,400 francs for the site, with the bulk of its actual cost, variously estimated between 1.8 and 3 million francs, being borne by the local ratepayers, who also financed special grants for each job created. In addition, the firm was charged exceptionally low water rates, and was exempted from local rates for five years.

70 There were two two-hour stoppages at the Bezons factory, where the CGT was the majority union. At the level of the CGE trust itself only financial support was organised; J. Capdevielle, *et al.*, op. cit., pp. 85–8.

71 Of twenty-one local committees of support with some degree of local municipal support in the four departments, ten were in left-wing municipalities, two in centre-led municipalities and nine in municipalities run by components of the presidential majority; ibid., pp. 71–8 and 165.

72 Ibid., p. 66.

73 Ibid., pp. 92–9.

74 On the 'Milk Strike', see *Le Monde*, May 1972, and J.-P. Le Dantec, op. cit., pp. 24–34 and 222–7.

75 R. Dulong, *La question bretonne*, op. cit., pp. 54–67 and 157–8.

76 On the terms of the contracts developed in both the cooperative and private sectors, see especially, C. Canevet, op. cit.; and B. Lambert, op. cit.

77 R. Dulong, *La question bretonne*, op. cit., p. 18.

78 Ibid., pp. 157–8.

9 The Anti-Nuclear Movement and the Rise of Political Ecology

TONY CHAFER
Lecturer in Languages and Area Studies
Portsmouth Polytechnic

On 6 March 1974 the Prime Minister, Pierre Messmer, announced that France was to embark upon the world's most ambitious civil nuclear programme, with 70 per cent of France's electricity (50,000 MW) to be generated in nuclear power stations by 1985 and two hundred nuclear power stations to be completed by the year 2000. While this did not mark the very beginning of the French anti-nuclear movement (France's first anti-nuclear demonstration had taken place at Fessenheim in Alsace on 12 April 1971 and had been followed by one at Bugey on 10 July 1971), it was certainly this announcement which gave the movement impetus and national importance. Henceforth the nuclear question was to be at the centre of the political and social stage and the anti-nuclear movement was to become a focus of dissent from the established order.

As it has gained in importance, the anti-nuclear movement has become the subject of much attention from, amongst others, politicians, scientists, journalists and sociologists. The aim of this chapter is not to examine the relative merits of the arguments for and against nuclear power but rather to study the emergence of the anti-nuclear movement as a focus of dissent from the established order and attempt an initial assessment of its significance and impact.

It must first be made clear, however, that I am concerned here exclusively with the movement against *civil* nuclear energy. The movement against nuclear arms has a separate existence and, as Claude Bourdet points out in a recent interview, many ecologists in France 'still do not believe that the nuclear bomb represents an immediate or urgent threat'.[1] The fact that the issues of civil and military applications of nuclear technology are perceived as separate issues by the anti-nuclear movement itself is further confirmed by the results of the meeting the Touraine group of sociologists arranged between members of the anti-nuclear movement and an army general.[2] As Touraine points out, the anti-nuclear militants themselves are led to make a clear distinction between the state, the military, international questions, national sovereignty and the bomb, on the one hand, and, on the other, those problems less directly linked with the state — the problems and conflicts of everyday life in peacetime, which are characteristic of a particular type of society and one of which is civil nuclear power.

As Brendan Prendiville points out in a recent review of Alain Touraine's *La prophétie antinucléaire*, the most comprehensive study, to date, of the French anti-nuclear movement: 'Possibly the most important single factor in the shaping of the present movement is the battle and eventual victory of the ecologists over the environmentalists. This battle gave birth to political ecology'.[3] In order to assess the significance of this, it will first be necessary to give a brief history of the anti-nuclear movement, so as to show how the focus of its opposition has changed and how it has played a central role in the emergence of political ecology. From a movement the sole argument of which appeared to be a principled refusal of nuclear energy based on fear due to the risks inherent in the nuclear cycle, the anti-nuclear movements has evolved into a movement which now provides a comprehensive social and political critique of the nuclear society and proposes an alternative model for the future development of a non-nuclear society.

The nuclear question is no longer simply a technical or scientific one between experts about how long fossil fuels will last or the true significance of the risks, real or imagined, of nuclear power. This evolution has already led, and will undoubtedly continue to lead, to important changes, both within the anti-nuclear movement itself and in the nature of the responses it demands from the established social and political institutions. An appreciation of these changes may help us to understand the reasons for the apparent lack of impact of the anti-nuclear movement on past Government policy and make possible some initial indications as to the likely future significance of the movement in the light of these developments and of the coming to power of a Socialist government in 1981.

I. The Emergence of Political Ecology: An Historical Outline

The word ecology was first used by a German scientist, E. Haeckel, in 1866 in his study of ecosystems, but the first interest in nature conservation in France dates back to the creation of the Société Nationale de Protection de la Nature in 1920 and it is not until the mid-1960s, with the emergence of *comités de défense de l'environnement*, that environmental issues begin to take on importance outside scientific circles.

The aim of most of these groups was confined to the elimination of some of the consequences of industrial society, but no attempt was made to put into question the type of society which had given rise to these problems. Their objectives were therefore specific and limited.

For the origins of political ecology, and of the anti-nuclear movement in particular, we must turn to the events of May 1968, one of the major currents of which is a critique of consumer society and a questioning of the objectives of a modern industrial society. As D. Simonnet puts it: 'The consumer society was the target of the *soixante-huitards*, who formulated the first political critiques of the ecological status quo by questioning the ends of industrial society and advocating a revolution of everyday life.'[4] Within the May movement there were, however, other equally important and often contradictory currents. There was the Marxist current with its critique of capitalist society, as expressed in particular by the Trotskyists and Maoists, for whom the May events were an opportunity to overthrow the bourgeois state and wrest economic and political power from the dominant capitalist class. There was also the anarchist current, with its stress on individual liberty and the autonomy of the individual against all forms of power and in particular that of the central state. The former aimed to control the state, the latter to destroy state power of any sort. The ideological divide between the Marxists and anarchist currents on the French left traditionally surfaces with renewed vigour at crisis points in French history: the events of 1848, 1871 and the arguments between the Surrealists and the Communists between the wars are but a few examples.

The anti-nuclear movement, with its origins in May 1968, contains within it and perpetuates elements of each of these currents: the Marxist critique of capitalist society, the anarchist critique of state power and the specifically 1968 critique of consumer society. In an important respect, the anti-nuclear movement can be seen as a further example of a time-honoured form of protest in France, a renewed expression of what Jack Hayward has called the 'dissentient France'.[5] It is the re-emergence of a counter political culture, in rebellion both against an authoritarian, alienating, over-centralised and over-hierarchical system, and against a society inegalitarian in terms of access to power as well as incomes and wealth, based on exploitative relationships between different social classes. These divergent currents, and the resistance of important elements of the environmentalist movement to the politicisation of ecological issues, are essential to an understanding of the weakness of the anti-nuclear movement. This will only begin to emerge clearly, however, after the demonstration against the project to build a fast-breeder reactor at Creys-Malville in July 1977.

In the meantime, awareness of environmental issues continued to grow, and many new environmentalist and ecologist organisations were created (up to around twenty per week according to Hayward).[6] The year 1970 was European Nature Conservation Year and a number of new associations were created during the year. The most notable of these were *Survivre et Vivre*, a grouping of radical scientists, and the *Comité de Sauvegarde de Fessenheim et de la Plaine du Rhin* (CSFR) which, as already mentioned, was later to organise France's first anti-nuclear demonstration at Fessenheim in 1971. The French arm of the international association Friends of the Earth, *Les Amis de la Terre*, was also formed in Paris in 1970. The year 1971 saw the creation of a *Ministère de la Protection de la Nature et de l'Environnement*, which Robert Poujade, France's first Environment Minister, was later to call *'le ministère de l'impossible'*. The activities of ecologists continued to grow, with the widely-reported demonstration against the extension of a military camp in the Larzac in November 1971 and the foundation of the first ecologist magazines: *Le Gueule Ouverte* in 1972 and *Le Sauvage* in 1973.

The activities of the ecologists took a new turn in March 1973, when the Alsace group *Ecologie et Survie* put forward a candidate at Mulhouse for the 1973 parliamentary elections. This marked the entry of the ecologists into the political arena and prepared the way for the agronomist René Dumont's campaign for the 1974 presidential elections. It was undoubtedly the announcement of France's nuclear programme in March 1974 that provided much of the impetus for the ecologists' decision to present a candidate at these elections. Although there was never any chance of Dumont being elected, his election campaign helped to focus attention on the ecological and anti-nuclear issues. However, while giving impetus to the movement, Dumont's campaign also highlighted splits within it. Many groups did not agree with the entry of ecology into the political arena and refused to support Dumont, preferring to confine their activity to local campaigns against specific developments such as a local construction project or power station. This split became even more evident at the ecologists' first national gathering at Bazoches in June 1974, at which no agreement was reached on proposals for a national structure. Despite this a national association, *Mouvement Ecologique*, was founded a few months later, although it was attacked by many ecologist groups for claiming to speak on behalf of the entire ecologist movement. Many did not, in fact, join it, and others that did later left.

These problems are indicative of the deep-seated fear within the movement of large structures and of any structure similar in type to that of a political party. Local groups jealously defended their autonomy and many ecologists remained extremely suspicious of traditional political parties and institutions.

During the 1970s opposition to nuclear power intensified and the PSU (the Unified Socialist Party) became the first political party to adopt an anti-nuclear position. An increasing number of petitions demanded a moratorium on the development of nuclear power, with the suspension of the Government's nuclear power programme in order to give time for a full and informed public debate on France's energy problem. This demand for a 'moratorium' was also taken up within the nuclear industry by members of France's second largest trade union, the CFDT (*Confédération Française Démocratique du Travail*) and a group of its members working in the French nuclear industry published in 1975 what is still the most thorough analysis in French of the whole nuclear question, *Le dossier électronucléaire*.[7] The adoption of an anti-nuclear stance by a political party, and the growing opposition to the Government's nuclear programme in parts of the trade union movement, are indicative of the increasingly political nature of the issue. The press statement issued by the CFDT on 12 May 1975, launching its book *Le dossier électronucléaire*, was significant in this respect in that it specifically stated that it was not opposed to the Government's nuclear programme through fear but 'because we reject the model of society which is implicit in the way nuclear power stations are run and the way they affect the wider society'.[8] It advocated an alternative energy policy which would be the result of a democratic debate and be based on the principle of a less centralised industrial society.

The first phase of the anti-nuclear movement's activity reached a peak with the demonstration at Creys-Malville on 31 July 1977, at which there were violent confrontations with the police and one demonstrator was killed. Certain commentators suggested that Malville represented a major defeat for the anti-nuclear movement and that, after the successes at the polls in the March 1977 municipal elections (in Paris, for example, they obtained an average of 10 per cent of the votes cast), their importance might now diminish. The struggle against the plan to build a nuclear power station at Plogoff in Brittany in 1980 shows that this judgement is a little premature, although the experience of Creys-Malville undoubtedly represents a turning point for the anti-nuclear movement, and its approach was to change significantly after July 1977.

Creys-Malville is the site chosen for France's first commercial fast-breeder reactor, '*Superphénix*'. Because of its sheer size and the increased risks involved, opposition to the fast-breeder reactor became a focus for the anti-nuclear movement and fifty thousand people gathered at the site to demonstrate their opposition to it. After the success of an earlier demonstration at Malville the year before, the anti-nuclear movement hoped to repeat its success in 1977. However, in the meantime, the movement had attracted new elements: 'Following the 1976 success, violent elements looking for a confrontation with the state came on the scene'.[9] The ecologists, who are dedicated to non-violence, became worried by the increasing influence of the extreme left (particularly Trotskyists and Maoists) in the *Comités Malville*, and the tactics of confrontation being adopted by them. It was this, combined with what they believed to be the unrealistic position on energy questions adopted by the ecologists, that led the PS (the Socialist Party) and the CFDT to refuse to take part in the Malville committees. The ecologists were opposed to nuclear power in principle, whereas the PS and CFDT, while opposed to the current Government programme, believed that the energy problem needed to be faced and alternative policies put forward.

The violence of the demonstration led to a profound feeling of disappointment and betrayal in the movement.[10] The extreme left, for whom the anti-nuclear movement was primarily a vehicle for the overthrow of the bourgeois state, had led the movement up a blind alley, and a reassessment of tactics and objectives was needed.

In fact, although the movement was still split between anarchists and Marxists, as well as between political ecologists and environmentalists who refused any political involvement, changes had already begun to take place as the issue was increasingly discussed in the political parties, in particular the PSU and PS, and in the CFDT. The split between those who refused to take part in elections or in any specifically political activity were criticised for their apolitical stance by the political ecologists, for whom elections were an ideal opportunity to give expression to, and popularise, the ecologists' ideas. This split in the movement resurfaced once again at the time of the 1978 parliamentary elections although the tide was already changing and, as C.-M. Vadrot pointed out in an article in March 1978, 'more and more ecologists are rejecting an apolitical stance'.[11] This claim was borne out by the new position adopted by the RAT (*Réseau des Amis de la Terre*, the body which groups together the local Friends of the Earth groups) in Paris, which issued a statement in 1978 favouring an alliance with other social movements such as the women's and regionalist movements, groups defending the rights of minorities, and innovatory movements such as Lip.[12] It was also borne out by certain developments in the provinces, a good example of which is Poitiers where the local Friends of the Earth association, the PSU, the MAN (*Mouvement pour un Alternatif Non-violent*) and ex-members of the local *Comité de Larzac* and *Comité de Malville*, joined together to present a *'Convergence Ecologie-Autogestion-Pouvoir Populaire'* candidate at the 1978 elections. This was an example of the RAT's new position being put into practice and was repeated in many other towns as the 'Convergence' was part of a national grouping called *Front Autogestionnaire: Droits des Femmes, Ecologie, Socialisme* which was formed to fight the 1978 elections and was supported by many local *Amis de la Terre* groups.

This strategy was, in a sense, a compromise between the apolitical stance of the environmentalists and the political ecologists in that this new strategy did not involve 'playing the electoral game' with the idea that it could win, nor simply to popularise its ideas. Nor was it allowing itself to be 'recuperated' by the traditional political parties. It envisaged participation in the elections with the objective of forging alliances with the other new social movements which might be expected to share its social aims. As such it was clearly taking a specific and distinctive stand in the social and political struggles of the time and indicated a desire on the party of many ecologists to break with the ambivalent attitudes and political positions the movement had often adopted in the past in its desire to avoid being identified either with the traditional left or the right. There were, then, already clear indications within the movement of the victory of the ecologists over the Marxists and anarchists, and of the political ecologists over the environmentalists.

II. The Anti-Nuclear Movement and the Touraine Group

The most important study of the anti-nuclear movement so far published is undoubtedly the one, already mentioned, by the Touraine group, *La prophétie antinucléaire*.[13] As Brendan Prendiville remarks, this is 'the first in-depth study of the anti-nuclear movement and its underlying motivations, and as such it is an important, if not indispensable, aid to understanding the many facets of the French anti-nuclear movement'.[14] It was undertaken in April and May 1978 and with the memory of Malville therefore still very strong in the minds of the anti-nuclear militants. It is of particular interest for two reasons: firstly, because the theoretical framework of Touraine's study provides a possible further basis for understanding the development and apparent weakness of the anti-nuclear movement; secondly, because the Touraine group's analysis and conclusions are based on the perceptions of anti-nuclear militants themselves, both in meetings with the researchers and in arranged meetings or 'confrontations' with representatives of the pro-nuclear lobby.

According to the Touraine group we are at present emerging from one type of society, industrial society, into a post-industrial, or what Touraine prefers to call 'programmed', society.[15] We may not be fully aware of this, as industrial society is still very much with us, and will be for a long time to come. The consequences are, however, extremely important, as the nature of class relations and of class conflict within a programmed society are fundamentally different from those that exist in industrial society. In the latter, the working class movement was the innovative social force which provided a counter-model to that of entrepreneurial capitalism — that was *'porteur d'avenir'* (literally, 'bearer of the future' — i.e. embodying in embryonic form a type of social relations which will be characteristic of the society of the future). However, as we emerge from an industrial society, the working class becomes increasingly institutionalised and concerned, on the one hand, with negotiating primarily sectional interests and, on the other, with primarily political action at the level of the state. In industrial society, capitalism was governed by the profit motive and work was organised accordingly. The working class, by challenging the capitalist's control of industry and the organisation of work in accordance with the Taylorian model, was putting into question the very system of class domination on which industrial society was based. In a programmed society, investment decisions are no longer dictated primarily by the profit motive and the demands of work organisation: 'What is specifically characteristic . . . of the programmed society is that the main form of investment is made at the level of production management and no longer at that of the organisation of labour, as was the case in industrial society'.[16] The class which holds the power of decision in such a society is the technocracy and the key social movement of the future will therefore be the one which challenges this claim. The central struggle will no longer be that which opposes capitalist and worker in the sphere of production; rather, it will be the resistance to technocratic domination wherever it manifests itself. At stake will be the control of knowledge, which is the basis of technocratic class domination — and not the control of the means of production, which was the basis for class domination in industrial society.

To attain the status of a social movement, as the working class movement did in industrial society, a movement must satisfy three conditions. It must, firstly, recognise what is at stake in its struggle — 'historicity' (*l'historicité*) — here, the control of the organisation of society. It must furthermore be able to identify its *adversary*, defined as the group or class which holds the power of decision in such a society and which therefore controls historicity. And finally it must have an identity; a social movement must have a *constituency* — in other words, it must represent a specific section or group in society.

In the view of the Touraine group it was the anti-nuclear movement which seemed to come closest to attaining the status of a social movement, and it was with this hypothesis in mind that they undertook their study. They justify this in two ways: firstly, historically, by referring to the working class movement: 'Perhaps this is because we still think of the working-class movement as our model, and because the struggle against the apparatus of production — especially of energy production — seems more fundamental to us than the rejection of the centralising state, student protest or the women's liberation movement'; they also justify their hypothesis by referring to the present and future importance of the energy issue and the scale of material and political resources that are mobilised by the nuclear power industry.[17]

If we accept Touraine's theory that we are now on the threshold of a new 'programmed' society, which we have not yet fully entered, then it would not be surprising if the social movements that are emblematic of this new society have difficulty in establishing themselves and identifying their adversary because the social struggles typical of this new society will be overlain with struggles that are typical of earlier, industrial, society. Touraine's study shows that this is, in fact, the case and some of the most vigorous opposition to the anti-nuclear movement comes from representatives of the traditional working class, in particular the Communist Party, certain elements of the PS and France's largest trade union, the CGT (*Confédération Générale du Travail*)[18] whose adherence to Marxist theories of unlimited productive forces is directly opposed to the ideas of the ecologist movement. This is clearly a central factor in the difficulty the anti-nuclear movement has experienced in gaining acceptance for its ideas among the traditional representatives of the working class and helps to account for its weakness.

The sociological method used by the Touraine group for the study of the new social movement is called *intervention sociologique*, the vocation of which is the study of society *in action*. It comprises four distinct phases. In the first, two *groupes d'intervention*, consisting of about ten members of the anti-nuclear movement, hold discussions with interlocutors of their own choice (allies, opponents, specialists, politicians, trade unionists, industrialists, ecologists, and so on). For this study, groups were formed in Paris and Grenoble. In the second phase, the two research workers in the groups encourage them to analyse their activities and aims. The researchers then establish a hypothesis, present it to the groups, pointing out what seems to be the highest possible significance of their struggles (*'le sens le plus élevé de leur action'*) and invite them to think of their action in these terms. The project does not stop here, however, and in the final phase, called *sociologie permanente*, the researchers discuss their conclusions with the original groups and with other anti-nuclear groups to see if their analysis can be of use to them or could become a programme for future action.[19] This is an ongoing process. The advantage of a study based on this method is that it studies the movement *in action*, in a situation of confrontation with its adversary. The divergent aims of different elements within the movement emerge clearly from these confrontations and some members of the groups actually depart before the end of the study because of deep-seated disagreements with other members of the group.

There are, as already indicated, many disparate elements within the anti-nuclear movement: ecologists, trade unionists, scientists, those who see the anti-nuclear movement as a pressure group involved primarily in a defensive local action, and those for whom the anti-nuclear movement represents the rejection of modern industrial society and the return to a simpler, community-based life. The last-mentioned leave the group at an early stage in the intervention. Their quest is individual rather than social and as such is in total contradiction with the principles on which the intervention is based — social actors in conflict with each other on a common ground for the control of historicity. Their behaviour reflects a refusal of conflict. As one says: 'Perhaps we can move more quickly if we keep things among ourselves'.[20] Those who see in the anti-nuclear movement basically a pressure group involved in a defensive, local action to prevent the building of a nuclear power station in their own backyard, but who would not object to it being built next door but one, are also rejected by the group. In the Paris group's meeting with a representative of the Nogent-sur-Seine anti-nuclear group who saw the movement in this light, the former were very critical. They effectively accused him of reacting in much the same way as if it had been a decision to build a new motorway or close a local school, seeing the problem in purely local terms and not questioning nuclear policy itself. The confrontation with the professional scientists became very technical and the anti-nuclear militants rapidly realised that the scientific arguments could not be the basis for a struggle that was basically political and social in nature.

The presence of so many different elements in the movement, with their diverse heritage, means that the problems experienced by the groups are, in themselves, not surprising. Several significant points do, however, emerge from the Touraine group's study. Firstly, it emerges that there is clearly ground for agreement for a unified movement between at least certain of its elements, and that, if the movement is to unite and be effective, the trade union members are going to play a key role both in this and in providing the links with the working class movement which are to be so important during the transition period between industrial and 'programmed' society. It is significant that the CFDT has never adopted an anti-nuclear position but has, instead, based its position on opposition to the *Government's* nuclear policy. The CFDT is thus not opposed to nuclear power *per se* but to a technocratic power which is imposing an all-nuclear policy with a minimum of public debate. Their adversary is of a social and political, not a technological, nature: '. . . the linkage between the cultural critique of the ecologists and defence against nuclear power stations can only be developed by constructing a political analysis'.[21] In order to succeed in this it is not sufficient for the movement simply to be opposed to nuclear power stations. It must also be innovatory and carry within itself new social and cultural values: 'At the same time that it is fighting technocracy, it will be creating new patterns or models of thinking of economic activity and of ethical conduct appropriate to post-industrial society'.[22] This, the Touraine group pointed out to the anti-nuclear militants, appeared to be *'le sens le plus élevé de leur action'*, but, as it also points out, it is far more difficult for a movement to establish itself when it is both anti-establishment (*contestataire*) and innovatory — a force of opposition *and* a carrier of new social and cultural values — than if it was indulging in activity of a more limited character, such as a trade union or pressure group which would more easily be able to define its strategy and tactics. However, the acceptance of this analysis by a number of the anti-nuclear militants, both trade unionists and ecologists, indicates that there is clearly the potential for a unified movement and leads the Touraine group to suggest that the anti-nuclear movement is at the *pre-*social movement stage — that it contains within itself the potential to become a key social movement of the future programmed society, but that it is too early to say definitely whether it will be able to fulfil this role.

III. Recent Developments: The Anti-Nuclear Movement After Touraine

If we accept Touraine's hypothesis and the conclusions he draws, then it will be of particular interest to examine developments in the movement since he undertook his study to see if there are signs of it developing beyond the pre-social movement stage. Has it been able to identify more clearly its adversary? Has it been able to articulate more coherently its alternative model for the future development of society?

In the Spring of 1979, two important events for the development of the anti-nuclear movement took place. Firstly, a number of ecologists who had taken part in the Touraine group's study presented a text to the RAT congress in Grenoble (28 April–1 May 1979) which marked a clear break with the tone of documents previously issued by *Amis de la Terre*. Instead of the usual rejection of industrial civilisation it stated: 'Our function is to open the way for anti-technocratic struggles, the current means of domination being the control of information and of technocracy. Our function is to be the new left, the one which will correspond to the conflicts of the future'.[23] The *Amis de la Terre*, traditionally hostile to this type of idea, listened not unfavourably on this occasion and, although the final document maintained the RAT's total opposition to nuclear power, it also contained a call for a national petition against nuclear power and authorised those who had presented the above-mentioned text to negotiate with the CFDT to see if there were possible grounds for agreement on the national petition. They were even authorised to make, if necessary, a major concession on the RAT's demand, hitherto central, for the closing down of the first stage of EDF's (*Electricité de France*) nuclear programme of thirty power stations. At its Congress at Brest (11–13 May 1979) the CFDT decided to make opposition to the Government's nuclear programme a central plank in its platform and this evidently helped to clear the way for agreement with the ecologists.

The petition was eventually launched on 25 June 1979 supported by, amongst others, the RAT, the CFDT, the PSU, the GSIEN (*Groupement de Scientifiques pour l'Information sur l'Energie Nucléaire*), the consumers' organisation UFC–Que Choisir? (*Union Fédérale des Consommateurs*), the MRG (*Mouvement des Radicaux de Gauche*) and, surprisingly, the Socialist Party, which had previously confined its opposition to the Government's nuclear policy to parliamentary action. Significantly, the petition did not express opposition to nuclear power *per se* but to the '*choix du "tout nucléaire" fait par le gouvernement*'. It demanded a full public debate and the making available of independent and decentralised information on the whole energy issue, on a new type of development based on the true needs of the workers and of local populations, on the conservation of scarce, non-renewable natural resources and on the job-creating possibilities of this alternative programme. The text, entitled 'Pour une autre politique de l'énergie: pour un débat démocratique sur l'énergie', was clearly a political initiative and an important break from the ecologists' traditional emphasis on creating an alternative life-style and culture.

In addition, although it was a national petition, the work involved in collecting the signatures had to be done at grassroots level and was an important incentive for regional and local coordination. There have been a number of significant new initiatives at local level since 1978; these initiatives have provided a basis for coordination between the different currents in the anti-nuclear movement. At Poitiers, for example, the plan to build a nuclear power station at Civaux led to the uniting of the more apolitical ecologists, such as the *Société pour la Protection de la Nature et de l'Environnement dans la Vienne* and the local *Amis de la Terre* group with the more political ecologists, many of whom were either members of the PSU or had supported the *Convergence* candidate in the parliamentary elections of March 1978.[24] At Plogoff in Brittany, the local population waged a long, much-publicised and eventually successful battle against the plan to build four nuclear power stations. This battle developed from a limited struggle against the plan to build a nuclear power station at Plogoff into a general struggle against the nuclear society and against the technocratic class which imposes nuclear power stations on an unwilling local population.

Indeed, the struggle at Plogoff became a new focus for the anti-nuclear movement and was, at least in part, responsible for providing the impetus for the creation of the *Projet Alter-Breton*, a comprehensive alternative energy strategy for Brittany. The *Projet Alter-Français* had been published in 1978 and proposed a comprehensive alternative, decentralised energy policy for France, based on a different sort of growth and consumption and on the use of renewable energy sources. The *Projet Alter-Breton* is a similar plan, but for Brittany alone, and was prepared by a group of mainly local scientists, supported by Breton ecologists and members of the PSU. The introduction to the report makes it clear that it is not of a purely technical nature: 'We are proposing an ALTERNATIVE solution, based on indefinitely renewable forms of energy, and compatible with another model of development — with a self-managing, ecological society'. Ecologist groups in Grenoble are also involved in producing an alternative regional energy plan, and one group, ARMOS (*Association de la Région de Malville Hostile à Super-Phénix*) has actually built a *maison autonome*, which is not connected to the national grid and which is being used locally to publicise the possibilities of local and decentralised renewable energy sources.[25] In fact, in preparations for the national petition, greater emphasis had been put on the need for regional energy plans than appeared in the final document, and this is clearly an important new aspect of the anti-nuclear struggle.

The anti-nuclear movement has come a long way from its original position of principled and uncompromising opposition to nuclear power, when its greatest weakness was its lack of an alternative strategy. It now has comprehensive and concrete proposals for an alternative economic and energy policy based on a different model for the future development of society. Ecology is no longer simply a science but a distinctive political creed and the developments within the anti-nuclear movement seem to suggest that Touraine's ideas have not fallen on entirely stony ground in the movement, and that some of his criteria for the creation of a social movement are beginning to be fulfilled. Two documents published in 1981 by *Amis de la Terre* groups in different parts of the country would seem to support this.

The first, 'Plogoff-Le Pellerin: même combat?', was published by the *Amis de la Terre* in Rennes. In this study it is clear that certain of Touraine's key ideas have made their mark. The anti-nuclear movement is described as the most important social movement to have grown out of May 1968, and the central change that has taken place in the movement is recognised: 'The anti-nuclear critique has come a long way. At both Le Pellerin and Plogoff, a simple "No to Nuclear Power" — a rejection of a Poujadist or similar type — has, at the end of a long process of learning and information on both sides, become a "No to Nuclear Power — here or anywhere else" '. In the second document, 'Accouchons! Le mouve-ment désiré',[26] written by two members of the *Amis de la Terre* at Lille, the influence of Touraine's ideas is even more evident. References to his ideas appear throughout the document and it is clear that Touraine's analysis has largely been accepted. The first chapter examines the reasons for the anti-nuclear movement's weakness, the second proposes a possible theoretical basis for future action, the third analyses the nature of class domination in a technocratic society, and the fourth chapter makes concrete proposals for the construction of a new opposition force, outside traditional political structures and able to challenge technocratic domina-tion in a programmed society. One particularly striking point is that it both recognises and attempts to explain the past weakness of the move-ment by the conflicting aims of its different elements — one of which readily adopted apocalyptic language, announcing the imminent collapse of civilisation and advocating a utopian reversion to a simpler life outside society, and the other of which was too ready to launch into ill-prepared electoral campaigns, without a proper debate and without any clear objectives. This analysis is of interest both because it is made by anti-nuclear militants themselves on the basis of their own experience and because it confirms points already made about the movements' diverse heritage and the disparate elements grouped within it. Each had its own drum to beat.

It is clear, then, that any comprehensive agreement on objectives and articulation of the movement's specific identity have up to now been virtually impossible, and that recognition of this within the movement is evidently essential if it is to be able to unite effectively behind an agreed programme. It is also clear that the movement has changed considerably since 1978. It is significant for example, as the Touraine group points out,[27] that after the accident in an American nuclear power station at Harrisburg on 28 March 1979, no new campaign was launched by French ecologists on the basis of the risks inherent in nuclear power. The French anti-nuclear movement, at least, had recognised that fear alone was not enough to gain support for its ideas in the population at large; however, it should not be concluded from this that the ecologist movement is now completely united. The difficulties experienced by the movement in reaching agreement on a 1981 presidential candidate, with many groups refusing even to take part in the whole procedure, are indicative of the deep-seated suspicion of traditional political institutions that is still very strong in the movement, and there are still many ecologists in local groups who dream of the utopian return to a simpler way of life and who totally reject Touraine's theories.

IV. The Socialists in Power

The Giscard Administration (1974–1981) had made the development of nuclear power, which it regarded as essential to France's future prosperity and national independence, a central plank in its economic strategy. It was clear that, despite Giscard d'Estaing's claim in the April 1974 presidential election campaign that 'Nuclear power stations will not be imposed on local populations who reject them', his Administration would not tolerate any questioning of its nuclear policy. The Socialist victory in the 1981 presidential and parliamentary elections therefore clearly raised some hopes among ecologists for a more sympathetic hearing for their ideas in the future, particularly as many ecologists had supported President Mitterrand in the second round of the presidential elections. Any optimism, however, was guarded as the PS had important pro-nuclear currents within it (notably the traditional left-wing faction CERES) and had never come out openly against nuclear power. Despite its support for the 1979 national petition, its opposition to the previous Government's nuclear policy had always focused on the means it employed to impose its policy rather than questioning the policy itself. François Mitterrand's own position has undoubtedly changed since his statement on Radio Monte-Carlo on 7 March 1974 that the recently announced Messmer nuclear programme was 'too little and too late' and that 'we must produce other sources of energy, especially in the nuclear field'[28] but his position is still most certainly not one of opposition to nuclear power and the only tangible concession made to the ecologists during his election campaign was the promise to cancel Plogoff.

At the time of writing this chapter (August 1981), the present position is, to say the least, unclear. A parliamentary debate of some sort is promised for October. In the meantime, the Council of Ministers on 30 July 1981 announced that plans for five nuclear power stations, in addition to Plogoff, had been 'suspended'; these are Civaux, Le Pellerin, Golfech, Cattenom and Chooz (see map). Work is to continue, however, on all those power stations on which work has started (except Golfech) and the

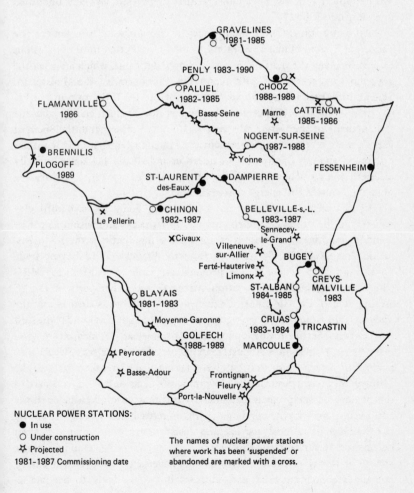

GRAVELINES
1981–1985

PENLY 1983–1990

PALUEL
1982–1985

CHOOZ
1988–1989

FLAMANVILLE
1986

Basse-Seine

Marne
CATTENOM
1985–1986

NOGENT-SUR-SEINE
1987–1988

BRENNILIS
PLOGOFF
1989

Yonne

FESSENHEIM

ST-LAURENT
des-Eaux

DAMPIERRE

CHINON
1982–1987

Le Pellerin

BELLEVILLE-s.-L.
1983–1987

Sennecey-
le-Grand

Civaux

Villeneuve-
sur-Allier

BUGEY

Ferté-Hauterive
Limonx

CREYS-
MALVILLE
1983

ST-ALBAN
1984–1985

BLAYAIS
1981–1983

Moyenne-Garonne

CRUAS
1983–1984

TRICASTIN

GOLFECH
1988–1989

MARCOULE

Peyrorade

Basse-Adour

Frontignan
Fleury
Port-la-Nouvelle

NUCLEAR POWER STATIONS:
● In use
○ Under construction
� Projected
1981–1987 Commissioning date

The names of nuclear power stations where work has been 'suspended' or abandoned are marked with a cross.

extension to the reprocessing plant at La Hague is to go ahead. As *Le Monde* (1 August 1981) pointed out, this does not in any way imply a major break with the previous Government's policy as over 50 per cent of France's electricity needs will still be met by nuclear-generated electricity in 1985. Furthermore, even without a change of Government, it is likely that some slowdown in the previous Government's programme would have been necessary. Doubts were already beginning to appear within the administration itself and an official report, prepared by the Energy Commission to the Eighth Plan under J.-M. Bloch-Lainé, raised severe doubts about the announcement of the Government's latest series of orders for nuclear power stations. This report, at first suppressed, was later published in expurgated form.[29]

In the meantime, Government policy is extremely unclear. On the one hand, the Energy Minister, Edmond Hervé, has said that local populations cannot be given the right of veto over energy decisions, which are a central government prerogative,[30] and Jean-Pierre Chevènement, the Minister for Science and Technology and spokesman for the CERES group in the PS, has pronounced his Government's support for nuclear energy and the development of the fast-breeder reactor.[31] On the other hand, the Socialist Party's most recent policy document, published in January 1981, contains a detailed analysis of the nuclear question and clearly favours a radically different energy policy based on a different sort of growth, diversification of energy sources and energy conservation.[32]

The Socialist Government is, then, clearly going to have difficulty reconciling the pro-nuclear elements within its ranks and within its parliamentary majority with those that are more sympathetic to the ecologists' ideas. The CGT, the FO (*Force Ouvrière*, France's third largest trade union) and parts of the PS are pro-nuclear, while the CFDT, the MRG (the Socialists' moderate coalition partners) and other parts of the PS are opposed to the Government's nuclear policy. What is clear is that the nuclear issue is not simply going to go away. The first clash under the new Government between riot police and anti-nuclear demonstrators took place at La Hague on 3 August 1981, while, during the same week, pro-nuclear CGT-led demonstrations were taking place in other parts of the country to protest against the Government's decision to suspend part of the nuclear power programme. The changes that have taken place in the anti-nuclear movement, combined with its refusal to be 'recuperated' by the traditional political parties and institutions, mean that, whatever defeats it may suffer in the short term, it is not going to give up its struggle and, as it identifies more clearly its true adversary — not nuclear energy but the technocratic class that imposes it — it is likely to become an increasingly effective force of opposition. As Laurent Samuel has pointed out,[33] the ecologists are the inheritors of the anarcho-syndicalist tradition and their natural allies are the PSU, the CFDT, and the non-violent and regionalist movements. If they can form an effective alliance with these groups, then their significance as a focus for dissent from the established order can only grow, although it will, as in the past, not be in conventional electoral terms.

Notes

1 C. Bourdet, interview with V.-C. Fišera, *Newsletter of the Association for the Study of Modern and Contemporary France*, no. 6 (July–August, 1981), p. 5.
2 Alain Touraine, *et al.*, *La prophétie antinucléaire* (Paris: Seuil, 1980), pp. 96–8.
3 B. Prendiville, review in *Journal of Area Studies*, no. 4 (Autumn, 1981), p. 38.
4 D. Simonnet, *Qu'est-ce que l'écologie?* (Paris: Hatier, 1979).
5 See chapter 1.
6 Ibid., p. 12.
7 Syndicat CFDT de l'Energie Atomique, *Le dossier électronucléaire* (Paris: Seuil, 1975; new edition, 1980).
8 See *Le Monde*, 15 May 1975.
9 Touraine, *et al.*, *La prophétie antinucléaire*, op. cit., p. 145.
10 See ibid., pp. 144–8.
11 C.-M. Vadrot, 'L'écologie n'est déjà plus ce qu'elle était', *Tribune Socialiste*, no. 777 (9–16 March 1978), p. 9.
12 The Lip factory in Besançon, threatened with closure by its owners, was taken over by the workers in 1973 and eventually reopened in 1974. For many, it became a symbol for opposition to the established order.
13 *La prophétie antinucléaire* is the third volume in a series of sociological studies by the Touraine group of the new French social movements. The first, *La voix et le regard* (Paris: Seuil, 1978) provides the methodological framework for the series. The second, *Lutte étudiante* (Paris: Seuil, 1978) is a study of the student movement and the fourth, *Le pays contre l'État* (Paris: Seuil, 1981), a study of the Occitan movement. Future volumes on the trade union and women's movements are projected.
14 loc. cit.
15 See Touraine, *La société post-industrielle* (Paris: Denoël, 1969), p. 7. Touraine prefers the word 'programmed' to 'post-industrial' because the former defines more clearly the nature of work and economic activity in such a society whereas the latter simply indicates the time-gap separating the two types of society.
16 Touraine, *La voix et le regard*, op. cit.
17 Touraine, *et al.*, *La prophétie antinucléaire*, op. cit., p. 11.
18 See, for example, the Touraine group's transcript of the confrontation between M. Briot, a representative of the CGT, and the Grenoble group, 15 May 1978. Briot stated that: 'The CGT begins with an analysis of the needs of the workers and of their role in the economy *given the economic apparatus which is currently available*. So far as the future is concerned, it will be impossible to do without nuclear energy'. See also the articles by Edmond Maire, leader of the CFDT, France's second largest trade union: 'Le mouvement ouvrier face aux idéologies de crise', *Le Monde*, 21 and 22 August 1980. These articles are particularly significant as the CFDT is a union which can usually be expected to be relatively

sympathetic to the new social movements. Yet, in these articles, he attacks the Touraine group and other theorists of post-industrial society such as Michel Bosquet (cf. his recent *Adieux au prolétariat* [Paris: Galilée, 1980]), for their premature announcement of the demise of the working class as a key social movement.

19 See *La prophétie antinucléaire*, op. cit., p. 339.
20 Ibid., p. 84.
21 Ibid., p. 299.
22 Ibid., p. 305.
23 Ibid., p. 284.
24 See E. Entwistle, *Les mouvements écologiques à Poitiers*, unpublished dissertation, Cambridgeshire College of Arts and Technology, 1980.
25 Y. Lers, ' "La maison autonome", défi des écolos de Malville', *Libération*, 31 July 1980, p. 7.
26 E. Delattre and P. Radanne, 'Accouchons! Le mouvement désiré', *L'Envert du Nord,* no. 26 (October, 1980).
27 See *La prophétie antinucléaire*, op. cit., pp. 282–4.
28 *Le Monde*, 9 March 1974.
29 See *Le Canard Enchaîné*, 29 April 1981, p. 4.
30 Interview with Edmond Hervé, *Le Monde*, 8 August 1981, pp. 1–2.
31 *Financial Times*, 18 August 1981, p. 2.
32 Parti Socialiste, *Energie: l'autre politique* (Paris: Club Socialiste du Livre, 1981).
33 In C.-M. Vadrot, *L'écologie: histoire d'une subversion* (Paris: Syros, 1978), p. 96, quoted by Hayward, loc. cit.

INDEX